Envisioning the Faculty for the Twenty-First Century

The American Campus

Harold S. Wechsler, Series Editor

The books in the American Campus series explore recent developments and public policy issues in higher education in the United States. Topics of interest include access to college, and college affordability; college retention, tenure and academic freedom; campus labor; the expansion and evolution of administrative posts and salaries; the crisis in the humanities and the arts; the corporate university and for-profit colleges; online education; controversy in sport programs; and gender, ethnic, racial, religious, and class dynamics and diversity. Books feature scholarship from a variety of disciplines in the humanities and social sciences.

Gordon Hutner and Feisal G. Mohamed, eds., *A New Deal for the Humanities: Liberal Arts and the Future of Public Higher Education*

Adrianna Kezar and Daniel Maxey, eds., *Envisioning the Faculty for the Twenty-First Century: Moving to a Mission-Oriented and Learner-Centered Model*

Scott Frickel, Mathieu Albert, and Barbara Prainsack, eds., *Investigating Interdisciplinary Collaboration: Theory and Practice across Disciplines*

Envisioning the Faculty for the Twenty-First Century

Moving to a Mission-Oriented and Learner-Centered Model

EDITED BY
ADRIANNA KEZAR
DANIEL MAXEY

RUTGERS UNIVERSITY PRESS

NEW BRUNSWICK, NEW JERSEY, AND LONDON

This publication was supported in part by the Eleanor J. and Jason F. Dreibelbis Fund.

Library of Congress Cataloging-in-Publication Data

Names: Kezar, Adrianna J., editor. | Maxey, Daniel, 1980– editor.

Title: Envisioning the faculty for the twenty-first century : moving to a mission-oriented and learner-centered model / edited by Adrianna Kezar and Daniel Maxey.

Description: New Brunswick, New Jersey : Rutgers University Press, 2016. | Series: The American campus | Includes bibliographical references and index.

Identifiers: LCCN 2015047304 | ISBN 9780813581002 (hardcover : alk. paper) | ISBN 9780813581019 (e-book (epub)) | ISBN 9780813581026 (e-book (web pdf))

Subjects: LCSH: College teachers—Tenure—United States. | Universities and colleges—United States—Faculty. | Education, Higher—United States—Administration.

Classification: LCC LB2335.7 .E68 2016 | DDC 378.1/22—dc23

LC record available at http://lccn.loc.gov/2015047304

A British Cataloging-in-Publication record for this book is available from the British Library.

Visit our website: http://rutgerspress.rutgers.edu

Manufactured in the United States of America

CONTENTS

PREFACE

This book emerged from our work as codirectors of the Delphi Project on the Changing Faculty and Student Success. This national project has partnered with more than forty higher education organizations representing diverse stakeholders to examine issues related to the changing composition of the faculty and its impact on student learning and the mission of higher education, as well as to develop potential solutions and alternatives to the current faculty model. We kicked off the project with a modified Policy Delphi study, an approach in which a group of experts is consulted and then brought together to help develop solutions to complex national problems. Following the study, the stakeholder groups continued to be involved with the project, contributing their ideas at various points in time to ongoing efforts to shape change and develop new models for the professoriate. In addition to the project's convening of higher education stakeholders and thought leaders, the editors have participated in numerous national conferences of stakeholder organizations, where we have made presentations and had opportunities to develop a broader sense of the challenges faced on campuses across the United States and abroad through dialogue with faculty members and administrators who face these challenges every day in their work.

Through this project, we have examined the impact of the devolution of the faculty into largely part-time and contingent appointments, unbundling of faculty roles, and other problems of deprofessionalization. The faculty workforce model that is in place today (that is, largely adjuncts) has not been intentionally designed and deployed with long-term institutional goals in mind. By collecting evidence about the ways that the changes in the faculty are affecting outcomes such as student retention, success, and graduation, we realized that we not only needed to point out the problems of the emerging model, but that we also had a responsibility to provide a constructive vision for the future. We have determined that a future vision needs to be grounded in an understanding of the types of faculty positions that are needed, as well as the roles of faculty members in serving our students, our institutions' missions, and the increasingly complex expectations of our society. As a result of this thinking, we recognized that the future faculty had to be grounded in student success and the other important missions of our institutions. These two principles undergirded much of our thinking throughout this book, including the contributions of the chapter authors that we invited to join the volume.

In the following chapters, we articulate a model for the future faculty, which is summarized and diagrammed in the final chapter. When we speak about a model, we do not mean a one-size-fits-all template with rigid criteria and prescriptions; rather, we refer to a collection of vital elements that make up a greater whole. Such a model and the elements that compose it frame important considerations that must be addressed, whether redesigning the faculty is a task taken on across the entire higher education enterprise in the United States or one addressed at an individual institution, and no matter what type of institution is involved. Models are used to help people know, understand, and replicate something. We also wanted to frame our book in terms of models of faculty work rather than roles alone, because roles speak to only a portion of the work of faculty members. A model can contain a broader set of categories such as new contract types, new approaches to work, and new values, not just a set of responsibilities as articulated under the notion of roles. The traditional faculty model is made up of various important concepts such as academic freedom; tenure; specialized knowledge; and multifaceted roles involving teaching, research, service, and other important functions—diverse concepts come together to compose this particular model of work. We want readers to step away from this book having acquired a better sense of ways to conceptualize the faculty role and, we hope, ways to replicate this new model in their institutions.

We see the need for new models of faculty work as being inherently tied to shifts that have occurred in the broader society. As institutions with diverse missions have emerged over the past four decades, a need for new faculty models has also emerged—new models that are tailored to best meet the needs of diverse institutional missions, the students served, and the different roles played by faculty. We encourage readers to realize that faculty models and roles have always been in flux. For example, over the past two hundred years, the faculty role has shifted dramatically from itinerant tutors, to pastoral and ministerial leaders, to purveyors of the classical curriculum, and to more specialized researchers under the current and dominant university model (Gehrke and Kezar 2015). What we commonly think of as the more traditional model of faculty was in place in any significant way only from 1940 to 1970. It was different prior to that time, and since then it has changed dramatically—most recently with the increase in contingent appointments, which now comprise a majority of the professorial positions. Unless there is more intentional planning, we worry about what may become of the faculty. We invite our readers to join us as partners in the effort to be more intentional and collaborative in forming a more viable and sustainable faculty model for the future.

REFERENCE

Gehrke, Sean, and Adrianna Kezar. 2015. "Unbundling the Faculty Role in Higher Education: Utilizing Historical, Theoretical, and Empirical Frameworks to Inform Future Research." In *Higher Education: Handbook of Theory and Research*, edited by Michael B. Paulsen, 93–150. New York: Springer.

ACKNOWLEDGMENTS

We would first like to express our gratitude to Susan Albertine, Caryn McTighe Musil, and the Association of American Colleges and Universities (AAC&U) for their partnership with the Delphi Project since its inception. AAC&U has provided exceptional leadership in advancing a thoughtful dialogue about the future of the faculty and helping shape the course of change. We would like to thank the thought leaders who participated in our May 30, 2014, convening at AAC&U's offices to discuss the future of the faculty. The ideas shared that day were integral to the formation of this volume and continue to guide the work we do in advocating for broader dialogue on this issue. We would also like to express our gratitude to the many non-tenure-track faculty members with whom we have worked over the past decade who have helped us to understand the imperative for changing the current model of faculty work, including Maria Maisto, our friend and partner at New Faculty Majority. Lastly, we would like to thank our families. Adrianna thanks her husband, Paul, and son, Tait. Daniel wishes to thank his parents, Dan and Jayne, and sister, Jess, for their support and encouragement over the past several years of transitions through career changes and graduate school.

PART ONE

The Context for a New Faculty Model

1

The Current Context for Faculty Work in Higher Education

Understanding the Forces Affecting Higher Education and the Changing Faculty

DANIEL MAXEY

ADRIANNA KEZAR

For nearly a hundred years, the dominant or "traditional" model of the faculty has been represented by full-time, tenure-track professors focused on a triad of responsibilities: for teaching, research, and service (Finkelstein and Schuster 2011; Kezar 2013). However, changes that have been afoot for several decades have begun to alter the essential nature of the professoriate and will continue to do so for the foreseeable future (Kezar and Sam 2010; Plater 1998). These changes have already affected the character of the professoriate in significant ways. Tenure-track jobs—once the most prevalent appointments on campuses—are being supplanted by an ever-rising number of full- and part-time non-tenure-track faculty positions. These contingent appointments now make up approximately 70 percent of faculty positions responsible for providing instruction in nonprofit higher education overall (National Center for Education Statistics 2013).[1] In addition to contingent appointments, professional unbundling has occurred: many faculty members have found themselves focusing primarily on either teaching or research (with no formal involvement in a service role) and having tenuous connections to the academic community on their own campuses and to other scholars in their disciplines more broadly. And although our institutions have retained a subset—albeit a shrinking one—of tenured and tenure-track faculty, there are signs of strain as these individuals take on an increasing and probably unsustainable level of responsibility for satisfying the multiple obligations of conducting research and providing administrative leadership and other forms of service for their institutions.

This introductory chapter will examine some of the main factors that have been the drivers of changes in the traditional faculty model over the past several decades, contributing to the rise in contingency and an unbundling of faculty roles. Understanding these factors and their continued effects is an important step toward coming up with faculty models that can best serve our institutions through the remainder of the twenty-first century and beyond. Changes in the composition of the faculty, the growing reliance on contingent labor, and the overall erosion of the academic profession have largely been the result of a haphazard response to a higher education landscape that is changing over time—a response that has lacked intentionality and planning for the long term. A number of factors are regularly cited as contributing to shifts in the composition of the faculty toward greater reliance on contingent positions: the massification of higher education, market fluctuations, economic concerns and uncertainty, corporatization, and technology and competition from for-profit institutions. These factors will be presented in detail below in this chapter.

But first, we will explain how the tenure-track model that we think of as traditional today is actually a more recent phenomenon, and we will provide a brief introduction to the non-tenure-track models that have emerged in recent decades to apply to a majority of the professoriate.

The "Traditional" Faculty Member: An Ever-Changing Model

It is important to recognize that even the "traditional" faculty model to which we refer here—the model largely characterized by full-time, tenure-track professors with obligations for research, teaching, and service—has not always been the dominant model in American higher education. Rather, the faculty model—its structure, composition, and roles—has continuously shifted to meet the changing needs of higher education and external conditions affecting the enterprise. That is, change has been a constant.

The traditional faculty model today bears little resemblance to that of the faculty of the earliest colonial colleges, for example. Faculty members in the colonial era were tutors who largely worked on contingent appointments. They provided students with general instruction and support for moral development; often they were clergy who were waiting for positions to open up in church parishes, so these positions were usually temporary. In the early 1800s, it became more common for institutions to employ permanent faculty members, as the need for more specialized professors in fields such as natural philosophy, divinity, and ancient languages increased. Then, from the 1890s into the first half of the 1900s, the rise of the modern university contributed to heightened expectations that faculty members would conduct research as a major part of their work. The model that emerged unbundled the advising, student development, and moral development components that were core attributes of the earlier tutor role and to a lesser degree the early permanent faculty role.[2] Faculty members were doing less of the day-to-day administrative work of their institutions (for example, registration), and they began to be more involved with institutional governance, research, and public service. As faculty became more professionalized, they felt it was important to have input into institutional matters related to the curriculum, educational policy, faculty personnel decisions, and the selection of academic administrators (Finkelstein 1997).

As responsibilities for some combination of teaching, research, and service became the norm for a larger subset of the faculty, the university model that has come to be known as traditional by today's standards took shape. Just as this model became fully implemented after World War II, an influx of new enrollments fueled unprecedented growth, introducing new types of institutions and further changes in roles, which will be discussed in more detail in the next section. The changes that have been seen in more recent years—characterized by rising numbers of contingent appointments and a continued unbundling of faculty roles—are just another development in a long history of faculty change. However, many of the changes that have been made over time have lacked intentionality; they have been reactive and short-sighted, and they have focused too little on long-term planning and sustainability. We have an opportunity now to strive to be more purposeful in designing—or redesigning—the faculty. How we respond to change today will affect the faculty for years to come. Priorities for the design of the faculty role for the twenty-first century compose the core themes of this volume.

Who Are Non-Tenure-Track Faculty?

The terms *non-tenure-track faculty* and *contingent faculty* are used interchangeably and commonly denote both full- and part-time academic staff who are not on the tenure track and not eligible to be considered for tenure. Part-time faculty are often referred to as *adjuncts*. It is important to understand that this is not a homogeneous group (see table 1.1). Individuals may have very different reasons for taking non-tenure-track jobs, and the nature of their work and working conditions can vary substantially, even on the same campus. In any event, although these individuals are not considered for tenure and may not be required or permitted to participate in the full range of teaching, research, and service tasks as tenure-track faculty, they are still faculty members. The work they do is tremendously important for the teaching and research missions of the institution. On some campuses, non-tenure-track faculty may teach a large share of the students enrolled in courses, particularly freshmen and sophomores or online students. They are often very committed to their field of study and to ensuring the success of the students they teach.

TABLE 1.1

Who Are Part- and Full-Time Non-Tenure-Track Faculty Members?

Part-time

Career enders	People who are retired or in the process of retiring. They may be faculty who decided to teach in retirement, or they may come from established careers outside of academia.
Specialists, experts, and professionals	Faculty who are employed full-time elsewhere, in a varied range of fields. They are hired for their specialized knowledge or success in certain fields, such as the arts or business. Often these individuals do not rely on the faculty positions for income but enjoy being involved in the academy and teaching.
Aspiring academics	Faculty members who are looking for a full-time or tenure-track position. So-called freeway fliers are a type of aspiring academic who typically teach at multiple institutions to create the equivalent of a full-time position.
Freelancers	People who typically have a job outside of academe and supplement their income with teaching. Some are also caretakers at home and prefer the flexibility of working part-time because of other demands.

Full-time

Teachers	People who spend over two-thirds of their time in instruction, with the rest of their time split between administrative tasks and research.
Researchers	People specifically hired to conduct research for over half their time, dividing the other half between instruction and administration.
Administrators	People who spend about half their time in administrative work (for example, as an associate dean) and the rest of the time in research and other activities.
Academic professionals	Full-time non-tenure-track faculty who spend half of their time on activities other than teaching, research, or administration. They are often lab technicians, programmers, or community service faculty members. Usually, they spend a quarter of their time teaching, depending on their qualifications.

Sources: Adapted from Baldwin and Chronister 2001; Gappa and Leslie 1993.

Although increases in part- and full-time non-tenure-track faculty are the largest change across higher education, other large-scale alternative models have developed in medical schools and for-profit institutions. A couple of other alternative models that have emerged are described in additional detail below in this chapter.

Adjunct or Part-Time Faculty

The most prevalent of the current faculty models is the *adjunct* or *part-time faculty member*. Because of individual circumstances, some part-time faculty members work only at one institution. However, they are more likely to have positions at multiple institutions and may aspire to full-time or tenure-track positions. In fact, research conducted by the Coalition on the Academic Workforce (2012) suggests that nearly three-quarters of part-time faculty members have sought full-time tenure-track positions and would accept such a position if it were offered at an institution where they currently teach. While adjuncts made up only a small portion of the workforce in 1970—approximately 20 percent—they now represent half of the faculty at nonprofit institutions of higher education (National Center for Education Statistics 2013; Schuster and Finkelstein 2006). Although a brief explanation of adjunct or part-time faculty is offered here, a more detailed description of some of the problems related to this model is offered in chapter 2.

Adjunct faculty are typically employed exclusively in teaching roles, hold short-term semester-to-semester contracts, and have limited involvement in decision making about curricula and other such matters, the life of the institution, and its long-term goals. Additionally, these positions often have lower status and pay and have been stripped of the job security, privileges, and forms of support (such as access to support staff, professional development, office space, and instructional resources) commonly associated with faculty on the tenure track. This model began to expand largely as a way to bring practitioner knowledge into the classroom in community colleges, so their short-term contracts were seen as relatively unproblematic for many years. However, the model has quickly expanded to become a low-cost and flexible way for institutions to meet demands for providing instruction without increasing costs—albeit with serious and negative implications for student learning outcomes.

Numerous studies have found the negative working conditions of these faculty to have a negative impact on student retention, transfer from two- to four-year institutions, and graduation or completion rates (Bettinger and Long 2010; Gross and Goldhaber 2009; Eagan and Jaeger 2009; Ehrenberg and Zhang 2004; Harrington and Schibik 2001; Jacoby 2006; Jaeger and Eagan 2009). Growing reliance on non-tenure-track faculty who receive little support and whose working conditions place limits on what they can do to support students is affecting student learning and success (Kezar and Maxey 2013 and 2015; Kezar, Maxey, and Badke 2013; Kezar and Sam 2010). The rising numbers of adjunct faculty are also affecting institutions in a variety of other ways (Kezar and Sam 2010). A sense of community and collegiality is lost when part-time faculty do not have the opportunity to interact with their colleagues or contribute to their departments through faculty meetings or other events. Faculty involvement in campus governance is at risk since part-time faculty—now the majority on many campuses—are often not permitted to participate. Academic freedom is eroded and threatened by the at-will nature of part-time faculty employment (American Association of University Professors 1986 and 1993). And institutional memory is lost with constant turnover. Perhaps most important, institutions are now often engaged in exploitative employment arrangements characterized by a growing number of faculty who cannot make enough money to survive, have no benefits, and lack a career path with opportunities for promotion (Coalition on the Academic Workforce 2012; Curtis 2005; Hollenshead et al. 2007; Kezar and Maxey 2015; Street et al. 2012; Toutkoushian and Bellas 2003).

Full-Time Non-Tenure-Track Faculty

Full-time non-tenure-track faculty may be referred to as *lecturers*, *instructors*, or *clinical faculty*. Titles and formal classifications may vary by campus and even among the numerous academic units at an institution. These people typically work at just one institution since they hold full-time appointments. Full-time non-tenure-track faculty now account for almost 20 percent of faculty among nonprofit higher education institutions. The job description of a full-time non-tenure-track faculty member is typically focused on only one part of the traditional faculty role (teaching, research, or service): roughly 70 percent of full-time non-tenure-track faculty are employed in positions where teaching is the focus (Lechuga 2006). However, full-time non-tenure-track faculty are increasingly being asked to perform additional service work, as the shrinking number of tenure-track faculty means that institutions and departments are unable to meet institutional service obligations (Hollenshead et al. 2007).

Full-time non-tenure-track faculty members are typically hired on an annual basis, but some have contracts for a period of three to five years. These longer contracts provide more job security than is commonly afforded to adjuncts, greater stability for planning courses and curricula, and additional time for carrying out service work. Studies of full-time non-tenure-track faculty members show that their working conditions tend to be closer to those of tenure-track faculty members (Baldwin and Chronister 2001; Baldwin and Wawrzynski 2011): they typically only have one institutional affiliation, are eligible for health and other benefits, have salaries that are closer to those of tenure-track faculty members, and are more knowledgeable about institutional goals and outcomes because they spend more time at the institution and are involved in its activities and decision making. Using this model has given institutions some additional flexibility to respond to fluctuations in enrollments, economic concerns, and declining state budget allocations.

Drivers of Change Affecting the Unraveling
of the Traditional Faculty Model

There is growing awareness among leaders throughout higher education of the mounting challenges provoked by a period of substantial change among the faculty for student learning and the sustainability of the enterprise (Kezar and Maxey 2015). However, there remains a fair amount of disagreement or confusion about the factors and forces that have contributed to changes in the faculty (Kezar and Sam 2010). Admittedly, a thorough explanation of how this shift has occurred, why, and exactly what caused it is difficult to produce; certainly, no single factor can be identified as being the cause for a shift from a mostly tenure-track faculty to an increasingly contingent one. However, we do not need to be able to point to a single "smoking gun." Rather, a review of major factors affecting higher education institutions over the past several decades can help us understand that a variety of factors have simultaneously shaped change and led us to our current conditions. The changes in faculty roles that have emerged have been the result of a haphazard response to this convergence of factors permeating the higher education environment over many years, instead of being part of a thoughtful and long-term strategic plan. Higher education leaders need to understand these changes and their effects on faculty models, while remaining cognizant of emerging challenges, to avoid repeating past mistakes and to effectively chart a new course forward.

Four main conditions are described as driving changes in the faculty workforce.[3] The first is the massification of higher education, which contributed significantly to overall enrollment growth and the introduction of new institutional types (Baldwin and Chronister 2001; Schell and Stock 2001). The second pertains to perceived and real enrollment fluctuations in institutions and individual fields of study. Third, there has been a dwindling of existing resources, particularly state budget allocations (Baldwin and Chronister 2001; Cross and Goldenberg 2009; Thedwall 2008). The fourth condition is the corporatization of higher education, which is believed to have influenced institutions' priorities and business models. Although these are some of the main factors, they are certainly not the only ones at play. The authors of the chapters that follow will offer their own insights about how other drivers of change, such as technology, have affected the faculty workforce.

The Massification of Higher Education: Rising
Enrollments and New Types of Institutions

The massification of higher education—the extension of the opportunity to attend college from an elite few to a larger cross-section of Americans—has been a major contributor to changes in the faculty since the mid-1900s. This change resulted in increasing enrollments and hastened the development of new types of institutions to meet a more diverse student population with varied interests and needs (Baldwin and Chronister 2001; Schell and Stock 2001). Student enrollments began rising with the implementation of the Servicemen's Readjustment Act, popularly known as the G.I. Bill, when the government began subsidizing the cost of educating soldiers returning from World War II (Schuster and Finkelstein 2006; Thedwall 2008). Years later, the civil rights movement led colleges and universities to enroll greater numbers of women, members of minority groups, and low-income students—groups whose members had not typically been able to access higher education before or whose representation on campuses had been very limited. These and other related changes resulted in a 500 percent increase in enrollments in the period 1945–75 (Thedwall 2008). These influxes of students threatened to overwhelm the capacity of institutions and their faculties, prompting institutions to hire more faculty members to help accommodate growing student bodies (Baldwin and Chronister 2001; Schuster and Finkelstein 2006).

The nature of these growing enrollments had another effect: it created the need for new types of institutions. The introduction of community colleges in the 1960s, for example, occurred as a response to changing demands for higher education. These institutions became access points for individuals who wanted to benefit from the opportunities offered by higher education but were unable or unwilling to pursue degrees at four-year institutions: most of these people were vocational students, part-time students, women, members of ethnic and racial minority groups, people with lower socioeconomic status, and students who were not prepared for university-level work (Brewster 2000; Cohen and Brawer 2008). Community colleges required different types of faculty members to meet their needs, and historically these institutions have employed the greatest percentages of non-tenure-track faculty, particularly part-time faculty. In many ways, compared to traditional four-year institutions, community colleges have been more limited in their options for accommodating their students, as they have had to cater to the needs of workforce development, keep tuition low, and have greater flexibility in hiring and scheduling (Brewster 2000; Christensen 2008; Cohen and Brawer 2008; Levin, Kater, and Wagoner 2006).

This shift in the faculty that largely began at community colleges introduced three main changes to the traditional faculty model, which began to spread to other institutions over time. First, rather than devoting time to research, community college faculty members were expected to spend most of their time teaching. Second, due to a greater emphasis on workforce development, some community college faculty members were professionals who had full-time jobs outside the institution; these individuals taught in part to help train the next generation of employees in their fields. This trend brought greater numbers of practitioners from professional fields into the faculty and meant that a growing segment of the faculty was employed on a part-time basis. Over time, hiring part-time instead of full-time faculty expanded and came to be seen as a signifi-cant way to keep costs under control (Anderson 2002; Gappa 1984): institutions were no longer just hiring practitioners to teach on a part-time basis, they were hiring academics on part-time appointments to cut expenses. Finally, com-munity colleges also would often employ individuals with a master's degree, rather than requiring someone to have a doctorate to join the faculty ranks (Cohen and Brawer 2008). These three types of changes represented significant departures from the traditional faculty model (Twombley and Townsend 2008). The trends that accompanied the introduction and development of community colleges eventually affected other types of institutions, too.

Market Fluctuations

Although enrollments in higher education have generally increased over time, institutions have sometimes encountered fluctuations; at times these fluctua-tions have been hard to predict. For example, during the economic recession of the late 1970s and early 1980s, many administrators anticipated that eco-nomic hardship would result in lower-than-normal enrollments. However, most overestimated the rate of decline in enrollments: typical enrollments actually increase during recessions. As a result, administrators often ended up hav-ing to hire additional faculty to meet their institutions' needs for instruction (Thedwall 2008). In addition to these broader fluctuations, periods of growth and decline in enrollments have also been encountered in particular fields of study such as the humanities, which have declined, and business and law, which have risen over the years (Baldwin and Chronister 2001). One area where fluctuations have been particularly noticeable in recent years is computer sci-ence (Lytle 2012): enrollments hit record levels in the early 2000s, then tapered off significantly to the lowest levels seen since the 1970s, and surged again in the past couple of years.

Market fluctuations have also prompted greater demands for flexibility. Depending on student enrollments, interest in a particular class, and unan-ticipated changes in budgets from one semester or academic year to the next, departments sometimes have had to make decisions to add or remove classes and thus instructors with little notice (Baldwin 1998; Gappa and Leslie 1993; Hollenshead et al. 2007; Tolbert 1998). Wary of economic uncertainty and the potential for fluctuations in enrollments, institutions started to expand their use of part-time faculty. At the same time, they also began to hire increasing numbers of faculty members on full-time non-tenure-track contracts to ensure that they could maintain the flexibility they desired to manage the academic workforce through periods of growth and decline.[4] Campus leaders began to question their ability to make long-term hiring commitments. Hiring contingent faculty, particularly part-time faculty who are hired on a semester-to-semester basis, allowed departments to respond more rapidly to any fluctuations in the market, whether they were the result of budget deficits or changes in demand. The ensuing decline in tenure-track positions left recent PhDs with fewer options, and many began turning to non-tenure-track positions to find work.

Economic Concerns: Uncertain Revenue Streams and Cost Concerns

Government appropriations for higher education have historically accounted for a large share of revenues at colleges and universities, particularly public institutions (Archibald and Feldman 2012). For a variety of reasons—including philosophically motivated changes in who should bear the burden of paying for higher education, economic crises such as the recent recession, and mandates for states to fund other government programs and services (for example, public-sector pensions, healthcare, and prisons)—the share of institutional budgets that comes from government has fluctuated but mostly declined substantially over the past few decades (Archibald and Feldman 2012; Marcucci and Johnstone 2007). Institutions have increased tuition and fees; they have also turned to private sources of revenue such as foundation grants, interest income from endowment fund investments, and charitable donations, although these sources of revenue have also proven to be unpredictable during periods of economic uncertainty. Ongoing public divestment of public institutions, pressure to slow the rate of growth in tuition increases, and greater competition for external funding has often meant that colleges and universities faced difficult decisions to offset those losses: institutions must make cuts, raise revenues, or both.

Most if not all scholars agree that economic factors play a very large role in the hiring of non-tenure-track faculty and the exploration of new workforce models (Baldwin and Chronister 2001; Benjamin 2002; Burgan 2006; Cross and Goldenberg 2009; Gappa and Leslie 1993; Hollenshead et al. 2007; Slaughter and Rhoades 2004). Roger Baldwin and Jay Chronister (2001) note that the reduction in government funding for higher education from the late 1980s to the 1990s was a major reason why institutions began to hire contingent faculty in greater numbers. While institutions were experiencing reductions in government allocations, the costs associated with maintaining a college or university were increasing. Institutions had to find new ways to address decreasing appropriations and rising costs. Institutions raised tuition, but they also needed to find a way to limit expenses without taking teachers out of the classroom (Baldwin and Chronister 2001). Hiring contingent faculty came to be seen as one way to reduce expenses, and there has continued to be a surplus of qualified individuals to fill these positions. For the price of one tenure-line faculty member, a college or university could afford to hire several adjunct faculty members and put more teachers in more classrooms, thus meeting the demands of increasing enrollment (Cross and Goldenberg 2009; Pratt 1997). In more recent years, particularly around the most recent recession, we have seen a continuation of this trend of hiring more faculty members off the tenure track.

Still, others suggest that any cost savings achieved by hiring more non-tenure-track faculty have merely been redirected to cover new or rising expenditures in other administrative areas rather than helping to reduce overall costs. Data from the Delta Cost Project have consistently demonstrated that expenditures on the academic mission and instruction as a share of institutional budgets have mostly remained flat—even declining at times—over the past thirty years, while expenses in other categories are increasing, sometimes dramatically.[5] For example, athletics programs continue to be a major draw on resources. The economic imperative to hire cheap faculty labor might instead be interpreted as a choice to pursue other institutional objectives, such as being more competitive in sports, research, or fundraising and marketing. This conclusion raises serious questions about the priorities of higher education institutions at a time when the public demands a greater emphasis on the quality of instruction and student outcomes.

Even as the United States recovers from the most recent recession, economic concerns persist for higher education institutions. Colleges and universities continue to be expected to do more with less; the tone in the current political climate nationally and in some states suggests reluctance to restore appropriations or invest additional funds in higher education after record cuts in funding have been seen in recent years. In addition, the rising cost of higher education for students and families nationally has recently reemerged as a major topic in the political and social discourse (Archibald and Feldman 2012). Students and families are concerned about how they will pay for an increasingly expensive college education, putting additional pressure on institutions to control costs. Elected officials across the political spectrum are also paying greater attention. Outside groups, from the media to foundations and the business community, have also joined the discussion. These pressures have made using increases in tuition to meet budget shortfalls a more difficult option than in the past, which in turn has caused institutions to seek new ways to cut costs.

Corporatization of Higher Education

Many observers note that over the past thirty years higher education has also been more heavily influenced by corporate or neoliberal values. These values altered expectations for institutions and the faculty. For example, boards of trustees, filled with corporate leaders, have asked institutions to consider new employment arrangements to reduce the bottom line. Throughout the 1980s and 1990s, and again in more recent years, corporations used employment models that were more dependent on contingent labor. Higher education institutions were increasingly expected to do the same. As a result of these new ideas, boards and other influential stakeholders also asked academic leaders to reconsider tenure and examine faculty productivity and workloads. Baldwin and Chronister (2001) note that for the first time in many years, institutions faced a loss of public trust in terms of faculty accountability, criticisms of tenure, and challenges to traditional faculty roles.

The shifts in faculty hiring and the current composition of the faculty are often believed to reflect the influence of a corporate or neoliberal value system among boards of trustees and other higher education leaders. These forces stimulated a surge in contingent appointments, a retraction of tenure, increased expectations for faculty productivity to obtain tenure, post-tenure review policies (in which a faculty member's productivity is evaluated even after he or she receives tenure), and more frequent evaluation. In addition to influencing changes in contract types and greater accountability for productivity, growing adherence to corporate values also prompted a reexamination of faculty priorities. For example, boards of trustees began questioning the value of emphasizing research over teaching, examining what they saw as low teaching loads for tenured and tenure-track faculty. Service and leadership work also began to be questioned. As a result, a narrower view of faculty roles—focused on teaching—was advanced. Corporate values about the division of labor suggested that unbundling faculty roles could be a more productive and efficient approach, leading to an increase in models characterized by teaching-only or research-only positions. This same corporate logic has been used to unbundle the teaching role into delivery, grading or assessment, and advising. In general, values of efficiency and productivity became dominant in rethinking and redefining faculty roles.

Recent surveys of college and university presidents have shown less support for tenure as it exists today and a desire for greater institutional flexibility around employment. In 2011, 35 percent of presidents said they would alter tenure policies, and 34 percent would increase teaching loads (Green, Jaschik, and Lederman 2011). And in 2013, 21 percent favored multiyear contracts over tenure, and 32 percent would shift more undergraduate teaching to adjuncts (Jaschik and Lederman 2013b). In surveys of chief academic officers conducted over the past several years, around two-thirds noted a preference for some sort of system of long-term contracts over the existing tenure system (Jaschik and Lederman 2013a, 2014 and 2015). While corporate values and a drive for a more accountable and productive model of faculty are likely to continue to shape the way academic institutions think about a faculty workforce model, this mindset could shift as leaders begin to understand the adverse effects of increasing contingency on institutions and student learning outcomes.

Although these are all issues that have already had an impact on the direction the faculty model has taken over the last several decades, each is expected to continue to affect changes in higher education for years to come—although it is unclear at what pace or to what end. Enrollments are likely to continue to increase as greater numbers of students seek higher education, with fluctuations occurring as students pursue degrees that will help them find the best jobs in a changing market. Economic pressures will continue to be a major factor in decisions about the direction of the faculty in the future. Institutions will face greater public pressure to control rising costs for attending a college or university and to increase productivity, exacerbating pressures created by public divestment and increasing competition for external funding. Faculty roles will almost certainly need to be reconsidered, with cost and productivity in mind, in an environment characterized by constrained resources and greater calls for accountability. Corporate or neoliberal values are so firmly entrenched that they will surely continue to influence priorities and business models. Other issues such as the rapid pace of technological change and the emergence of new, disruptive business models that will compete with traditional models are likely to bring about many as yet unanticipated changes for higher education and the faculty in the coming years. Therefore, it is likely that the need for the development of new faculty models will persist in the foreseeable future.

New Faculty Workforce Models

Given all these various pressures for change, one might imagine that several alternative faculty models to the current tenure-track model have been developed to accommodate the range of factors and forces described above, as well as other emerging or evolving issues such as internationalization and technology, which are discussed by other authors in this volume. In fact, four main models have emerged as alternatives to the tenure-track model and have achieved sector-level scale: the use of adjuncts, full-time non-tenure-track faculty, and clinical faculty within medical schools, and the online or for-profit model. The adjunct and full-time non-tenure-track models were introduced above in this chapter; the remaining two will be discussed briefly below. While each has emerged as a response or, perhaps more appropriately, a reaction to one or more of the external factors and forces described above (for example, the emerging use of adjuncts in response to the demand for a less costly and more flexible workforce), with the exception of the medical school model none has been intentionally designed and deployed with long-term institutional goals in mind. The other three models can largely be interpreted as devolutions of the traditional tenure-track faculty model. We describe these models to convey some of the changes that have occurred so far. Chapter 2 will consider some additional criticisms of the current adjunct and tenure-track models, including how they fail to meet the current needs and missions of institutions, and the need for new thinking about the future of the professoriate.

Although the rise of part- and full-time non-tenure-track faculty models described above reflects the largest shift across higher education, other large-scale alternative models have developed in medical schools and for-profit institutions. To be clear, some more isolated experimental models that deviate from the traditional tenure-track model have also emerged at some institutions, which might be used in forming new models in the future. In addition to the non-tenure-track faculty models described above, the following examples represent two of the most widespread current alternatives to the tenure-track faculty model.

Medical School Models

Although most institutions have reacted to changes in the higher education landscape in a haphazard fashion, medical schools have been tinkering with their own faculty model to address various challenges (the factors that were described above and others unique to the medical field) for several years. Many medical schools have adopted a model that most closely resembles the full-time non-tenure-track model, but there are some unique features with regard to how it is commonly deployed in medical schools (Jones and Gold 2001; Kezar 2013). Medical school faculty appointments are categorized into three main tracks—research, education, and clinical—to better meet the mission of medical schools (Bunton and Mallon 2007); there are also combined tracks where faculty perform some combination of these functions. Research faculty members' work is largely focused on knowledge generation; education or teaching faculty members are charged with providing instruction; and clinical faculty members maintain their own medical practice but often also teach on a part-time basis.

All of the tracks are afforded equal status, and medical schools have worked to redefine cultural norms that often prioritized research and clinical practice over teaching. Faculty on all three tracks are also included in governance and given voting rights. They all receive appropriate support and equitable compensation and benefits, although there are often different systems for evaluation and promotion. However, traditional tenure has largely been reserved for only a small number of faculty members conducting basic science research. This model is described in greater detail in chapter 5.

The Online or For-Profit Faculty Model

The faculty model in for-profit education makes greater use of technology and unbundles the teaching role with the objective of maximizing cost effectiveness: functions that can be carried out by technology or by nonfaculty employees for the sake of cost savings or effectiveness are split from faculty roles. Faculty members with more traditional roles are considered to be too expensive to have a central role (de Boer et al. 2002; Howell, Williams, and Lindsay 2003; Howell et al. 2004; Paulson 2002). The online or for-profit faculty model has the following characteristics (Lechuga 2006): Nearly all faculty are hired on a part-time basis, with very limited numbers of full-time faculty employed to develop courses and fulfill administrative duties. There is usually no faculty involvement in governance, service, or research. Faculty members typically have limited or no disciplinary ties or expertise, and often a doctorate is not a primary criterion in hiring decisions (a master's degree or field experience is accepted instead). Faculty members are hired on performance-based contracts measured by student evaluations, but they occasionally receive peer evaluations as well. And since for-profit institutions have been particularly responsive to market fluctuations, positions may be created or eliminated as demand for employees in different fields rises or falls.

Vernon Smith (2008) describes the model as a sort of virtual assembly line: rather than having faculty members develop and deliver entire courses, teaching is commonly broken into eight different functions that are carried out by a variety of employees with specialized roles. The functions include instructional design (technology and graphics experts), subject matter (faculty members), development (graphic designers, web designers, web programmers, and editors), delivery (networking, technology, and learning help desks), interaction (faculty, although this is often outsourced to tutors), grading (peers and tutors), improvement (instructional design and faculty), and advising (student services, tutors, and specialist leads).

Even among for-profit institutions and other online providers, varying levels of unbundling can be identified in examples from different institutions. The University of Phoenix uses faculty to design courses and staff to deliver and assess them. Western Governors University uses external providers for the development and assessment of courses (providers that are often staffed with faculty) and tutors to provide student support and advising (Paulson 2002). Coursera's massive open online courses (MOOCs) represent yet another approach, in which a small number of faculty members design and deliver courses, but assessment and advising is assigned to peers and tutors. The important point is that unbundling of teaching in various for-profit institutions and different online configurations is occurring in many ways, and there is no single faculty workforce model in this sector.

Conclusion

The forces and factors that have shaped the faculty over the past several decades will almost certainly continue to influence changes for years to come. How we respond, collectively or in our individual institutions, will affect the course of future changes for faculty models, roles, and expectations. Most of the changes that have occurred to date have been the result of short-sighted and reactive, rather than intentional, efforts. The growth of part-time faculty, for example, started as a means of bringing professional expertise into the classroom, but it has turned into a way for campuses to increase their reliance on cheap and flexible employees—without considering the implications of a lack of support and other practices on student learning and other aspects of institutional missions. In some more isolated cases, though, experimental models have emerged that might be described as having been more thoughtful adaptations.[6] Although they are similar to the changes described here in that they deviate from the traditional model, they represent a reimagining of contracts and faculty roles that have managed to avoid some of the problems associated with the more typical sort of non-tenure-track faculty that have become prominent on other campuses (Chait and Ford 1982). These experiments have sought to address overall factors affecting higher education and unique institutional circumstances through innovation. Although institutions across the entire sector have experienced the same overarching forces and pressures, the outcomes are often very different.

Existing experiments might not always provide a neat template for changes on other campuses, but the mere fact that alternatives are possible ought to inspire us to seek a more deliberate, rather than a reactive, course. We can create faculty models for the future that respond to environmental challenges but that also—and more importantly—enhance scholarship and student success; effectively serve unique institutional missions and disciplinary differences; promote faculty professionalism, satisfaction, and productivity; and honor the core values of the academic profession. There is little doubt that to bring about more purposeful change as we proceed, we will need to be more attentive to the forces and factors that have shaped the faculty over the past several decades and be aware of additional challenges that have yet to emerge. The future of the faculty—its structure, composition, positions and contracts, and responsibilities—can be shaped more purposefully to be responsive to changing environmental conditions, while also ensuring that the needs of institutions, as well as their students and faculties, are met. This book addresses a wide range of issues that will need to be considered in undertaking this monumental change, whether it occurs on the scale of the full higher education sector or on individual campuses.

NOTES

1. Although the proportions of tenure-track and non-tenure-track appointments vary by institution type, fewer than 50 percent of faculty members in each category of institution in the United States (public, private, community colleges, research universities, and so on) are on the tenure track or have already received tenure (Kezar and Maxey 2012).

2. The responsibilities that had formerly been conducted by the tutors needed to be addressed, and this led to the emergence of the student personnel movement (Rentz and Howard-Hamilton 2011).

3. This section draws on prior publications by the authors, including a report on changing faculty workforce models prepared for the TIAA-CREF Research Institute and resources for the Delphi Project on the Changing Faculty and Student Success. See Kezar 2013 and Kezar and Maxey 2015.

4. The actual effect of market fluctuations as a reason for growing reliance on contingent faculty is difficult to determine. Several of the areas where the use of non-
tenure-track positions has grown—for example, liberal arts fields like mathematics
and composition—have more stable enrollments than others. Thus, we are somewhat
skeptical that the claim that non-tenure-track faculty are employed to respond to
short-term fluctuations in enrollments, which is frequently made by administrators,
holds true in all cases.

5. For more information, see Delta Cost Project 2015.

6. For examples of more experimental models, see Kezar 2013 and Kezar and Maxey 2015.

REFERENCES

American Association of University Professors. 1986. *Statement on Full-Time Non-Tenure-Track Appointments.* Washington: American Association of University Professors.

———. 1993. *The Status of Non-Tenure-Track Faculty.* Washington: American Association of University Professors.

Anderson, Eugene L. 2002. *The New Professoriate: Characteristics, Contributions, and Compensation.* Washington: American Council on Education.

Archibald, Robert B., and David H. Feldman. 2012. "Explaining Increases in Higher Education Costs." *Journal of Higher Education* 79 (3): 268–95.

Baldwin, Roger G. 1998. "Technology's Impact on Faculty Life and Work." *New Directions for Teaching and Learning* 1998 (76): 7–21.

Baldwin, Roger G., and Jay L. Chronister. 2001. *Teaching without Tenure.* Baltimore, MD: Johns Hopkins University Press.

Baldwin, Roger G., and Matthew R. Wawrzynski. 2011. "Contingent Faculty as Teachers: What We Know; What We Need to Know." *American Behavioral Scientist* 55 (11): 1485–509.

Benjamin, Emelia. 2002. "How Overreliance on Non-Tenure-Track Appointments Diminishes Faculty Involvement in Student Learning." *Peer Review* 5 (1): 4–10.

Bettinger, Eric, and Bridget T. Long. 2010. "Does Cheaper Mean Better? The Impact of Using Adjunct Instructors on Student Outcomes." *Review of Economics and Statistics* 92 (3): 598–613.

Brewster, David. 2000. "The Use of Part-Time Faculty in the Community Colleges." *Inquiry* 5 (1): 66–76.

Bunton, Sarah A., and William Mallon. 2007. "The Continued Evolution of Faculty Appointment and Tenure Policies at U.S. Medical Schools." *Academic Medicine* 82 (3): 281–89.

Burgan, Mary. 2006. *What Ever Happened to the Faculty? Drift and Decision in Higher Education.* Baltimore, MD: Johns Hopkins University Press.

Chait, Richard P., and Andrew P. Ford. 1982. *Beyond Traditional Tenure: A Guide to Sound Policies and Practices.* San Francisco: Jossey-Bass.

Christensen, Chad. 2008. "The Employment of Part-Time Faculty at Community Colleges." *New Directions for Higher Education* 2008 (143): 29–36.

Coalition on the Academic Workforce. 2012. "A Portrait of Part-Time Faculty Members: A Summary of Findings on Part-Time Faculty Respondents to the Coalition on the Academic Workforce Survey of Contingent Faculty Members and Instructors." Accessed December 6, 2015. http://www.academicworkforce.org/CAW_portrait_2012.pdf.

Cohen, Arthur M., and Florence B. Brawer. 2008. *The American Community College.* San Francisco: Jossey-Bass.

Cross, John G., and Edie N. Goldenberg. 2009. *Off-Track Profs: Nontenured Teachers in Higher Education*. Cambridge, MA: MIT Press.

Curtis, John. 2005. "Inequities Persist for Women and Non-Tenure-Track Faculty: Economic Status of the Profession 2004–5." *Academe* 91 (2): 19–98.

De Boer, Harry, Jeroen Huisman, Anne Klemperer, Barend van der Meulen, Guy Neave, Henno Theisens, and Marijk van der Wende. 2002. *Academia in the 21st Century: An Analysis of Trends and Perspectives in Higher Education and Research*. The Hague: Adviesradd voor het Wetenschaps en Technologiebeleid.

Delta Cost Project. 2015. Home page. Accessed December 6, 2015. http://www .deltacostproject.org/.

Eagan, M. Kevin, and Audrey J. Jaeger. 2009. "Effects of Exposure to Part-Time Faculty on Community College Transfer." *Research in Higher Education* 2009 (50): 168 88.

Ehrenberg, Richard L., and Lin Zhang. 2004. *Do Tenured and Non-Tenure Track Faculty Matter?* Working Paper No. 10695. Cambridge, MA: National Bureau of Economic Research.

Finkelstein, Martin J. 1997. "From Tutor to Specialized Scholar: Academic Professionalization in Eighteenth and Nineteenth Century America." In *The History of Higher Education*, edited by Lester F. Goodchild and Harold S. Wechsler, 99–121. 2nd ed. Boston: Pearson Custom.

Finkelstein, Martin J., and Jack H. Schuster. 2011. *A New Higher Education: The "Next Model" Takes Shape*. New York: TIAA-CREF Institute.

Gappa, Judith M. 1984. *Part-Time Faculty: Higher Education at a Crossroads*. ASHE-ERIC Higher Education Report 84 (3). Washington: Association for the Study of Higher Education.

Gappa, Judith M., and David W. Leslie. 1993. *The Invisible Faculty: Improving the Status of Part-Timers in Higher Education*. San Francisco: Jossey-Bass.

Green, Kesten C., Scott Jaschik, and David Lederman. 2011. *Presidential Perspectives: The 2011 Inside Higher Ed Survey of College and University Presidents*. Washington: Inside Higher Ed.

Gross, Betheny, and Dan Goldhaber. 2009. *Community College Transfer and Articulation Policies: Looking Beneath the Surface*. Seattle, WA: Center on Reinventing Public Education.

Harrington, Charles, and Timothy Schibik. 2001. *Caveat Emptor: Is There a Relationship between Part-Time Faculty Utilization and Student Learning Retention?* Professional File No. 91. Tallahassee: Association for Institutional Research.

Hollenshead, Carol, Jean Waltman, Louise August, Jeanne Miller, Gilia Smith, and Allison Bell. 2007. *Making the Best of Both Worlds: Findings from a National Institution-Level Survey on Non-Tenure-Track Faculty*. Ann Arbor, MI: Center for the Education of Women.

Howell, Scott L., Farhad Saba, Nathan K. Lindsay, and Peter B. Williams. 2004. "Seven Strategies for Enabling Faculty Success in Distance Education." *Internet & Higher Education* 7 (1): 33–49.

Howell, Scott L., Peter B. Williams, and Nathan K. Lindsay. 2003. "Thirty-Two Trends Affecting Distance Education: An Informed Foundation for Strategic Planning." *Online Journal of Distance Learning Administration* 6 (3): 1–18. Accessed February 13, 2016. http://www.westga.edu/~distance/ojdla/fall63/howell63.html.

Jacoby, Daniel. 2006. "The Effects of Part-Time Faculty Employment on Community College Graduation Rates." *Journal of Higher Education* 77 (6): 1081–103.

Jaeger, Audrey J., and M. Kevin Eagan. 2009. "Unintended Consequences: Examining the Effect of Part-Time Faculty Members on Associate's Degree Completion." *Community College Review* 36 (3): 167–94.

Jaschik, Scott, and David Lederman. 2013a. *The 2013 Inside Higher Ed Survey of College & University Chief Academic Officers*. Washington: Inside Higher Ed.

———. 2013b. *The 2013 Inside Higher Ed Survey of College & University Presidents.* Washington: Inside Higher Ed.

———. 2014. *The 2014 Inside Higher Ed Survey of College & University Chief Academic Officers.* Washington: Inside Higher Ed.

———. 2015. *The 2015 Inside Higher Ed Survey of College & University Chief Academic Officers.* Washington: Inside Higher Ed.

Jones, Robert F., and Jennifer S. Gold. 2001. "The Present and Future of Appointment, Tenure, and Compensation Policies for Medical School Clinical Faculty." *Academic Medicine* 76 (10): 993–1004.

Kezar, Adrianna. 2013. *Changing Faculty Workforce Models.* Washington: TIAA-CREF Research Institute.

Kezar, Adrianna, and Daniel Maxey. 2012. *National Trends for Faculty Composition over Time.* Los Angeles: Delphi Project on the Changing Faculty and Student Success.

———. 2013. *Review of Selected Policies and Practices and Connections to Student Learning.* Los Angeles: Delphi Project on the Changing Faculty and Student Success.

———. 2015. *Adapting by Design: Creating Faculty Roles and Defining Faculty Work to Ensure an Intentional Future for Colleges and Universities.* Los Angeles: Delphi Project on the Changing Faculty and Student Success.

Kezar, Adrianna, Daniel Maxey, and Lara Badke. 2013. *The Imperative for Change: Fostering Understanding of the Necessity of Changing Non-Tenure Track Faculty Policies and Practices.* Los Angeles: Delphi Project on the Changing Faculty and Student Success.

Kezar, Adrianna, and Cecile Sam. 2010. *Understanding the New Majority: Contingent Faculty in Higher Education.* ASHE Higher Education Report 36 (4). Hoboken, NJ: Jossey-Bass.

Lechuga, Vicente M. 2006. *The Changing Landscape of the Academic Profession: The Culture of Faculty at For-Profit Colleges and Universities.* New York: Routledge.

Levin, John S., Susan Kater, and Richard L. Wagoner. 2006. *Community College Faculty: At Work in the New Economy.* New York: Palgrave Macmillan.

Lytle, Ryan. 2012. *Computer Science Continues Growth on College Campuses.* Washington: U.S. News and World Report.

Marcucci, Pamela N., and Bruce D. Johnstone. 2007. "Tuition Fee Policies in a Comparative Perspective: Theoretical and Political Rationales." *Journal of Higher Education Policy and Management* 29 (1): 25–40.

National Center for Education Statistics. 2013. *Integrated Postsecondary Education Data System.* Washington: Department of Education.

Paulson, Karen. 2002. "Reconfiguring Faculty Roles for Virtual Settings." *Journal of Higher Education* 73 (1): 123–40.

Plater, William. 1998. "Using Tenure: Citizenship within the New Academic Workforce." *American Behavioral Scientist* 41 (5): 680–715.

Pratt, Lawrence R. 1997. "Disposable Faculty: Part-Time Exploitation as Management Strategy." In *Will Teach for Food: Academic Labor in Crisis*, edited by Cary Nelson, 264–77. Minneapolis: University of Minnesota Press.

Rentz, Audrey L., and Mary Howard-Hamilton. 2011. "Student Affairs: An Historical Perspective." In *Rentz's Student Affairs Practice in Higher Education*, edited by Naijian Zhang, 30–62. 4th ed. Springfield, IL: Charles C. Thomas.

Schell, Eileen, and Patricia Stock, eds. 2001. *Moving a Mountain: Transforming the Role of Nontenure-Track Faculty in Composition Studies and Higher Education.* Urbana, IL: National Council of Teachers in English.

Schuster, Jack H., and Martin J. Finkelstein. 2006. *The American Faculty: The Restructuring of Academic Work and Careers.* Baltimore, MD: Johns Hopkins University Press.

Slaughter, Sheila, and Gary Rhoades. 2004. *Academic Capitalism and the New Economy: Markets, State, and Higher Education.* Baltimore, MD: Johns Hopkins University Press.

Smith, Vernon C. 2008. "The Unbundling and Rebundling of the Faculty Role in E-Learning Community College Courses." PhD diss., University of Arizona.

Street, Steve, Maria Maisto, Esther Merves, and Gary Rhoades. 2012. *Who Is Professor 'Staff'? and How Can This Person Teach So Many Classes?* Center for the Future of Higher Education.

Thedwall, Kate. 2008. "Non-Tenure-Track Faculty: Rising Numbers, Lost Opportunities." *New Directions for Higher Education* 2008 (143):11–19.

Tolbert, Pamela S. 1998. "Two-Tiered Faculty Systems and Organizational Outcomes." *New Directions for Higher Education* 1998 (104):71–80.

Toutkoushian, Robert K., and Marcia L. Bellas. 2003. "The Effects of Part-Time Employment and Gender on Faculty Earnings and Satisfaction: Evidence from the NSOPF: 93." *Journal of Higher Education* 74 (2): 172–95.

Twombley, Susan, and Barbara K. Townsend. 2008. "Community College Faculty: What We Know and Need to Know." *Community College Review* 36 (1): 5–24.

2

Recognizing the Need for a New Faculty Model

ADRIANNA KEZAR

DANIEL MAXEY

In the previous chapter we described a variety of external changes and pressures that suggest we need to reconsider the faculty model. In this chapter, we explore why faculty matter to student success to provide a rationale for why going through the difficult work of creating new models is so important. In addition, we review existing critiques of current faculty models that also demonstrate the need for change. We review evidence that campuses are failing to make the best use of faculty—both tenure-track and non-tenure-track—to attain institutional goals and optimize student learning outcomes. Many stakeholders both inside and outside of the academy sense that we may need a new faculty model; however, the hard work of conceptualizing such a model is unlikely to become a priority. There are two reasons for this. First, without a deeper understanding of the problems with the existing dominant tenure-track and adjunct models, there seems to be no urgency. Second, many leaders today are not knowledgeable about why faculty matter so much to the learning mission of the institution. This chapter is aimed at opening the reader up to new possibilities by discussing the problems that have emerged with existing roles and models and that require a vigorous response. As the reader will see, these problems are significant, systemic, and not going away. They represent deep and critical flaws that suggest the current faculty models are broken and in need of revision. This chapter also outlines these problems to demonstrate and develop an awareness among leaders so we can try to avoid perpetuating these issues in future models. Only by seeing the consequences of the failed design can we develop a better, more robust approach.

First, we demonstrate why faculty matter for student learning and for our enterprise and why focusing on faculty models is so important. In K–12 educational policymaking, teachers are typically regarded as central to promoting student learning and success (Darling-Hammond 1999 and 2008). As a result, teacher education programs, standards and certification for teachers, and professional development receive a great deal of attention (Darling-Hammond 1999 and 2008; Elmore 1996). It is accepted that teachers matter to student learning and that student success is dependent on teacher performance. The same assumptions are not made in higher education. We believe that the lack of consideration of the central role of the faculty in facilitating learning is not without consequence and that it is a key reason why the faculty role was allowed to devolve in the manner it has. In our work bringing together accreditors, academic leaders, policymakers, and other important constituent groups in higher education (Delphi Project on the Changing Faculty and Student Success 2014), we have observed that there is not a well-grounded understanding of the research on faculty members' impact on students or a clearly articulated rationale for why faculty are important to student outcomes and learning. Yet a substantial body of research that has been conducted over a span of more than fifty years demonstrates that faculty-student interaction is a key factor in promoting student success—particularly among those students who are most in need of support, such as first-generation college students. This research is consistent, is pervasive, and has informed the development of major surveys and projects in higher education, but it has not typically been mentioned in discussions about appropriate faculty models. A brief summary of this research will help readers see why the work of rethinking faculty roles is so crucial.

Second, we summarize empirical studies by educational researchers over the past two decades that demonstrate the problems associated with increasing contingency and the adjunct faculty model. While this body of research is more limited, studies have also identified problems with the tenure-track faculty model, particularly in relationship to supporting innovation in teaching and supporting student success.

We acknowledge that some campuses have had success with the adjunct and tenure-track models, but on the whole, current faculty models have problems. If these problems are not addressed, they will threaten the integrity of the academic enterprise. By examining the ethical and functional shortcomings of our current arrangements, it will become more apparent why we need to conceive a vision—or visions—for new faculty models and roles, and perhaps even the academic profession as a whole. By sorting through the mess we are in, we can begin to develop models that will value the contributions of all faculty members, provide adequate support, respond to the needs of institutions and their internal and external stakeholders, and address the various forces and environmental challenges that will continue to affect the higher education sector.

Faculty Matter to Student Outcomes and Institutional Missions

Some leaders may question whether an investment in faculty matters at all. These skeptics might believe that a focus on creating a supportive learning

environment is more important than taking up the difficult challenge of revising faculty roles. Certainly, other areas are easier to address: changes in advising or technology, for example, might be implemented more quickly. While
these changes are also important, if they are the only ones made and the faculty
role is not considered, it is unlikely the learning environment will improve
markedly. This is a path some institutions are following. We are convinced that
only making these changes is a serious mistake. A strong educational environment, particularly one in which optimal teaching and learning take place,
requires faculty who can engage students. In the following sections, we present
the accumulated research on why faculty matter so much to student outcomes
and success.

The Importance of Faculty-Student Interactions

Interactions between faculty members and students have long been documented
as one of the main educational practices affecting the quality of students' learning and their educational experiences (Chickering and Gamson 1987; Kuh 1995;
Kuh, Bridges, and Hayek 2006; Light 2001). Such interactions have been found
to foster a host of positive outcomes, such as students' increased persistence
and completion rates; higher grade-point averages (GPAs) and standardized
test scores; and development of leadership, critical thinking, sense of worth,
career and graduate school aspiration, and self-confidence. As Bradley Cox and
coauthors note, "no shortage exists of empirical studies of the nature, quality,
and frequency of faculty-student contact and their [sic] educational consequences for students" (2010, 768).

Faculty-student interaction overlaps with a range of other positive
instructional practices that have been proven to promote student success,
such as academic challenge, active and collaborative learning, high-impact
practices (for example, undergraduate research and service learning) and
other enriching experiences such as study abroad, and the existence of a
supportive campus environment. Yet studies repeatedly demonstrate an
independent impact associated with faculty-student interactions alone.
Additionally, in a study examining historical findings about faculty-student
interactions between 1950 and 2000, George Kuh and Shouping Hu (2001)
found that the positive outcomes associated with frequent and high-quality
contact between students and their professors remained relevant even as
campus and student demographics changed over time. Hundreds of quantitative and qualitative studies have probed the educational outcomes of
faculty-student interactions and found that a generally positive relationship
exists (Kuh 1995).[1]

Studies show better learning outcomes for students who have more frequent and high-quality interactions with faculty members in a variety of ways,

including being a guest in a professor's home, working on a research project with a faculty member, talking with instructors outside of class, or serving on committees or campus organizations with faculty (Astin 1993; Kuh 2003; Kuh and Hu 2001). In fact, Kuh and coauthors conclude: "In general, for most students most of the time, the more interaction with faculty the better. Both substantive in-class and social out-of-class contacts with faculty members appear to positively influence (though indirectly) what students get from their college experience, their views of the college environment (especially the quality of personal relations), and their satisfaction" (Kuh, Bridges, and Hayek 2006, 41).

Research has associated faculty-student interactions with a number of additional outcomes, many of which correspond to the goals of major initiatives to improve student learning and success. One of the strongest findings in research has been the relationship between faculty-student interactions and persistence toward degree completion (Braxton, Bray, and Berger 2000; Johnson 1997; Lundquist, Spalding, and Landrum 2003; Wang and Grimes 2001), which has been a perennial concern among the public and policymakers. One of the factors that we know decreases dropout rates and increases persistence is the amount of time that students interact with faculty and the quality of these relationships (Braxton, Bray, and Berger 2000; Johnson 1997; Lundquist, Spalding, and Landrum 2003). Studies have also associated frequent and high-quality interactions with other common measures of student success, such as students' GPAs (Anaya 1992; Anaya and Cole 2001; Carini, Kuh, and Klein 2006) and performance on standardized tests (Anaya 1992). These interactions have been found to have a more pronounced positive influence on students with lower SAT scores (Anaya and Cole 2001).

Researchers have also explored more specific cognitive and affective outcomes that are fostered by faculty-student interactions. For example, studies have found faculty-student interactions to be associated with leadership ability and development (Sax, Bryant, and Harper 2005); critical thinking and problem solving (Bjorklund, Parente, and Sathianathan 2002; Carini, Kuh, and Klein 2006); self-authorship, or the ability to define one's capacity and identity (Wawrzynski and Pizzolato 2006); better communication skills (Bjorkland, Parente, and Sathiyananthan 2002); sense of purpose (Martin 2000); and character development (Jenney 2011). While we need more research that investigates precisely how faculty affect specific types of learning outcomes such as critical thinking, the current studies suggest that high-quality faculty-student interactions make a difference not just in outcomes such as persistence, graduation rates, and performance in classes and on standardized tests, but also in the breadth and depth of types of learning that occur among students.

Faculty Impact on Students of Color and First-Generation Students

Although interactions and relationships with faculty members are strong predictors of learning among all groups of students, they have been found to be strongest among students of color and first-generation college students (Lundberg and Schreiner 2004). Given the significant changes in demographics nationally, these findings should be heeded by campus leaders. No other factor plays as strong a role in persistence for students of color, making this a particularly important finding for our colleges and universities, which are serving increasingly diverse student bodies (Allen 1992). Students note that faculty interactions encourage them to engage more with learning, try harder, and meet high academic expectations (Anaya and Cole 2001). Studies that specifically examined the effects of interactions for Latina/o and African American students found that students who perceived their professors as accessible and supportive as a result of their positive interactions reported higher levels of academic achievement (Allen 1992; Anaya and Cole 2001; Himelhoch et al. 1997). For example, Sharon Fries-Britt and Bridget Turner (2002) found that students attending historically black colleges and universities (HBCUs) attributed their success to the encouragement and support they received from faculty and staff. Similarly, research by Boulaloy Dayton and others (2004) suggests that strong relationships with faculty and staff contribute to Latina/o students' sense of belonging and their feeling that they are valued and matter in the community. Additionally, Catherine T. Amelink (2005) found that first-generation students who reported positive interactions with faculty were more likely to experience academic success (for example, to have satisfactory GPAs and persistence) and were more satisfied with their academic experience.

The Depth and Quality of Faculty Interactions

Earlier studies on faculty-student interactions focused on the number of contact incidents and found more frequent interactions to be related to more positive outcomes for students (Pascarella and Terenzini 1978). In recent years, however, studies have found that the depth and quality of the relationships is more important to the type and strength of outcomes. Studies of students' development of higher-order cognitive skills also suggest that the purpose and quality of faculty–student interactions may be more important than their frequency (Cox et al. 2010). Marisol Arredondo (1995) found that interactions that were deeper and more meaningful—such as working with a faculty member on a research project, spending time with a faculty member outside of class in a social situation, or having a conversation about careers and future plans—are important in promoting positive student outcomes. These outcomes include increased motivation and persistence, higher aspirations, and greater achievement. Various programs that are identified with student success often build in this type of deep and meaningful faculty mentoring, such as undergraduate research programs, course-connected internships, and faculty members' serving as advisors for student clubs (Christie 2013; Hurtado et al. 2011). Other studies demonstrated that more tutorial-style classes, in which faculty meet with students individually and interact with them each week, are also associated with greater student learning (Smallwood 2002).

Interactions with a substantive focus appear to have a greater impact on knowledge acquisition and skill development, for example, than do more casual, less-focused contacts (see, for example, Kuh and Hu 2001). However, studies have found that even informal and infrequent contact is associated with persistence, increased graduation rates, and student development (Komarraju, Musulkin, and Bhattacharya 2010). These lesser types of interaction include talking after class about academic or personal issues, occasional greetings, and receiving advice about a major or job. Research helps us understand what constitutes a high-quality faculty interaction or relationship—whether the source is formal or informal contacts or a combination of the two. Studies have specifically identified four qualities of a high-quality interaction: faculty members were approachable and personable; faculty members had enthusiasm and passion for their work; faculty members cared about students personally; and faculty members served as role models and mentors (Alderman 2008).

Institutional Factors Shape Positive Faculty-Student Interactions

Robert Blackburn and Janet Lawrence (1995) and James Fairweather (1996 and 2002) provide caveats to the findings about student-faculty interactions by demonstrating how institutional factors and role construction can limit their positive impacts. As we will highlight below with the tenure-track and adjunct models, the way institutions implement faculty models can affect whether positive student outcomes result. The Blackburn and Lawrence model, in particular, provides a framework for understanding how the institutional environment (for example, resources, mission, and composition of the student body) affects faculty roles and expectations (such as faculty norms, educational practices, behaviors, and productivity). We argue that the lack of intentional design of strong faculty models aimed at improving student outcomes has led to a degradation in the value proposition of what faculty can offer for student learning.

Critiques of the Adjunct Faculty Model

Given the importance of the faculty to student learning, one would assume that there has been a thoughtful development of faculty models that support student learning and institutional mission, as Blackburn and Lawrence (1995) suggest is so critical to garnering these benefits. However, instead of a thoughtful faculty role design, the random expansion of the adjunct model has proven to pose serious problems for optimizing faculty-student interactions.

The numbers of adjunct faculty have grown over several decades, and the group has become the largest subset of the faculty—comprising approximately half of the instructional faculty at nonprofit institutions nationally (Kezar and Maxey 2015). So it seems important to address the problems with this model first.

The original reason for hiring adjunct faculty was to facilitate opportunities for practitioners to contribute to the education of students in a field of study, particularly in professional or vocational programs.[2] Adjunct faculty seem appropriate for this purpose: individuals with practical, real-world experience and knowledge from the field are employed to help enrich the educational experience and quality for students, supplementing the work of the permanent faculty (Kezar 2013). Individuals would be hired on short-term contracts; receive modest compensation and no benefits—an honorarium, in effect; and would not be involved in service tasks, campus governance, or decision making about curricula and other such matters. Since individuals holding these positions would typically have jobs outside of the institution, issues like job security, a living wage, a lack of access to benefits, and exclusion from decision making would not be problems (Kezar and Sam 2010).

This is not how things have played out, however. Although the sort of adjunct faculty member described in the preceding paragraph is often still used (particularly in professional education programs) and makes great contributions to the educational missions of institutions, the adjunct model has been expanded and exploited as a way to provide instruction to students at the lowest possible cost (Kezar 2013). A positive and useful model for involving people who could contribute practical knowledge and experience to the education of the next generation became strained over time. Critics of the adjunct model contend that this growth and change in the purposes of the adjunct model has occurred without much apparent concern for how working conditions affect instructional quality (Bettinger and Long 2010; Eagan and Jaegar 2008; Ehrenberg and Zhang 2005; Gross and Goldhaber 2009). These positions have increasingly been used to provide administrators with greater flexibility over the faculty workforce and to provide instruction to students without the long-term obligations associated with hiring tenure-track faculty, such as providing access to professional development opportunities, office space and instructional resources, and inclusion in decision making (Kezar 2013). Since these new adjuncts were not full-time professionals working in other fields, most of them wanted a full-time role and were barely making a living from their positions. A recent national study found that over three-quarters of adjunct faculty desired a full-time position (Eagan, Jaeger, and Grantham 2015). The low wages and the lack of job security and benefits became problematic (Kezar 2013). Furthermore, with large numbers of adjuncts in departments and institutions, fewer faculty are now available to be involved in governance; meet with students to answer questions, provide feedback on assignments, or mentor them about career options; plan the curriculum; or perform other traditional faculty roles. The adjunct model serves an important role when used judiciously and sparingly; however, it is clear that these positions have generally come to be abused and have deviated from their original purposes.

Several problems have been identified with an overreliance on the adjunct faculty model that can inform future efforts to develop appropriate faculty models. Studies suggest that increasing numbers of non-tenure-track faculty in higher education are negatively affecting student success outcomes—leading, for example, to lower graduation rates, decreased persistence, diminished transfer rates between two- and four-year institutions, and greater attrition for students in their first year (Bettinger and Long 2010; Eagan and Jaegar 2008; Ehrenberg and Zhang 2005; Gross and Goldhaber 2009; Harrington and Schibik 2001; Jacoby 2006; Jaegar and Eagan 2009). But the committed educators serving as adjunct faculty are not to blame for these adverse effects on student learning. Rather, poor working conditions and a lack of support diminish their capacity to provide a high-quality learning environment and experience for students. These poor working conditions include having little or no orientation, input on course and curriculum design, knowledge of departmental or programmatic learning goals, access to resources such as sample syllabi or textbooks, and office space or pay for office hours, as well as a lack of job security, inequitable compensation and access to benefits, and last-minute hiring (which interferes with stability and planning) (Baldwin and Chronister 2001; Gappa and Leslie 1993). Certainly the type of meaningful faculty-student interactions described in the first part of this chapter are largely impossible to create with most adjunct positions. These are just a few of the problems that exist. The cumulative effect of these poor working conditions constrains individual instructors' abilities to have important faculty-student interactions and apply their many talents, creativity, and subject knowledge to maximum effect inside and outside the classroom (Baldwin and Wawrzynski 2011; Eagan and Jaeger 2008; Jacoby 2006; Umbach 2007).[3]

Second, many institutions do not provide professional development opportunities for adjunct faculty members, which limits their access to and practice of effective pedagogies, high-impact practices, and innovative strategies to promote student learning. It also limits their ability to stay current on knowledge in their disciplines (Baldwin and Chronister 2001; Gappa and Leslie 1993; Kezar and Sam 2010). Recent national data suggest that less than 30 percent of adjunct faculty had access to professional development (Coalition on the Academic Workforce 2012). This not only constrains their ability to offer the very best educational experience for their students, a goal to which they are often very committed, but also shapes their ability to succeed when they apply for tenure-track positions. Even less common than professional development on campus is for adjunct faculty to be eligible for or receive funds to travel off campus for conferences, workshops, or to conduct research (Baldwin and Chronister 2001; Gappa and Leslie 1993). And even when professional development is available to adjunct faculty, it is typically offered at times when they are unable to participate or they are not paid for their time—thus, to participate they have to do so on their own time and at their own expense (Baldwin and Chronister 2001; Gappa and Leslie 1993; Kezar and Sam 2010).

The results of this lack of professional development are clearly demonstrated by empirical research. Roger Baldwin and Matthew Wawrzynski (2011) found that adjuncts tend to use less student-centered and active teaching approaches. These approaches are associated with greater learning, so adjuncts' using them less compromises student learning. They also found that adjuncts used fewer high-impact teaching practices associated with greater learning, such as service learning, undergraduate research, and study abroad. Paul Umbach (2007) found that tenure-track faculty were also more likely to use student-centered and engaging practices than adjuncts. Umbach's earlier studies also showed that faculty who use student-centered teaching approaches—getting to know students and having more frequent and substantive interactions with them—is one of the key ways that faculty can have a positive impact on student outcomes (Umbach and Wawrzynski 2005). While these studies do not identify why adjuncts use these positive teaching approaches less often, it is likely that their contracts and work arrangements exclude them from participating in the professional development, mentoring, and interactions with colleagues that would result in their adoption of better teaching practices. Some of these studies have also found that overreliance on student evaluations makes adjuncts wary of experimenting with new teaching methods. When faculty are provided with these opportunities, research has suggested that they have a positive impact. For example, another recent study of full-time non-tenure-track faculty by David Figlio, Morton Schapiro, and Kevin Soter (2013) found that non-tenure-track faculty members who are well supported (with paid office hours and access to an office and professional development) and use strong teaching practices produce student outcomes that are comparable to those of tenure-track faculty members.

Third, the presence of large numbers of adjuncts has created a strain on those responsible for departmental work and has resulted in inequities for adjuncts, who are typically excluded from involvement in the life of the department and campus. Adjuncts also receive inadequate support from their institutions and departments in terms of basic orientation, mentoring, and supplies such as sample syllabi to complete their work, all of which are critical to developing a strong learning environment (Baldwin and Chronister 2001; Gappa and Leslie 1993). They are also excluded from activities such as governance and service. As a result of this exclusion, tenure-track faculty workloads are increasing in areas of governance and leadership, departmental work is not advanced, curricula remain outdated, new faculty must fend for themselves, and potential innovations are ignored (Schuster and Finkelstein 2006). Departments are also missing out on opportunities to draw on adjuncts' expertise and knowledge from the field, which could help innovate the curriculum and support students (Baldwin and Chronister 2001; Gappa and Leslie 1993; Kezar and Sam 2010).

Fourth, adjunct faculty receive little, if any, constructive evaluation of their work to assess their effectiveness and allow them opportunities to improve. Usually, the only feedback adjunct faculty receive about their teaching comes from student evaluations (Baldwin and Chronister 2001; Kezar 2013; Marits 1996). Institutions commonly require favorable student evaluations to rehire adjunct faculty. This reliance on student evaluations has often made adjuncts wary of holding students to high standards, grading rigorously, giving difficult assignments, and experimenting with their teaching (Kezar and Sam 2010). Adjunct faculty typically do not benefit from formal or informal evaluations from department chairs or faculty colleagues, such as mentors who observe and provide feedback about their instruction and possible areas for improvement. Adjuncts are thus denied the opportunity to enhance their performance or make improvements to the courses that they teach. Also, because adjunct faculty contracts are largely dependent on student evaluations, research has shown that even when they receive professional development they are unlikely to implement it for fear of a decline in evaluations that would jeopardize their further employment (Rutz et al. 2012). The use of pedagogies that improve student learning are often resisted by students at first because they are used to more passive pedagogies, and that resistance results in lower faculty evaluations (Smith 1988).

Fifth, since adjunct faculty members are often not included in orientation programs, faculty meetings, and decision making, they may not possess important information about academic policies and practices, programs available to students, the curriculum, or overall learning goals for their departments and institutions (Baldwin and Chronister 2001; Gappa and Leslie 1993; Kezar and Sam 2010). As the numbers of adjunct faculty continue to increase, there are fewer faculty members who understand the learning goals of their academic programs and institutions, as well as how those are related to the curriculum (Kezar and Sam 2010). Although accreditors continue to press for the development of policies, practices, and curricula that foster student learning outcomes, we are decreasing our capacity to both develop and support the attainment of learning goals by excluding this important and growing segment of the faculty from participating in these activities.

Sixth, a lack of job security contributes to higher rates of turnover and a lack of stability for academic programs and their students. There is often no process in place to ensure that adjunct faculty will be rehired or to notify them in advance of contract renewal, even when they perform in an excellent manner

(Coalition on the Academic Workforce 2012; Gappa and Leslie 1993; Hollenshead et al. 2007). In any given semester, adjunct faculty may not know whether they will have work for the next semester, which may cause them to seek other employment. They can also be terminated or their appointments can be discontinued for no reason and with very little notice. The high turnover rate for adjuncts affects students' abilities to find mentors and to develop relationships with faculty members that are critical to student learning and self-efficacy; it also creates difficulties in such key activities as students' obtaining letters of recommendation or help with job placement (Benjamin 2003). The turnover also interferes with the formation and vitality of a community of scholars at an institution, particularly at institutions with very large numbers of part-time employees.

Seventh, the adjunct faculty model views faculty members merely as a tool for facilitating content delivery, downplaying the important contributions of educators to student learning—which is to the detriment of the faculty and the students whose learning they support. The move away from a stable faculty that is knowledgeable about the entire curricular and programmatic experience is also changing the profession to one aimed more at information delivery. Adjunct faculty are limited in their ability to connect larger student learning outcomes like critical thinking, writing, and quantitative reasoning in their discrete courses; they are largely unaware of broader program, department, or college learning goals. Instead, classes are seen as discrete learning opportunities where particular content is delivered. Some worry that as the scholarly component of faculty roles declines, there will be a breakdown between idea generation and delivery (Schuster and Finkelstein 2006). When faculty members maintain a scholarly role, they keep up with new knowledge and imagine how they can contribute to furthering knowledge and understanding, even if conducting research is not their main role. However, we have little history to inform an understanding of how faculty will perform when they are no longer considered to be scholars and are completely disconnected from knowledge generation.

Eighth, the professionalism of the faculty role has been degraded. With its lower pay, lack of job security, inadequate professional development, and lack of input on the curriculum, adjunct faculty work is no longer a profession (Rhoades 1998). This professional degradation will make faculty work overall less attractive over time and affect the capability of the academy to attract talented individuals to pursue faculty jobs. In the future, this will have an impact on the quality of students entering graduate school and the overall professoriate and should be of major concern to leaders within the enterprise.

Ninth, the use of the adjunct model to generate cost savings has resulted in inequities in compensation, access to benefits, and working conditions. Adjunct faculty members are customarily paid significantly less than other faculty members for the same work, and they are typically not even given access to health benefits (Coalition on the Academic Workforce 2012; Curtis 2005; Hollenshead et al. 2007; Toutkoushian and Bellas 2003). This inequity means that faculty are being paid dramatically different wages ($2,700 per class for adjuncts versus $10,000 for tenure-track faculty) for largely the same work. Besides raising the question of why individuals do not receive at least roughly the same pay for largely equal work (even if adjunct faculty and their tenure-track counterparts have different credentials, which may or may not be the case), this inequity raises serious ethical concerns for the academy. The main reasons for hiring adjunct faculty have shifted from occasionally using a working professional in the classroom (the original model for why they were hired) to creating a cheap, flexible, and expendable faculty workforce.

There is a great need to address the effects of growing reliance on adjuncts in higher education. Continuing along the course we are on has the potential to diminish the success of numerous efforts across higher education to improve student learning and outcomes and to achieve the completion agenda by retaining and graduating more students. A growing volume of reports and empirical research, summarized above, is contributing to greater awareness of these problems. This growing body of research has the potential to lead to action, but as yet it has not succeeded in producing comprehensive changes to the roles of adjunct faculty or in stimulating a broader conversation about our faculty models. Even though research and advocacy efforts have started to expose problems associated with practices related to the use of adjuncts, efforts to change them are few and isolated. In fact, engaging more stakeholders is one reason for the creation of this book. Many campus stakeholder groups still do not understand that problems exist (Cross and Goldenberg 2011). For example, a recent survey of college and university trustees indicated that two-thirds of trustees have not discussed issues related to adjunct employment status (Association of Governing Boards of Universities and Colleges 2014). Yet there are clear reasons to be concerned about the policies and practices related to adjunct faculty. The concerns outlined above demonstrate the need for the leaders of our institutions to systematically review the current adjunct faculty model when considering changes to the faculty model to ensure that new policies and practices are designed to be equitable. Furthermore, faculty roles and related policies and practices should be examined with their impact on student learning and other aspects of the institutional mission in mind.

Critiques of the Traditional Tenure-Track Model

While the adjunct model has been critiqued and has received much attention in recent years, there are also long-standing concerns with the tenure-track model that new models of the faculty role could also address. Major concerns about the once dominant tenure-track faculty model have led to its decreased popularity and a decline in the percentage of tenure-track faculty in academe as a whole.

First, a disproportionate emphasis on conducting research and publishing has essentially downplayed the importance of teaching, which is a core part of the mission of most institutions (Fairweather 1996). Today's tenure-track faculty roles, which have been influenced the most by the university faculty model that rose to dominance in the period after World War II, typically emphasize responsibilities for research and publication—even at institutions that claim to have a strong mission for teaching (Massy and Zemsky 1994). While there have been numerous calls (including Ernest Boyer's oft-noted *Scholarship Reconsidered* [1990]) for expanding or reconsidering the role orientations and rewards for tenure-track faculty to include more attention to teaching or civic engagement, the attention of tenure-track faculty has largely remained focused on traditional forms of research and publication because these are the activities that are valued and validated by current rewards schemes.

Second, tenure does not allow for flexibility in hiring to teach new fields or to account for market fluctuations. The lifetime protections of tenure have made it difficult for institutions to adjust the size and expense of the academic workforce to respond to enrollment fluctuations, growth of new fields, or declining enrollments in certain areas (Baldwin and Chronister 2001; Kezar 2013). Granting tenure involves institutions' committing to pay the salary and benefits of faculty members for an indefinite period of time—sometimes for decades, since there is no mandatory retirement age. Facing declining state appropriations and periods of economic hardship, leaders of many institutions have found the tenure system to be misaligned with current economic realities in higher education (Baldwin and Chronister 2001; Kezar 2013). Proposals for term tenure (tenure that is only for a certain length of time) and other alterations to make the model more workable have had little uptake (O'Meara and Rice 2005).

Third, there is limited emphasis on teaching and learning or on incentives to improve and innovate teaching in the current tenure-track model (Fairweather 1996; O'Meara and Rice 2005; Schuster and Finkelstein 2006). There has long been concern that tenure-track faculty are not sufficiently focused on student learning and outcomes and are not motivated to innovate their teaching (Fairweather 1996). As technology emerges as an important tool that can facilitate more active learning, critics worry that tenure-track faculty do not have incentives to adopt new technologies that might help them focus on innovating their teaching. As a result, important practices that we know are aligned with student learning are slow to be adopted, such as high-impact practices. Tenure has repeatedly emerged in studies as a reason for why teaching innovations do not spread (Austin 2011).

Fourth, little attention has been paid to other important scholarly roles that faculty can play in service, civic engagement, and local leadership. Faculty on the tenure track, which privileges research, express concern that they cannot perform other important activities related to student learning or the institutional mission because doing so may jeopardize their efforts to obtain tenure. Many institutions have a mission of outreach or community engagement, but tenure-track roles and rewards are structured in such a way that most faculty are leery of getting involved in service learning; community-based research; or partnerships with local nonprofits, agencies, and businesses. Particularly at institutions where research and scholarship are a major function or role, critics worry that scholarship is defined too narrowly as only empirical research published in peer-reviewed journals (Boyer 1990; O'Meara and Rice 2005). For example, Boyer (1990) argued that there are various forms of scholarship, and some are more aligned with the teaching-oriented or local or regional educational institutions that have burgeoned since World War II. In addition, applied research to support local communities, community-based research, and the scholarship of teaching (research focused on one's own teaching to improve one's practice) have been suggested as key areas that are more appropriate for certain institutions with a mission focused on service and teaching (Boyer 1990). There has also been concern about whether existing faculty roles give faculty members enough flexibility to commit to performing service roles, contribute to civic engagement, and provide leadership in support of higher education's public-service mission and purpose. Leaders in civic engagement initiatives aimed at meeting higher education's goals for developing citizens and democratic behaviors often register concern about whether traditional tenure-track faculty roles are defined in ways that support work in the community (Shaker 2014).

Fifth, faculty who are not yet tenured but who are on the tenure track (probationary faculty) often feel constrained in what they can focus on. Many faculty members have voiced concern that they must emphasize research and publication while compromising teaching to gain tenure (Fairweather 1996; O'Meara and Rice 2005; Rhoades 1998). While pursuing tenure, many faculty feel they cannot attend to priorities that they believe are important; they find themselves influenced by the priorities of faculty who already have tenure and will judge their advancement and promotion. Even once faculty are tenured, associate professors still feel pressure to conform to standards of more senior faculty and may downplay important advising, outreach, service, leadership, or teaching activities in pursuit of goals that are deemed to be more important by their colleagues.

A major concern about maintaining the tenure system is its protection of academic freedom. In recent years, there has been acknowledgment that academic freedom can likely be protected without tenure as it is conceived today. Those involved in initiatives and experiments at Evergreen State College and Hampshire College, for example, have pointed out that faculty members' academic freedom can be protected without tenure through other institutional policies (Chait and Trower 1997). Some commentators have challenged the necessary connection between the concepts of academic freedom and tenure, which are related but not synonymous (Byrne 1997). Institutions with no tenure system or a mix of tenured and untenured appointments have found ways to address the vulnerabilities associated with the absence of tenure protections through academic freedom policies and to establish clear procedures for addressing potential violations of academic freedom, although these arrangements often require a great deal of trust between the faculty and the administration.

Various efforts over time have tried to address these criticisms. For example, the Preparing Future Faculty project of the Association of American Colleges and Universities and the Council of Graduate Schools attempted to educate graduate students about the full scope of faculty roles and responsibilities and broader notions of scholarship, as well as providing them with experiences that helped them understand the differences in mission and faculty roles that exist across various types of institutions. Boyer's *Scholarship Reconsidered* (1990) was another well-known and ambitious project that sought to expand the definition of scholarship to include a greater emphasis on engagement, applied research, and teaching. Both efforts were aimed primarily at tenure-track faculty. These efforts have resulted in some important changes, but since this work has occurred, the faculty composition has changed dramatically. These issues need to be addressed anew in the current context and in light of the full assortment of concerns related to both traditional faculty models and the newer adjunct model.

Moving Forward with Intentionally Designed Faculty Models

For too long, we have taken for granted that our leaders understand the value that faculty add to learning in postsecondary institutions and the important role they have in our core academic mission. We need to remind ourselves of the critical role that faculty play in student learning and other outcomes and work to design faculty roles that best support these significant outcomes. In addition to student success, our primary institutional mission, current faculty positions also affect other important outcomes such as institutional governance, leadership, and community engagement. We also need to be active critics of existing models that have long not served students as well as they could and to challenge our colleagues who support models of faculty work that do not meet institutional goals or support positive student outcomes.

The rest of this book focuses on what changes can be made to faculty roles and how to intentionally design them in ways that support student success and meet other institutional outcomes, as well as addressing the challenges described in chapter 1. For example, Eugene Rice's chapter wrestles with how we can maintain the professionalism of faculty roles even as institutions move away from the tenure that has long protected that professional status; KerryAnn O'Meara and Lauren DeCrosta examine the way faculty roles can be more differentiated and made flexible enough to serve both institutional and organizational needs; several chapters discuss the need for faculty roles to focus much more on student learning and advising and mentoring students; and others explore the need for greater collaboration between faculty to serve institutional and departmental missions, and even the broader societal mission of higher education.

NOTES

1. It is important to note that the studies described controlled for characteristics of incoming students and other college experiences. However, there is no way to control for students who perform well or who are inclined to persist tending to seek out more faculty interactions. Also, the effects of student-faculty interaction are conditional. For example, students who were better prepared academically and who devoted more effort to their studies interacted more frequently with faculty members. It is not clear whether this is because such students were more assertive in seeking out faculty members or because faculty members invited students who performed well academically to make contact (for example, writing laudatory comments in the margins of a student's paper suggesting they talk further about the topic) (Kuh and Hu 2001).

2. This section draws largely from a report by the authors (Kezar and Maxey 2015).

3. For additional information on research about the adverse impacts of adjunct faculty working conditions on student success, see Kezar, Maxey, and Badke 2013; Kezar and Maxey 2013.

REFERENCES

Alderman, Rosalind V. 2008. "Faculty and Student Out-of-Classroom Interaction: Student Perceptions of Quality of Interaction." PhD diss., Texas A&M University.

Allen, Walter R. 1992. "The Color of Success: African-American College Student Outcomes at Predominantly White and Historically Black Public Colleges and Universities." *Harvard Educational Review* 62 (1): 26–44.

Amelink, Catherine T. 2005. "Predicting Academic Success among First-Year, First Generation Students." PhD diss., Virginia Polytechnic Institute and State University.

Anaya, Guadalupe. 1992. "Cognitive Development among College Undergraduates." PhD diss., University of California, Los Angeles.

Anaya, Guadalupe, and Darnell G. Cole. 2001. "Latina/o Student Achievement: Exploring the Influence of Student-Faculty Interactions on College Grades." *Journal of College Student Development* 42 (1): 611–22.

Arredondo, Marisol. 1995. "Faculty-Student Interaction: Uncovering the Types of Interactions That Raise Undergraduate Degree Aspirations." Paper presented at the annual meeting of the Association for the Study of Higher Education, Orlando, FL, November.

Association of Governing Boards of Universities and Colleges. 2014. "Survey Results: Adjunct Faculty Unions [Infographic]." *AGB Blog*, April 8. Accessed December 6, 2015. http://agb.org/blog/2014/04/08/survey-results-adjunct-faculty-unions-infographic.

Astin, Alexander W. 1993. *What Matters in College? Four Critical Years Revisited.* San Francisco: Jossey-Bass.

Austin, Ann E. 2011. *Promoting Evidence-Based Change in Undergraduate Science Education.* Washington: National Academies National Research Council Board on Science Education.

Baldwin, Roger G., and Jay L. Chronister. 2001. *Teaching without Tenure: Policies and Practices for a New Era.* Baltimore, MD: Johns Hopkins University Press.

Baldwin, Roger G., and Matthew R. Wawrzynski. 2011. "Contingent Faculty as Teachers: What We Know; What We Need to Know." *American Behavioral Scientist* 55 (11): 1485–509.

Benjamin, Ernst, ed. 2003. "Exploring the Role of Contingent Instructional Staff in Undergraduate Learning." Special issue, *New Directions for Higher Education* 9 (123).

Bettinger, Eric P., and Bridget Terry Long. 2010. "Does Cheaper Mean Better? The Impact of Using Adjunct Instructors on Student Outcomes." *Review of Economics and Statistics* 92 (3): 598–613.

Bjorklund, Stefani A., John M. Parente, and Dhushy Sathianathan. 2002. "Effects of Faculty Interaction and Feedback on Gains in Student Skills." Paper presented at the 32nd Annual Frontiers in Education Conference, Boston, November.

Blackburn, Robert T., and Janet H. Lawrence. 1995. *Faculty at Work: Motivation, Expectation, Satisfaction.* Baltimore, MD: Johns Hopkins University Press.

Boyer, Ernest L. 1990. *Scholarship Reconsidered: Priorities of the Professoriate.* San Francisco: Jossey-Bass.

Braxton, John M., Nathaniel J. Bray, and Joseph B. Berger. 2000. "Faculty Teaching Skills and Their Influence on the College Student Departure Process." *Journal of College Student Development* 41 (2): 215–27.

Byrne, J. Peter. 1997. "Academic Freedom without Tenure?" New Pathways: Faculty Career and Employment for the 21st Century Working Paper Series, Inquiry 5. Washington: American Association for Higher Education.

Carini, Robert M., George D. Kuh, and Stephen P. Klein. 2006. "Student Engagement and Student Learning: Testing the Linkages." *Research in Higher Education* 47 (1): 1–32.

Chait, Richard, and Cathy Ann Trower. 1997. "Where Tenure Does Not Reign: Colleges with Contract Systems." New Pathways: Faculty Career and Employment for the 21st Century Working Paper Series, Inquiry 3. Washington: American Association for Higher Education.

Chickering, Arthur W., and Zelda F. Gamson. 1987. "Seven Principles for Good Practice in Undergraduate Education." *AAHE Bulletin* 39 (7): 37.

Christie, Barbara. 2013. "The Importance of Faculty-Student Connections in STEM Disciplines: A Literature Review." *Journal of STEM Education* 14 (3): 22–26.

Coalition on the Academic Workforce. 2012. "A Portrait of Part-Time Faculty Members: A Summary of Findings on Part-Time Faculty Respondents to the Coalition on the Academic Workforce Survey of Contingent Faculty Members and Instructors." Accessed December 6, 2015. http://www.academicworkforce.org/CAW_portrait_2012.pdf.

Cox, Bradley E., Kadian L. McIntosh, Patrick T. Terenzini, Robert D. Reason, and Brenda R. L. Quaye. 2010. "Pedagogical Signals of Faculty Approachability: Factors Shaping Faculty-Student Interaction Outside the Classroom." *Research in Higher Education* 51 (8): 767–88.

Cross, John G., and Edie N. Goldenberg. 2011. *Off-Track Profs: Nontenured Teachers in Higher Education.* Cambridge, MA: MIT Press.

Curtis, John W. 2005. "Inequities Persist for Women and Non-Tenure-Track Faculty: Economic Status of the Profession, 2004–05." *Academe,* 91 (2): 19–98.

Darling-Hammond, Linda. 1999. *Teacher Quality and Student Achievement: A Review of State Policy Evidence.* Seattle: Center for the Study of Teaching and Policy, University of Washington.

———. 2008. "Teacher Learning That Supports Student Learning." *Teaching for Intelligence* 2:91–100.

Dayton, Boulaloy, Nancy Gonzalez-Vasquez, Carla R. Martinez, and Caryn Plum. 2004. "Hispanic-Serving Institutions through the Eyes of Students and Administrators." *New Directions for Student Services* 2004 (105): 29–40.

Delphi Project on the Changing Faculty and Student Success. 2014. Home page. Accessed December 6, 2105. http://www.thechangingfaculty.org.

Eagan, M. Kevin, and Audrey J. Jaeger. 2008. "Effects of Exposure to Part-Time Faculty on Community College Transfer." *Research in Higher Education* 50 (2): 361–65.

Eagan, M. Kevin, Audrey J. Jaeger, and Ashley Grantham. 2015. "Supporting the Academic Majority: Policies and Practices Related to Part-Time Faculty's Job Satisfaction." *Journal of Higher Education* 86 (3): 448–83.

Ehrenberg, Ronald G., and Liang Zhang. 2005. "Do Tenured and Tenure-Track Faculty Matter?" *Journal of Human Resources* 40 (3): 647–59.

Elmore, Richard F. 1996. "Getting to Scale with Good Educational Practice." *Harvard Educational Review* 66 (1): 1–27.

Fairweather, James S. 1996. *Faculty Work and Public Trust: Restoring the Value of Teaching and Public Service in American Academic Life.* Needham Heights, MA: Allyn and Bacon.

———. 2002. "The Mythologies of Faculty Productivity: Implications for Institutional Policy and Decision Making." *Journal of Higher Education* 73 (1): 26–48.

Figlio, David N., Morton O. Schapiro, and Kevin B. Soter. 2013. *Are Tenure Track Professors Better Teachers?* Working Paper No. w19406. Cambridge, MA: National Bureau of Economic Research.

Fries-Britt, Sharon, and Bridget Turner. 2002. "Uneven Stories: Successful Black Collegians at a Black and a White Campus." *Review of Higher Education* 25 (3): 315–30.

Gappa, Judith M., and David W. Leslie. 1993. *The Invisible Faculty: Improving the Status of Part-Timers in Higher Education.* San Francisco: Jossey-Bass.

Gross, Betheny, and Daniel D. Goldhaber. 2009. *Community College Transfer and Articulation Policies: Looking beneath the Surface.* Working Paper No. 2009-1. Seattle, WA: Center on Reinventing Public Education.

Harrington, Charles, and Timothy Schibik. 2001. *Caveat Emptor: Is There a Relationship between Part-Time Faculty Utilization and Student Learning Retention?* Professional File No. 91. Tallahassee: Association for Institutional Research.

Himelhoch, Carol R., Adriana Nichols, Steven R. Ball, and Lana C. Black. 1997. "A Comparative Study of the Factors Which Predict Persistence for African American Students at Historically Black Institutions and Predominantly White Institutions." Paper presented at the annual meeting of the Association for the Study of Higher Education, Albuquerque, NM, November.

Hollenshead, Carol, Jean Waltman, Louise August, Jeanne Miller, Gilia Smith, and Allison Bell. 2007. *Making the Best of Both Worlds: Findings from a National Institution-Level Survey on Non-Tenure-Track Faculty.* Ann Arbor, MI: Center for the Education of Women.

Hurtado, Sylvia, Kevin M. Eagan, Minh K. Tran, Christopher B. Newman, Mitchell J. Chang, and Paolo Velasco. 2011. "We Do Science Here: Underrepresented Students' Interactions with Faculty in Different College Contexts." *Journal of Social Issues* 67 (3): 553–79.

Jacoby, Daniel. 2006. "Effects of Part-Time Faculty Employment on Community College Graduation Rates." *Journal of Higher Education* 77 (6): 1081–103.

Jaeger, Audrey J., and M. Kevin Eagan. 2009. "Unintended Consequences: Examining the Effect of Part-Time Faculty Members on Associate's Degree Completion." *Community College Review* 36 (3): 167–94.

Jenney, T. J. 2011. "The Holistic Development of College Students: Spirituality as a Predictor of College Student's Pro-Social Character Development." *Culture & Religion Review Journal* 2011 (4): 56–145.

Johnson, Judith L. 1997. "Commuter College Students: What Factors Determine Who Will Persist and Who Will Drop Out?" *College Student Journal* 31 (3): 323–33.

Kezar, Adrianna. 2013. *Embracing Non-Tenure Track Faculty: Changing Campuses for the New Faculty Majority.* New York: Routledge.

———. 2015. *Adapting by Design: Creating Faculty Roles and Defining Faculty Work to Ensure an Intentional Future for Colleges and Universities.* Los Angeles: Delphi Project on the Changing Faculty and Student Success.

Kezar, Adrianna, and Lara Badke. 2013. *The Imperative for Change: Fostering Understanding of the Necessity of Changing Non-Tenure Track Faculty Policies and Practices.* Los Angeles: Delphi Project on the Changing Faculty and Student Success.

Kezar, Adrianna, and Daniel Maxey. 2013. *Review of Selected Policies and Practices and Connections to Student Learning.* Los Angeles: Delphi Project on the Changing Faculty and Student Success.

Kezar, Adrianna, and Cecile Sam. 2010. *Understanding the New Majority: Contingent Faculty in Higher Education.* ASHE Higher Education Report 36 (4). Hoboken, NJ: Jossey-Bass.

Komarraju, Meera, Sergey Musulkin, and Gargi Bhattacharya. 2010. "Role of Student-Faculty Interactions in Developing College Students' Academic Self-Concept, Motivation, and Achievement." *Journal of College Student Development* 51 (3): 332–42.

Kuh, George D. 1995. "The Other Curriculum: Out-of-Class Experiences Associated with Student Learning and Personal Development." *Journal of Higher Education* 66 (2): 123–55.

———. 2003. "What We're Learning about Student Engagement from NSSE: Benchmarks for Effective Educational practices." *Change* 35 (2): 24–32.

Kuh, George D., Brian Bridges, and John C. Hayek. 2006. *What Matters to Student Success?* Washington: National Postsecondary Education Cooperative.

Kuh, George D., and Shouping Hu. 2001. "The Effects of Student-Faculty Interaction in the 1990's." *Review of Higher Education* 24 (3): 309–32.

Light, Richard J. 2001. *Making the Most of College: Students Speak their Minds.* Cambridge, MA: Harvard University Press.

Lundberg, Carol A., and Laurie A. Schreiner. 2004. "Quality and Frequency of Faculty-Student Interaction as Predictors of Learning: An Analysis by Student Race/Ethnicity." *Journal of College Student Development* 45 (5): 549–65.

Lundquist, Cara, Rebecca J. Spalding, and R. Eric Landrum. 2003. "College Student's Thoughts about Leaving the University: The Impact of Faculty Attitudes and Behaviors." *College Student Retention Research, Theory & Practice* 4 (2): 123–33.

Marits, Edward J. 1996. "Professional Development of Adjunct Faculty." In *The Adjunct Faculty Handbook,* edited by Virginia Bianco-Mathis and Neal Chalofsky, 221–26. Thousand Oaks, CA: Sage.

Martin, Linda M. 2000. "The Relationship of College Experiences to Psychosocial Outcomes in Students." *Journal of College Student Development* 41 (3): 292–301.

Massy, William F., and Robert Zemsky. 1994. "Faculty Discretionary Time: Departments and the Academic Ratchet." *Journal of Higher Education* 65 (1):1–22.

O'Meara, KerryAnn, and R. Eugene Rice. 2005. *Faculty Priorities Reconsidered: Rewarding Multiple Forms of Scholarship.* San Francisco: Jossey-Bass.

Pascarella, Ernest T. 1980. "Student-Faculty Informal Contact and College Outcomes." *Review of Educational Research* 50 (4): 545–95.

Pascarella, Ernest T., and Patrick T. Terenzini. 1978. "Student-Faculty Informal Relationships and Freshman Year Educational Outcomes." *Journal of Educational Research* 71 (4): 183–89.

Rhoades, Gary. 1998. *Managed Professionals: Unionized Faculty and Restructuring Academic Labor.* Albany: State University of New York Press.

Rutz, Carol, William Condon, Ellen R. Iverson, Cathryn A. Manduca, and Gudrun Willett. 2012. "Faculty Professional Development and Student Learning: What Is the Relationship?" *Change* 44 (3): 40–47.

Sax, Linda J., Alyssa N. Bryant, and Casandra E. Harper. 2005. "The Differential Effects of Student-Faculty Interaction on College Outcomes for Women and Men." *Journal of College Student Development* 46 (6): 642–57.

Schuster, Jack H., and Martin J. Finkelstein. 2006. *The American Faculty: The Restructuring of Academic Work and Careers.* Baltimore, MD: Johns Hopkins University Press.

Shaker, Genevieve, ed. 2014. *Faculty Work and the Public Good.* New York: Teachers College Press.

Smallwood, Scott. 2002. "Me and My Professor: Oxford Style Tutorials." *Chronicle of Higher Education*, February 15.

Smith, Barbara Leigh. 1988. "The Washington Center: A Grass Roots Approach to Faculty Development and Curricular Reform." *To Improve the Academy*, paper 158.

Toutkoushian, Robert K., and Marcia L. Bellas. 2003. "The Effects of Part-Time Employment and Gender on Faculty Earnings and Satisfaction: Evidence from the NSOPF: 93." *Journal of Higher Education* 74 (2): 172–95.

Umbach, Paul D. 2007. "How Effective Are They? Exploring the Impact of Contingent Faculty on Undergraduate Education." *Review of Higher Education* 30 (2): 91–123.

Umbach, Paul D., and Matthew R. Wawrzynski. 2005. "Faculty Do Matter: The Role of College Faculty in Student Learning and Engagement." *Research in Higher Education* 46 (2): 153–84.

Wang, Huiming, and Judith Wilson Grimes. 2001. "A Systematic Approach to Assessing Retention Programs: Identifying Critical Points for Meaningful Interventions and Validating Outcomes Assessment." *College Student Retention Research, Theory & Practice* 2 (1): 59–68.

Wawrzynski, Matthew R., and Jane Elizabeth Pizzolato. 2006. "Predicting Needs: A Longitudinal Investigation of the Relation between Student Characteristics, Academic Paths, and Self-Authorship." *Journal of College Student Development* 47 (6): 677–92.

PART TWO

Ideas for a New Faculty Model

3

An Emerging Consensus about New Faculty Roles

Results of a National Study of Higher Education Stakeholders

ADRIANNA KEZAR

ELIZABETH HOLCOMBE

DANIEL MAXEY

One of the reasons why new faculty models have not emerged is that there has been little discussion or perceived agreement about what future faculty roles might be. To exacerbate these problems, stereotypes that different stakeholder groups have of each other often prevent meaningful discussion. Faculty commonly believe that administrators want to eradicate tenure and make all faculty part-time and deprofessionalized, whereas administrators believe that faculty are intractably attached to tenure and unwilling to examine any other possible arrangements. Certainly these stereotypes are based on some real practices, as shown by statements from the American Association of University Professors (AAUP) about the eradication of tenure and various administrators' repeated decisions to hire fewer tenure-track faculty and enormous numbers of part-time faculty over the past several decades (Kezar and Sam 2010). We do not mean to belittle these perspectives or suggest that they are not based on some evidence. However, in our conversations with various stakeholder groups over the past decade we have come to see that these stereotypes and perspectives may be overstated, and that levels of agreement about future directions for faculty might be higher than some groups in the academic enterprise think.

To test these assumptions, we developed a survey and administered it to some key stakeholder groups in higher education: disciplinary societies; groups that represent part- and full-time non-tenure-track and tenure-track faculty; academic unions; groups representing academic leaders (provosts and deans), such as the American Council on Education, Council of Independent Colleges, and Council of Colleges of Arts and Sciences;

policymaking groups such as the State Higher Education Executive Officers; board members; and accreditors. In this chapter, we present the results of this survey, which suggest several key areas of agreement in thinking about future faculty roles. We first present some information about the background of the survey.

Survey Study

To better understand higher education stakeholders' perspectives about future faculty models, we developed and conducted a survey in the fall of 2014 and spring of 2015. We first reviewed the literature on new faculty models and new employment models in other professional fields and then identified examples of new faculty models on campuses that could inform the survey design. We collected potential alternative models to test, some theoretical and some already existing in the field. These models included creativity contracts, Ernest Boyer's work on *Scholarship Reconsidered* (1990), Evergreen State's interdisciplinary model, and alternative faculty models in medical schools (see chapter 5).

Our goal was to get various key stakeholders to envision the future of the faculty and to see if we might build consensus around a more effective model that could meet the needs of faculty, administrators, institutions, and students. Our survey included thirty-nine items focused on eight key areas related to faculty roles: faculty pathways; contracts; unbundling of faculty roles; status in the academic community; faculty development, promotion, and evaluation; flexibility; collaboration and community engagement; and public good roles. The survey was designed to capture whether stakeholders found the models presented to be both attractive and feasible: we wanted to know both whether they found the model a positive future direction and whether they thought it might be possible to implement it. We also gave respondents the opportunity to provide open-ended responses in every section of the survey, with the particular goal of understanding any gaps between attractiveness and feasibility. We received several thousand comments in response.

Our total sample consisted of 1,553 respondents (see table 3.1). We conducted descriptive and trend data analysis about similarities and differences in stakeholder views. We also examined for differences by institutional type (for example, public versus private institutions, and two-year versus four-year ones). In this chapter, we do not review differences by institutional type, though there were actually very few such differences. We also analyzed the open-ended survey responses, which as noted above numbered in the thousands. Open-ended responses were particularly important in understanding the gaps between attractiveness and feasibility of the faculty models in the survey.

TABLE 3.1

Survey Respondents by Stakeholder Group

Stakeholder group	No. of respondents
Accreditors	23
Deans	81
Faculty: tenured or tenure-track	904
Faculty: full-time non-tenure-track	199
Faculty: part-time non-tenure-track	131
Governing board members	20
Provosts	188
State higher education executive officers	7
TOTAL	1,553

In addition, the open-ended comments helped us understand the attractiveness or lack of appeal of certain aspects of the models.

An Emerging Consensus

Restoring Professionalism to the Faculty Role

The greatest consensus in our survey had to do with the idea that the faculty role should remain a professional one. Professionals are typically defined as individuals who are involved in decision making, have ongoing professional development, and have some level of autonomy (Gappa, Austin, and Trice 2007; Sullivan 2005. In higher education, professionalism has been related to academic freedom, which has historically been linked to tenure. Related to the notion of professionalism is the idea that a faculty role should be a career. Careers are typically characterized as having promotion opportunities, job security, defined expectations and rigorous evaluation, decent compensation, and ongoing learning (Sullivan 2005). Given the way that faculty goals have been redefined in recent years, we wanted to explore whether there was agreement around this idea of retaining (or restoring) the professional status and career role of faculty. With the exception of tenure, which we discuss in the final section of this chapter, there was great support for all areas related to the professionalism of the faculty role.

There was almost uniform agreement among all stakeholders in our survey on all the items related to ensuring that faculty members have academic freedom, equitable compensation and access to benefits, involvement in shared governance, access to resources needed to perform their role, opportunities for promotion, clearly defined expectations and evaluation criteria, clear notification of contract renewal as well as grievance processes, and continuous professional development. This level of support is at odds with hiring practices over the past twenty years that have moved away from the professionalization of faculty. Currently, many faculty have no academic freedom, poor pay, no opportunities for promotion, no involvement in shared governance, no access to professional development, limited or no evaluation, and little access to basic information or the tools they need to do their work (Gappa, Austin, and Trice 2007; Kezar and Sam 2010).

Given the overwhelming support by all stakeholders for the restoration of professionalism to the faculty role, with academic freedom and the other benefits mentioned above, it seems important to have meaningful discussions about why our practices fall so short of what we believe should be occurring. Perhaps there should also be discussions about what it means to have a professional role and a career in today's environment, and how that role and career might look different than they did in the past. One potential difference that comes to mind is related to faculty autonomy, which has traditionally given faculty members the freedom to define their own research agendas and work activities, along with a host of other conditions; in practice, however, faculty autonomy has often come at the expense of student success, the creation of quality learning environments, meaningful service, and strong research outcomes (Boyer 1990; Shaker 2014). Faculty as professionals in today's environment may need to emphasize working collectively toward community, institutional, or departmental goals, since it is unclear how well autonomy has served the academic enterprise as a whole. Redefining aspects of what it means to be a professional in academia might help muster greater support for the professional faculty role moving forward.

A Way Forward: Reduce Dependence on Part-Time Faculty by Focusing on Full-Time Employment

Stakeholders' strong agreement with proposals about restoring the professionalism of the faculty role is likely to be a result of the increasing deprofessionalization of the faculty role in practice over the past several decades, mentioned above and throughout this book. Specifically, the number of part-time faculty has increased across all institutional types over the past three decades, and those faculty now make up over 50 percent of instructional faculty nationally (National Center for Education Statistics 2013). Our survey responses suggest that there is significant agreement across all groups that we should increase the use of full-time non-tenure-track appointments to reduce the reliance on part-time faculty. This agreement represents an opportunity and points to a key area in which to begin discussions of changes in the current system. Increasing full-time non-tenure track appointments could be a good step toward restoring professionalism to the faculty role. Open-ended comments support these findings and suggest that academic leaders are beginning to think strategically about hiring more full-time faculty. Current full-time non-tenure track faculty members themselves also commented about the value of their positions, which have some of the hallmarks of professionalism and career described above. One full-time non-tenure-track faculty member said: "I hold a non-tenurable, full-time, continuing position, with health and retirement benefits. It isn't perfect, but it is a pretty darn good situation. I'm also more fortunate than most anyone else I know who is not on a tenure track."

Another creative way of moving away from the part-time faculty model would be to have more consortium agreements through which several institutions would jointly employ a single part-time faculty member so that person could have a full-time teaching position. Our survey respondents strongly supported this proposal, though many noted its limitations for certain institutions—such as those that are geographically isolated. For other institutions, consortium agreements could represent a creative alternative when hiring full-time faculty is not realistic, such as in a very specialized curricular area or for a very small program. For those situations in which faculty may be employed for their narrow expertise, consortium arrangements could provide a more ethical and professional employment model while reducing some of the negative effects associated with large numbers of part-time faculty.

Differentiated Faculty Roles

A broad consensus also emerged around the idea of creating more differentiated faculty roles. This idea emerges from the fact that different institutions have different missions, and that even single institutions have departments or programs that are each targeted at different aspects of the university's mission. Such diversity is one of the hallmarks of the American higher education system. Despite this diversity, the faculty role has historically been defined largely by a single model: tenured; research-oriented even at institutions that do not have a research mission; but simultaneously involved in teaching, research, and service. Stakeholders in our survey recognized this apparent disconnect between institutional diversity and a limited model for faculty work and agreed that faculty work should be more differentiated in the future.

We asked specifically about the attractiveness of the model in Boyer's *Scholarship Reconsidered* (1990), in which scholarship is more broadly defined to encompass teaching and research on teaching, institutional service and community engagement, and more varied forms of research that include synthesis and applied research as well as the more traditionally common pure "discovery" research. Parts of Boyer's proposal have already been adopted across the higher education enterprise, although in varying degrees from one institution to the next. The data from our survey suggest that there is strong agreement that an effort to continue working toward the ideal set forth by Boyer should be a priority.

We also asked about creativity contracts, which give faculty members opportunities to experience highly customized and continuously changing roles. Creativity contracts allow faculty to customize the way they focus their work based on both their expertise and institutional needs. For example, early in a faculty member's career she may want to focus on research, but later she may find herself interested in focusing on teaching, and perhaps later still choose to engage in scholarship on teaching. Each group agreed that giving faculty members the ability to negotiate their involvement in a variety of roles over the course of their careers is an important feature to consider for future faculty models, rather than the narrower foci and largely unchanging roles that are part of current faculty work today.

In addition, there was strong support from stakeholders for providing multiple pathways or tracks for faculty members to pursue appointments that focus their primary, long-term responsibilities in a particular area, such as research, teaching, or professional or clinical practice. This option would be more fixed than the creativity contracts described above, but it would still provide an alternative to the dominant research role that has characterized the faculty of the past and would be aligned with the value that stakeholders place on more differentiated faculty models. This value is seen again in response to a survey question asking about adding teaching-only tenured positions to the faculty. There was support for this proposition as well, though it is important to note that tenure-track faculty and provosts were less supportive than other groups.

Lastly, there was general agreement that institutions should revise their incentive and reward structures and policies to better reflect these different institutional priorities. More customized reward structures could be aligned with teaching, research, or community service and engagement profiles. Again, this supports the ideas of greater differentiation and changing institutional structures to support that differentiation.

Each of the stakeholder groups that we surveyed seemed to agree that a more flexible faculty role will be important to the faculty of the future rather than the very narrow and singular track that is part of current roles. However, it is important to note that while all groups supported differentiation, they were not supportive of unbundling the faculty role in other ways that have been emerging across the academic enterprise. For example, there was no interest across any of the stakeholder groups in having more educational professionals such as so-called paraprofessionals supporting teaching or instruction, or for the teaching role to be unbundled and distributed among curriculum developers, course designers, and outcomes assessment offices. These responses and accompanying comments indicate that increasing the differentiation of faculty roles must be undertaken with care: the faculty role must not become so fragmented that it loses its focus on teaching—one of the key ways in which it supports institutional missions.

The Importance of Teaching

Responses to several propositions supported an increased emphasis on the role of faculty as teachers, including the creation of teaching-only tenure-track positions, supporting ongoing professional development in pedagogy and teaching practice, and fostering a greater faculty focus on teaching and student development. Teaching is a key part of every institution's mission, and the faculty role of the future must make space to emphasize and honor the teaching role to a greater degree. Proposals to this effect, including introducing teaching-only tenure positions, have been circulated in recent years (Bérubé and Ruth 2015), and our findings suggest that exploring these options and further developing this idea might be a worthwhile endeavor.

Scholarship as a Core Element of New Faculty Roles

Despite the strong support that we found for increased differentiation in faculty roles, our survey responses indicated that scholarship must remain a core element of the faculty role regardless of how differentiated roles become. There was strong interest in supporting all faculty who teach, regardless of rank or contract type, to conduct scholarship. This blend of teaching and scholarship is at the core of what makes the faculty role unique and distinguishes it both from teaching at the K–12 level and from pure research. One comment from a state higher education executive officer helped bring home the importance of this issue: "Teaching faculty have to have some way to stay current. 'Scholarship' as it is traditionally defined is probably not the best way to insure [sic] this happens, but something needs to take its place. While participation in research may not be the best way to keep faculty up-to-date, it does help."

We see scholarship as a continuous process of learning, so that faculty continue to hone their expertise and specialization over the course of their career. Like the notion of being a professional, being a scholar may need some redefinition moving forward, and the interest of our respondents in many proposals related to Boyer's *Scholarship Reconsidered* (1990) suggests that there is a potential base of support for this redefinition. Scholarship could be defined more broadly as gaining expertise in how people learn and the best ways to teach or expertise in working with community groups to solve complex problems, in addition to the traditional form of expertise related to conducting a particular type of research. We hope to encourage discussions about the various ways for faculty to have a scholarly role regardless of their particular focus or specialty.

Flexibility

In addition to the more differentiated or flexible faculty roles described above, stakeholders indicated that more flexible working arrangements could be an attractive component of future faculty models. Traditional faculty careers have been designed in a very linear and singular fashion: tenure-track faculty members typically proceed through seven years to tenure and then have opportunities for promotions at standardized intervals. Individuals often need—and desire—more flexible arrangements to meet their various personal and professional responsibilities, particularly to seek greater work-life balance or to respond to life challenges that demand their attention. There was broad support for granting greater flexibility for tenure-track faculty members' pathways, such as allowing them to stop the tenure clock or move to part-time appointments while caring for children and other family members. There was also support for greater flexibility for faculty to address personal needs on campus by offering access to a variety of services such as child care, dry cleaners, or meal plans. These types of arrangements are becoming more common in other sectors, such as the technology sector, to boost morale and allow employees to channel more energy into their work. Offering such flexibility could allow faculty members to meet personal and professional obligations while also improving overall faculty productivity and benefiting the mission and operations of the institution.

Collaboration and Community Engagement

In recent years there has been concern about whether faculty are connected enough to their local, regional, and state communities and are supporting public interests more broadly (Shaker 2014). Historically, faculty have had an uneven connection to external communities. Land grant institutions have a long history of engaging with local communities in the areas of extension, agriculture, and local service, but many other institutions have remained largely disconnected from their communities (Shaker 2014). We asked survey respondents about collaboration because there have been increasing calls for more interdisciplinary work and collaboration among faculty in their teaching, research, and important regional service (Kezar and Lester 2009).

Given higher education's historically uneven connection to the community, the near universal agreement across stakeholder groups about the importance of community outreach and partnerships was quite striking. All groups generally supported increasing the amount of faculty members' collaboration and community engagement. Support was strongest across all groups for interdisciplinary collaborations and community engagement through activities such as service learning, participatory research, and voluntary service. Academic leaders and policymakers were extremely supportive of faculty engagement with external groups. Faculty were less supportive of this idea than other stakeholders, although they still supported it. In addition, all stakeholder groups saw a greater role for faculty in collaborating across the institution. This suggests a change in current faculty arrangements, which are mostly embedded in their disciplinary contexts.

The Faculty and the Public Good

As institutions focus more on instrumental goals of credentialing students, generating revenue, and winning grants, we thought it was important to explore if stakeholders—particularly board members, policymakers, and academic leaders—felt that faculty should still play a role in serving the public good. Traditionally, this role has been defined by core areas such as being a social critic, conducting research on controversial issues, developing citizenship among students, making research available to the public, and supporting low-income and first-generation college students (Kezar, Chambers, and Burkhardt 2005).

There was near-universal agreement among stakeholder groups that faculty should be encouraged to support low-income and first-generation college students. While not explicitly stated in the survey item, ways that faculty could provide such support include sponsoring undergraduate research, mentoring, and participating in bridge programs or first-year college experiences. There was also relatively strong support for faculty to be encouraged and rewarded for playing a role as social critics and doing research on controversial issues. While there was less support for other proposals related to the public good, such as fostering citizenship among students and conducting more open-access research, the open-ended comments we received suggested that our questions may not have captured many of the local ways that serving the public good is defined. It is important that individual institutions explore how faculty roles are defined in ways that serve the public good.

Feasibility

In addition to evaluating the attractiveness of aspects of new faculty models, groups were also asked to consider whether a particular practice was feasible. There were practices that many stakeholder groups considered feasible, such as those related to professionalizing the faculty and to faculty development, promotion, and evaluation. For example, most groups agreed on the attractiveness and feasibility of ensuring that all faculty members have access to the tools and information necessary to do their jobs, clearly defined expectations and evaluation criteria, and clear terms for contract renewal or termination and processes for addressing grievances and violations of academic freedom. In other words, most stakeholders surveyed believe that these basic requirements of faculty working conditions are both necessary and feasible to implement. However, other areas of the survey revealed gaps between stakeholders' interest in a particular statement and their belief that it would be feasible to implement. We found feasibility gaps in some of the survey items that garnered the highest levels of support, such as creativity contracts, Boyer's model, consortium arrangements, and other proposals related to flexibility. The open-ended responses suggested that the main reasons feasibility fell below attractiveness for these items were due to concerns about their logistical complexities or budgetary implications:

> For small liberal arts colleges like mine, the options that require specialization of roles and those that require frequent renegotiation would present both logistical and political problems.
>
> —Comment from a provost

> Unfortunately the Boyer model is incredibly hard to operationalize and can easily become an "anything goes" approach.
>
> —Comment from a dean

> At our public institution, it would be difficult to find the money for most of these things. Great ideas, probably impossible to implement.
>
> —Comment from a part-time non-tenure-track faculty member

Surely any major changes to the faculty role will have logistical complexities and budgetary implications. However, as discussed elsewhere in this book, financial constraints might be less salient than is widely thought, and campuses have dealt with equally complex problems related to multiple and differentiated faculty roles in the past. It appears that the bureaucratic complexity of new faculty models is an issue that needs more research and visionary thinking among academic leaders. This issue should be prioritized so that viable approaches can be developed.

Some Hot-Button Issues to Consider

While we wanted to focus our chapter on those areas where there were points of consensus, there were also some items on the survey where stakeholders were much more divided. It is important to briefly mention them, as they may be hot-button issues that campus leaders should be sure to address carefully. At a minimum, these are areas to be aware of because they may spark difficult discussions.

There were several proposals about which stakeholders disagreed. Tenured faculty and deans saw phasing out tenure as a very negative proposition, while non-tenure-track faculty and other groups saw it as either attractive or neutral. It is not surprising that there were very different perspectives, given stakeholders' different relationships to and experiences with tenure.

A second proposal that generated mixed levels of support was the idea of differentiated faculty roles being associated with particular institutional types: for example, all liberal arts college faculty would focus chiefly on teaching, and all research university faculty would focus mostly on research. While board members and state-level policymakers indicated some support for this idea, most institutional stakeholders rejected it, indicating concerns about exacerbating existing institutional hierarchies or competitions for status.

A third area of disagreement was having faculty more closely align their work to departmental and institutional needs rather than faculty career goals. Board members, policymakers, and academic leaders were in favor of this, while faculty of all types opposed it. As noted above, there is a lot of data suggesting that not having faculty work collaboratively has been detrimental to efforts to attain institutional and departmental goals, so this is likely an area that needs to be addressed. However, faculty autonomy has long been an important value in academe. Conversations about future faculty roles need to take into consideration this historical vestige while also including arguments about why more alignment with department and institutional goals might be important.

One additional proposal that was not an area of disagreement but was notable for its universal lack of support was termed tenure appointments, in which a faculty member would be given tenure but for only a certain amount of time, such as fifteen to twenty years. We feel that this is still a viable option and one way to save tenure from being eradicated, but the open-ended survey comments suggested it is not well understood. Some faculty indicated concerns that it would effectively do away with tenure, while other stakeholders noted that it is too like the current tenure system to be a feasible alternative.

Conclusion

Despite some of the hot-button issues noted above, there appear to be many areas of agreement about future faculty roles that provide a way forward. Campus leaders need to make it a priority to reprofessionalize faculty roles, as this is the greatest area of agreement among stakeholders. One way of reprofessionalizing is to move from relying on part-time faculty to more full-time employment models. There are a variety of ways to conduct this work, including hiring full-time non-tenure-track faculty, hiring more tenure-track faculty, and creating consortium arrangements to fully employ part-time faculty.

Additionally, there is clear support for greater flexibility and differentiation of roles, though there is some concern about differentiation being determined by institutional type or leading to an erosion of the core elements of teaching and scholarship. The importance of agreement around differentiation is that it allows faculty members to have much more expansive roles that match the broad mission and goals of the higher education enterprise. This bodes well for the enterprise, which has long had very differentiated missions and goals but a singular faculty model. The strong support for maintaining a scholarly role for all faculty suggests that we need some deep thinking about ways to support faculty learning and expertise that goes beyond involvement in disciplinary societies, which are currently the main avenue for scholarly development. Or it may mean that disciplinary societies need to change to match the new and different needs of faculty who may not conduct scholarship as discovery in the same way as they have in the past.

The embracing of collaborative work and community engagement is aligned with recent changes in the environment in which academic work takes place. It is encouraging to see the agreement among stakeholders and suggests clear areas for redesigning faculty roles. And while the role of increasing the public good was not universally approved or as attractive as the roles related to collaborative work or community engagement, it still remains an area that many stakeholders feel is important to the overall faculty role. We suspect that this issue is more locally defined than our global questions were able to capture.

In the end, we feel our survey suggests that productive conversations about faculty roles are possible and that stakeholders have much more in common than they disagree about regarding the way forward. Stakeholders are willing to address the problems noted in chapter 2, including the deprofessionaliza-tion of faculty in the adjunct model, the need for more full-time faculty, the importance of faculty positions aimed at teaching and of differentiated faculty roles to meet higher education's diverse missions, and altered incentives and reward structures. What we need now are courageous stakeholders to lead such conversations so that we can move from the poor models of faculty that have emerged over the past two decades to more efficacious models that support student learning, institutional missions, and faculty vitality. Many detailed rec-ommendations for what this might look like are presented in the chapters that follow. Join us in exploring what the professional faculty career of the future might look like, how collaboration may become more prominent, and how we might better support students through a greater faculty role in advising or as pedagogical experts.

REFERENCES

Bérubé, Michael, and Jennifer Ruth. 2015. *The Humanities, Higher Education, and Academic Freedom: Three Necessary Arguments*. London: Palgrave Macmillan.

Boyer, Ernest L. 1990. *Scholarship Reconsidered: Priorities of the Professoriate*. San Francisco: Jossey-Bass.

Gappa, Judith M., Ann E. Austin, and Andrea G. Trice. 2007. *Rethinking Faculty Work: Higher Education's Strategic Imperative*. San Francisco: Jossey-Bass.

Kezar, Adrianna, Anthony C. Chambers, and John C. Burkhardt, eds. 2005. *Higher Education for the Public Good: Emerging Voices from a National Movement*. San Francisco: Jossey-Bass.

Kezar, Adrianna, and Jamie Lester. 2009. *Organizing for Collaboration in Higher Education: A Guide for Campus Leaders*. San Francisco: Jossey-Bass.

Kezar, Adrianna, and Cecile Sam. 2010. *Understanding the New Majority: Contingent Faculty in Higher Education*. ASHE Higher Education Report 36 (4). Hoboken, NJ: Jossey-Bass.

National Center for Education Statistics. 2013. *Integrated Postsecondary Education Data System*. Washington: Department of Education.

Shaker, Genevieve, ed. 2014. *Faculty Work and the Public Good*. New York: Teachers College Press.

Sullivan, William M. 2005. *Work and Integrity: The Crisis and Promise of Professionalism in America*. San Francisco: Jossey-Bass.

4

Core Principles for Faculty Models and the Importance of Community

ANN E. AUSTIN

ANDREA G. TRICE

For anyone who is looking for challenge and opportunity, higher education is the place to be in the early decades of the twenty-first century. A long list of forces and factors are pressing on higher education institutions and transforming the nature of academic work. These include demands from societal stakeholders for heightened accountability and productivity, volatile fiscal constraints, a changing student body bringing a range of needs and expectations to their academic pursuits, the deepening of knowledge about human learning, the burgeoning research supporting calls for pedagogies that encourage active learning, the possibilities as well as uncertainties accompanying the availability of new technologies, the exponential rate of knowledge expansion, and the opportunities for global connections that enrich research and teaching. As the workforce that carries out the missions of higher education institutions, the faculty is directly affected by these forces and factors. Along with changes in the nature, pace, location, and organization of academic work, a dramatic shift is occurring in the structure of academic appointments. The traditional tenure-track faculty appointment is no longer the norm. Academic appointment patterns across institutional types are shifting from full-time tenure-track positions toward part-time, fixed-term, contingent, and renewable non-tenure-track positions.

The creativity and commitment of faculty members and the quality of their work are essential factors in the ability of universities and colleges to fulfill the responsibilities to society represented in their missions. The faculty of an institution is the means through which its missions are accomplished. Envisioning models of faculty work for the twenty-first century that are workable, attractive, and effective is a critically important undertaking for everyone involved in the higher education enterprise today. In today's context, full-time tenure-track positions exist alongside a variety of non-tenure-track and part-time arrangements, and such an array of appointment types is likely to characterize the professoriate of the future. Thus, envisioning an approach to faculty work that is relevant to the changing context and future developments is a compelling issue. A few years ago, we took up this task, along with our colleague Judith Gappa, in our book *Rethinking Faculty Work: Higher Education's Strategic Imperative*. We wrote that "rethinking faculty work and workplaces is the wise strategic choice for colleges and university in the twenty-first century. The work of the faculty is essential to the excellence and effectiveness of higher education institutions," with their missions of creating new knowledge, supporting and facilitating student learning, and applying cutting-edge knowledge to the vexing problems confronting society (Gappa, Austin, and Trice 2007, 11).

Our work explored new approaches to and models for faculty careers and workplaces in the twenty-first century, given the diversity of faculty characteristics, the major shifts in faculty appointment types, and the new challenges and expectations affecting the nature of faculty work. We examined ways in which the structure of academic work could simultaneously support both institutional missions in service to society and the needs of individual faculty members. To help us in rethinking approaches to faculty work and envisioning new ones, we sought out and highlighted innovative institutional policies and practices that other institutions grappling with this issue could use as models. The project resulted in our developing a "Framework of Essential Elements" for institutional use in creating new approaches to faculty work (Gappa, Austin, and Trice 2007, 234), an extensive array of specific institutional examples of ways to create approaches and models for faculty work that address a range of appointment types (including full-time and part-time, as well as tenure-track, permanent, and temporary appointments), and an argument for the development of a reciprocal contract to define faculty work across flexible appointment types. Throughout our work, we were informed by several guiding principles: (1) a commitment to including key features of academic work that historically have contributed to the respect accorded faculty members in American higher education; (2) recognition that to be relevant and useful, any framework must address the diversity of individuals and appointment types now characterizing faculty work in US higher education and likely to do so in the future; (3) attention to the literature on the sociology of work and to research on work satisfaction, morale, organizational commitment, and productivity, as well as to the literature specifically on faculty work and careers; (4) interest in developing a framework that would be useful to higher education institutions immediately, while also being sufficiently robust and flexible to be relevant in coming years as new challenges and changes confront higher education institutions; and (5) responsiveness to the suggestions of higher education scholars, institutional

leaders, and faculty members who contributed to the refinement and validation of our framework.

We do not believe a single model of faculty work for the twenty-first century is likely to emerge or is reasonable in the dynamic higher education environment. Thus, rather than a single model, we offered a framework for faculty
work that highlights essential elements that we argued should be incorporated
into all types of faculty appointments, providing the key ingredients for supporting faculty members in doing work that both meets their personal needs
and interests and is relevant to the missions of the institutions they serve. The
resulting framework recognized the complex array of faculty appointments that
have emerged and that we expect will continue to characterize work within
academe, and it called for the incorporation of the essential elements into the
work of each faculty member, regardless of appointment type. This approach
is a vision for how faculty work can be organized as higher education moves
forward; it is not a description of higher education at present, at least not for
many faculty members. Using the framework as a guide, institutions can create
a range of arrangements for faculty work that are appropriate for their particular faculty members and their institutional contexts and missions.

Drawing on our earlier work as well as our ongoing thinking, this chapter
is organized in the following way:

- First, we propose that new approaches to faculty work be based on a fresh
  conceptualization of the relationship between the faculty member and the
  employing institution, defined as a reciprocal, two-way relationship that
  includes benefits and responsibilities for both the individual faculty
  member and the institution and that is relevant for all faculty members,
  regardless of employment type.
- Second, we explain the "Framework of Essential Elements" to be provided in
  faculty work, offering it as a set of underlying core principles relevant to all
  approaches to or models of faculty work that may emerge. We offer practical
  examples of ways in which each essential element can be used to create an
  array of approaches to faculty work (including full-time and part-time positions, as well as a range of tenure-track and non-tenure-track appointments).
  If institutions incorporated these elements into all faculty appointments
  (which is far from the current situation in US higher education), both diverse
  institutional priorities and individual faculty interests would be served.
- Third, we envision that the new reciprocal contract between faculty
  members and employing institutions would involve collective action and
  collaborative communities, rather than the more typical individualistic
  approaches to faculty work that are currently prevalent in academe. Such
  collaborative action, we suggest, is at the heart of the efforts needed to
  bring about a major shift in approaches to faculty work. Furthermore,

a workplace in which faculty members work collaboratively and each enjoys the essential elements of academic work, regardless of his or her appointment type, is likely to contribute to faculty satisfaction and institutional commitment and, thus, to the greater fulfillment of institutions' missions in service to society.

Defining a New Relationship between Faculty Member and Employing Institution

For many years, the ideal faculty employment situation has been defined by the notion of the tenure relationship, which was codified in a statement of the American Association of University Professors (1940). At the center of tenure is an understood, reciprocal, and mutually beneficial relationship between faculty members and the institutions that employ them. In our book, we explained: "Tenured faculty members were guaranteed job security, autonomy in the exercise of their responsibilities, and academic freedom at their institutions. In exchange, faculty members made long-term commitments to their institutions, used their intellectual capital for the benefit of their academic communities and society, and assumed responsibility for academic decision making in an environment of shared governance" (Gappa, Austin, and Trice 2007, 129–30). While we greatly value the tenure relationship, we also recognize that the percentage of faculty members who enjoy such a relationship is declining significantly. The likelihood of a national swing back to a highly tenured faculty is small. Rather, we are seeing the bifurcation of the faculty into those who enjoy the benefits of tenure and those who do not. In such a scenario, those without tenure face job uncertainty and instability, lack of protections for academic freedom, and minimal levels of workplace support and benefits.

Recognizing the reality of this shift away from tenure-track positions toward contract and short-term positions, we have grappled with ways to preserve the key elements intended to be protected by tenure, including academic freedom and some degree of job security, for the many faculty members in full-time and part-time positions that are not defined by the tenure relationship. We have offered a new conceptualization of the relationship that defines faculty work, one that requires responsibility from and provides benefits to both individual faculty members and their employing institutions (Gappa, Austin, and Trice 2007). For those without tenure, this relationship would be defined not by the expectations and guidelines of the tenure system, but by a commitment on the part of the individual faculty member and the employing institution to reciprocal responsibilities and mutual support. In other words, such a relationship would emphasize that, while employed by a university or college, faculty members have a responsibility to support their institutions' missions in service to society through their creativity, intellectual contributions, good work, and participation in institutional governance. The responsibility of the higher education institution, in turn, is to provide respect, protections for academic freedom and autonomy, opportunities for collegiality, flexibility, and job security for the defined time period of the faculty member's employment contract. Ideally, this relationship would involve multiyear contracts (for those in full-time or part-time positions), rather than very short-term employment. Institutions would also have the responsibility to enhance the likelihood of faculty members' job security by offering them professional development opportunities that would deepen and expand their professional skills. This new relationship would be characterized by both reciprocity and mutuality—that is, it would provide benefits for faculty employee and employing institution, while also requiring them to honor their mutual responsibilities. Such a conceptualization of the defining relationship between faculty member and employing institution would also contribute to a collaborative and collegial approach to the work within academic units in colleges and universities, since each faculty member would be recognized as making an important contribution to the collective responsibilities of fulfilling institutional missions.

Respect is at the heart of the reciprocal and mutual relationship that we recommend should define faculty work in the twenty-first century. We define *respect* as "the basic human valuing of every faculty member" (Gappa, Austin, and Trice 2007, 139), and we assert that respect is an entitlement that should be enjoyed by every employee in any workplace. The placement of respect as the core essential element is informed by theories of motivation and job satisfaction (Alderfer 1972; Herzberg 1966; Maslow 1970) that explain the importance of intrinsic factors in how employees assess their work satisfaction. Additionally, research on work in the corporate sector points to respect as a foundational need of employees (Campbell and Koblenz 1997). Employees expect respect, and without a culture of respect in a workplace, other benefits cannot be fully appreciated. In academe, for example, research on part-time faculty shows that they often do not feel respected and valued; the absence of respect undermines their sense of belonging and satisfaction and contributes to feelings of marginalization (Gappa and Leslie 1993; Kezar and Sam 2011). The reciprocal and mutually beneficial relationship that we advocate would diminish the frustrations and perceptions of not being valued that many part-time faculty and non-tenure-track faculty sometimes feel.

In twenty-first-century academe, how might a culture of respect be cultivated in a university or college and used as the core principle underlying a new relationship, regardless of appointment type, between the faculty member and the employing institution? In *Rethinking Faculty Work* (Gappa, Austin, and Trice 2007), we suggested several ways in which higher education institutions can highlight respect as a core institutional value and can monitor its presence in the campus culture. Of particular importance, institutional leaders should articulate respect as a core institutional value and something that each member of the community can expect to receive and, conversely, should give to all colleagues. Institutional leaders could also ensure that decisions and policies exemplify a culture with respect at its core and could explicitly explain and highlight how institutional actions, policies, and processes advance the core value of respect.

Consideration of what is implied in position titles is another strategy to advance respect as a core institutional value that is simultaneously explicit, strategic, symbolic, and practical. For example, while the use of the term *contingent faculty member* is widespread, we have argued that other terms such as *fixed-term faculty member* are likely to convey greater respect (Gappa, Austin, and Trice 2007), and we suggest that institutions review the terms and titles they use. Another way to express respect for each faculty member, regardless of appointment type, is to ensure that the accomplishments of all colleagues are recognized through awards, news articles, and announcements. We also suggest that faculty members, again regardless of appointment type, should have appropriate opportunities to voice their perspectives on institutional governance at levels and in ways appropriate to their level of involvement in institutional work. While institutional leaders set the tone and often can influence policies and decisions, faculty members themselves (especially those in tenure-track and permanent positions) have a significant responsibility for establishing a culture of collegial respect as they engage in daily work and interactions.

Essential Elements of Faculty Work

While the framework for faculty work in the twenty-first century that we advocate is predicated on the notion of respect, it also highlights five other essential elements of faculty work that constitute the glue connecting faculty members and institutions in reciprocal relationships that advance both institutional missions in service to society and faculty well-being (Gappa, Austin, and Trice 2007). The presence of these five elements across all appointment types, building on respect, creates the necessary conditions to enable faculty members to develop and express their intellectual talents in ways that contribute to institutional quality, effectiveness, and excellence—institutional characteristics that are necessary for fulfilling institutional missions to the broader society. These five elements are academic freedom, flexibility, collegiality, professional development, and equity, and they have long been valued by faculty members holding tenure-track positions. However, as academic work changes and faculty members hold various types of appointments, we assert that renewed commitment to these elements would ensure that all faculty members—regardless of appointment type—are supported in their work, feel part of a ccommunity that shares responsibility for achieving institutional missions, and have the opportunity to participate in a reciprocal relationship such as the one that has defined faculty employment (albeit through tenure) in academe for many years.

The sections below describe the essential elements, which are presented more extensively in *Rethinking Faculty Work* (Gappa, Austin, and Trice 2007). We discuss how each element can be integrated into the complex and diverse range of faculty appointment types to simultaneously support the needs of individual faculty members and ensure a vibrant academic workforce capable of fulfilling the missions of the institutions in which its members serve. Figure 4.1 highlights the essential elements and shows that institutional characteristics and individual faculty characteristics contribute to the particular configuration of faculty work that is optimal in each context.

Employment Equity

Perceiving that one is being treated fairly and equitably is important for employees everywhere, but it is especially key in academe, where each faculty member may have a somewhat different set of responsibilities. Thus, employment equity is one of the essential elements of academic work that should be part of every appointment. We have defined equity as "the right of every faculty member (regardless of appointment type or time base) to be treated fairly in regard to all aspects of his or her employment by the institution and its departments, to have access to the tools necessary to do his or her job, and to have status as a fully-fledged, albeit necessarily different, member of the faculty" (Gappa, Austin, and Trice 2007, 140).

Equity must be integrated into all types of faculty work. The work and lives of faculty members are affected by a number of institutional policies, such as those addressing probationary periods, evaluation, peer review, compensation, benefits, and opportunities for advancement and professional learning. Equity across an institution is supported and protected by explicit guidelines and policies that define and govern these aspects of academic work and that include provisions for each employment type. In addition to guidelines and policies, achieving and protecting equity in the academic workplace also requires commitment to consistent implementation.

Faculty members in part-time and temporary positions often experience a lack of equity, especially in regard to space, support services, and equipment. For example, some part-time faculty members are not provided with office space they can use to meet with students or prepare for class, a condition of employment that full-time and permanent faculty routinely enjoy. As noted above, the presence of the essential elements serves both the needs of the individual faculty member and the priorities of the institution. The lack of office space for part-time faculty, which constitutes a violation of the essential element of equity, not only puts a burden on faculty members trying to do their work, but it also diminishes the institution's commitment to educational

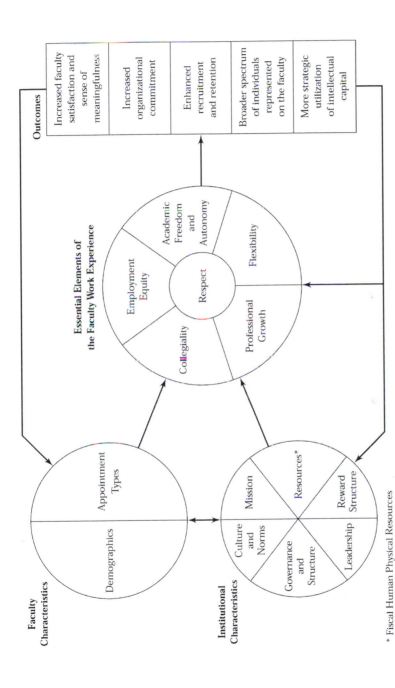

Faculty Characteristics

Demographics

Appointment Types

Institutional Characteristics

Culture and Norms

Mission

Resources*

Governance and Structure

Leadership

Reward Structure

Essential Elements of the Faculty Work Experience

Respect

Employment Equity

Academic Freedom and Autonomy

Flexibility

Professional Growth

Collegiality

Outcomes

Increased faculty satisfaction and sense of meaningfulness

Increased organizational commitment

Enhanced recruitment and retention

Broader spectrum of individuals represented on the faculty

More strategic utilization of intellectual capital

* Fiscal Human Physical Resources

FIGURE 4.1 The Essential Elements of Faculty Work

Reprinted from Gappa, Austin, and Trice 2007, 134. This material is reproduced with permission of John Wiley & Sons, Inc.

quality when students cannot easily meet and discuss their work in a confi-
dential setting with their teachers. Striving to include equity in the academic
workplace for all faculty members, in all appointment types, contributes to
both educational excellence and faculty satisfaction and creates work units in
which each faculty member feels valued.

Academic Freedom

Academic freedom historically has been a core value in academe, involving
"the norms and values that protect each faculty member's freedom of intellectual expression and inquiry" (Gappa, Austin, and Trice 2007, 226). Academic
freedom protects faculty members' freedom to teach as they choose in their
areas of expertise, to conduct research and publish on issues pertaining to their
expertise, and to enjoy their rights of free speech as citizens. Academic freedom
also has been implicitly associated with an expectation of autonomy, in which
faculty members decide and manage the details of how they do their teaching
and research. Commitment to the value of academic freedom both allows individual faculty members to be able to pursue work in their areas of expertise
and ensures that society at large has the benefits of creative and open thought
and intellectual contributions. Historically, academic freedom has been protected by the tenure process. The challenge now, as other faculty employment
arrangements emerge in academe, is to find ways to ensure that academic freedom continues to be protected as a core value and mode of work for all those
serving in faculty roles. Ensuring the excellence of teaching and the creativity of
the research process requires policies that foster and protect academic freedom
as a core right of all faculty members, regardless of appointment type.

Academic freedom is an essential element in all types of faculty work. In
Rethinking Faculty Work, we proposed a three-pronged approach to protect
academic freedom. First, we recommended that institutions should extend
the protections of academic freedom to all their faculty members by "clearly
defin[ing] what constitutes academic freedom, and includ[ing] the definition in
the contracts for contract-renewable and fixed-term academic appointments"
(Gappa, Austin, and Trice 2007, 228). Second, faculty members in all appointment types must understand what academic freedom is, what its related rights
and duties are, and what implications it has for all aspects of their work while
they are employed at the institution. Orientation programs should explicitly
address academic freedom, and given the nature of changing conditions in
faculty work, universities and colleges should consider organizing periodic
opportunities for their institutional communities to revisit their understanding of the meanings and responsibilities associated with academic freedom.
These issues could be addressed in convocations and unit-level discussions.
Third, higher education institutions should establish specific procedures for
handling complaints about and alleged violations of academic freedom, and

such procedures should explicitly state that they apply to and address the circumstances of faculty members in all appointment types. Guidelines might discuss the procedures for renewing or deciding not to renew the appointments of fixed-term and contract-renewable faculty, and provisions for grievance procedures should be available to every faculty member.

Academic freedom is essential to ensuring excellence in the quality of academic work and to supporting the professional lives of faculty members, whether they hold part-time or full-time positions; or permanent, renewable, or fixed-term positions. However, since academic freedom has been closely connected with tenure, protecting this concept requires careful thinking and commitment by faculty members and academic leaders as employment arrangements diversify in academe. We see the protection of this core concept and the development of related institutional policies and processes as critically important during this time of change in the nature of academic work.

Flexibility

Another key element in faculty work, especially in workplaces that employ academics in a range of appointment types, is flexibility. This element can be understood as "a way to define how and when work gets done and how careers are organized" (Healy n.d.). More specifically, in regard to academic employees, we defined flexibility as "the ability of faculty members to construct work arrangements to maximize their contributions to their institution as well as the meaningfulness of their work and personal lives" (Gappa, Austin, and Trice 2007, 141). Flexibility involves the ability to adjust one's daily or long-term schedule (such as shifting between part- and full-time employment), to shift between appointment types (such as between tenure-track and contract-renewable appointments), and to have the option of leaving or reentering the faculty career (for example, if family responsibilities require a significant period of absence). Arrangements need to honor both the needs of the institution and those of the individual. A workplace that honors flexibility as a principle in faculty work provides options and avenues for faculty members to work out arrangements that benefit both the individual employee and the institution.

The rationale for incorporating flexibility into all types of academic appointments is related to both individual and institutional benefits. For the institution, policies providing flexibility strengthen institutional recruitment and retention efforts, helping make the institution attractive to excellent candidates (Gappa, Austin, and Trice 2007). We are aware of a highly accomplished academic couple in which both partners are very competitive in the employment market, who indicated that they were specifically looking for institutions that had well-articulated policies for flexibility and dual career appointments. Flexibility also helps individuals who have multiple personal responsibilities to manage in addition to accomplishing their academic work by enhancing both their well-being and productivity (Gappa, Austin, and Trice 2007). Many academic employees today do not fit the model of the so-called ideal worker (a term discussed by many authors, such as William Whyte [1956] and Joan Williams [2001]). The ideal worker is available to focus all of his or her time on work while the partner or spouse manages the household and personal responsibilities. Rather, in today's workplace, both women and men are managing personal responsibilities, such as child or elder care. Overall, however, women continue to handle such family responsibilities at a much greater rate than men (Williams 2001), and, in the case of faculty, a higher proportion of women than men have indicated that their responsibilities contribute to their stress (Lindholm et al. 2002), Policies providing flexibility contribute to creating workplaces that help both male and female academics handle the complex responsibilities of their lives, and that enable departments and other academic units to accomplish their missions and responsibilities while honoring the individual needs and circumstances of their faculty members.

Flexibility is an element that must be integrated into all types of faculty work. One way to do this is to move from emphasizing time spent on work to focusing on the nature of goals met or output produced (Bailyn 1993; Gappa, Austin, and Trice 2007). In universities and colleges, the primary way in which flexibility is enacted is through policies that recognize that faculty members also have personal responsibilities by providing options for addressing and juggling both personal and professional duties. These options include leaves that help faculty members when they face periods of personal or family-related need, such as maternity, parental, and family leave options (beyond what is required under the 1993 Family and Medical Leave Act) for those giving birth or providing care for children new to a family, or caring for family members in serious health situations. For example, some institutions offer options for parental leave or modified duties for employees who are the sole or primary caregivers for new babies and automatic extensions to the tenure clock when a faculty member takes a personal leave.

Another approach to flexibility involves reduced-load appointments, flexible time bases, and job-sharing options. A flexible time-base policy enables faculty members in full-time positions to adjust the nature of their commitment to a part-time arrangement for a particular period of time, with the option of returning to full time when their circumstances change. However, such arrangements understandably need to factor in institutional needs and constraints in addition to faculty preferences and circumstances. At some institutions, such as Amherst College, faculty members who teach at least half time but less than full time are eligible for tenure under the same kinds of qualitative standards as their full-time colleagues. Policies that support job sharing, career breaks, and delayed entry into a career (for example, for someone who has taken time away from work for health or family reasons) are additional strategies for supporting flexibility in academic work. In addition to policies defining employment options, institutions can also provide services that help faculty manage work-life responsibilities, such as on-site child care or referrals to community resources; elder care guidance and resources; web-based resource lists pertaining to personal and family issues; and services and resources pertaining to financial planning, health needs, and meal planning.

Providing policies, services, and resources that aid employees in addressing work-life issues is a very useful strategy for enhancing the quality and effectiveness of academic workplaces. Of particular importance is ensuring that faculty members across all employment types have access to such resources. At the same time, faculty members need to recognize that institutional and community needs must be factored in along with individual needs. If flexible policies are to work effectively, faculty members and administrative leaders must commit themselves to collaborative decision making and providing mutual support.

Professional Growth

All faculty members need to be vibrant, adaptable, and up-to-date in their knowledge of their fields and of pedagogical and research practice in their areas of specialty. As an essential element of academic work, professional growth refers to "opportunities that enable faculty members to broaden their knowledge, abilities, and skills, to address challenges, concerns, and needs, and to find deeper satisfaction in their work" (Gappa, Austin, and Trice 2007, 141). Opportunities to engage in professional growth strengthen a faculty member's sense of professional identity and convey the commitment of the institution to investing in them as members of the community whose talents are valued and supported. Thus, when a university or college encourages and supports opportunities for faculty members in all appointment types—full or part time; permanent, fixed term, or on a short-term contract—to engage in ongoing professional growth, the institution is conveying a strategic message to faculty members about how they are viewed. Faculty members who feel valued and who are supported in advancing their professional talents and knowledge are well positioned to contribute to the quality and excellence of the institution in pursuing its missions.

Professional development is an essential element that should be integrated into all types of faculty work. Institutional efforts to provide professional development opportunities can take several forms. First, institutional leaders can ensure that all faculty members have the information that they need about performing their responsibilities and about the resources available to help them in their work. For example, a part-time faculty member teaching a single course needs to know (just as a full-time faculty member does) how the course fits into the broader curriculum, what resources are available to help with curriculum design and other questions, the characteristics and expectations of the students, what technological strategies are expected or might be used, and what pedagogical and technological resources are available to assist him or her. Institutional leaders can also provide professional development opportunities through assignments to committees or task forces and other responsibilities. In engaging in such work as curriculum design, for example, faculty members connect with other colleagues, encounter new perspectives, and gain knowledge and experience that constitute professional development. The judicious use of assignments by institutional leaders can help ensure that faculty members across appointment types have an array of opportunities through which to learn and to participate in fulfilling institutional work and addressing individual aspirations. Another strategy is to organize specific collegial interactions and collaborations such as coteaching, which enable groups or small teams of faculty to learn from each other. Various innovative approaches to mentoring are used on many campuses, including collaborative mentoring teams and mentoring committees involving peers and near peers as well as senior advisors, as well as more traditional two-person relationships. Another way to promote professional growth is the use of individualized growth plans, through which faculty members assess their strengths and areas for growth, propose paths through which to address priorities for growth over three or four years, and discuss with a chair or dean how individual interests and institutional priorities can be aligned and supported.

Professional development needs to be integrated into the work of all faculty members, and in the changing context for higher education in the twenty-first century, ongoing learning will be essential for everyone in a faculty role. Institutions will need to consider the particular needs of faculty members based on career stage, responsibilities, and appointment type. The opportunity for faculty members to stay current, cultivate innovative approaches, and share ideas with colleagues is a necessary ingredient in a model of academic work that befits the challenges facing higher education today.

Collegiality

The fifth element needed in any framework for faculty work in the twenty-first century is collegiality. We have defined *collegiality* as "opportunities for faculty members to feel that they belong to a mutually respectful community of colleagues who value their unique contributions to their institutions and who are concerned about their overall well-being" (Gappa, Austin, and Trice 2007, 142). Collegial interactions help faculty members feel that they belong, and a sense of belonging and feeling connected contributes to satisfaction and morale (Rice and Austin 1988) and greater likelihood of wanting to remain at the institution (Barnes, Agago, and Coombs 1998). Faculty members themselves report valuing and seeking collegiality (Boice 1992; Rice, Sorcinelli, and Austin 2000; Tierney and Bensimon 1996).

In higher education today, various factors undermine opportunities to nurture collegiality, including the many demands on faculty members' time; technology that makes it possible for faculty to work away from campus, which diminishes easy daily interactions; and the diversity of faculty in terms of age, background, and appointment type. In this context, collegiality needs to be cultivated more actively than may have been necessary in the past. In fact, the factors mitigating collegiality may make especially important the project of building what William Tierney (1993) has described as multicultural campus communities characterized by mutual respect and caring.

Collegiality is an essential element that must be integrated into all types of faculty work. How can collegiality, along with mutual respect and caring, be cultivated so that it is embedded into a faculty model for today and the future? Faculty members themselves must hold each other responsible for expressing mutual respect in all their interactions and for modeling ways to interact and even engage in vigorous debate while maintaining mutual civility. Collegiality can also be nurtured by such practical strategies as finding appropriate ways—commensurate with their appointment types—to include the diverse range of faculty members in institutional governance, including faculty senates and advisory groups and, where appropriate, search committees. Practically speaking, an employment model responsive to the complexities of faculty appointments in the twenty-first century would offer provisions for all faculty members, as appropriate for their circumstances and responsibilities, to have library privileges, orientation, office space, parking, and access to institutional facilities and support resources. Cultivating and conveying collegiality should be an ongoing, dynamic characteristic of a university or college. If it is to be part of the employment model for all faculty members, institutional leaders and faculty members will need to work together to consider effective ways that are relevant to the institution's culture and resources to nurture this essential element of the faculty experience.

A Vision of Academic Work as Collegial, Collaborative, and Community-Based

In contrast to common perspectives on academic work, the vision we offer of academic work—in which each faculty member, regardless of appointment type, participates in a reciprocal and mutually beneficial relationship with the employing institution—suggests a collaborative and community-based approach to academic work. Higher education institutions in the United States have traditionally emphasized individual success. During the second half of the twentieth century, the evaluation and reward systems increasingly emphasized the ability of individual faculty members to succeed in negotiating the tenure process and gaining a reputation by developing individual records of success

(Geiger 1999; Thelin 2011). Sizable research teams have been common in some science and engineering fields for years, and interdisciplinary work is becoming more usual as researchers tackle complex societal problems. However, until recently at many institutions, and even today at others, collaboration generally has not been encouraged or rewarded by the evaluation and reward processes and may actually have been discouraged (Austin and Baldwin 1991). In fact, co- or multiauthored publications have sometimes counted as less than single-authored publications in tenure and evaluation processes.

Alongside tenure practices that have emphasized the success of individual faculty members, employment trends in academe in recent years have created a situation of inequity, in which some faculty members are fortunate enough to find coveted, well-supported, prestigious tenure-track positions and others try to cobble together work involving multiple positions, accompanied by low compensation, little job security, and inadequate resources to support their teaching and research appropriately. These current employment trends in academe in the United States may lead to a bifurcated faculty, in which relatively few faculty members enjoy permanent positions with extensive support and benefits, and a much larger majority experience uncertain employment associated with far less attractive benefits (Kezar and Sam 2010 and 2011). This path is typically not productive or beneficial for faculty members. Nor, in the long term, is it healthy for the quality, excellence, and productivity of US higher education institutions in their efforts to pursue their missions of teaching, research, and outreach.

The vision and framework we offer are based on a different understanding of faculty work and an alternative way to think about organizing and supporting the work done in universities and colleges in support of their missions. The new vision for organizing academic work that we suggest would require departments and other academic units to recognize a collective responsibility for achieving their missions. That is, rather than perceiving the work activities of individual faculty members as separate and unique contributions, a more effective and productive way to serve both institutional missions and individual interests would be to think of the faculty in a unit as a collaborative group working together toward common goals. Each faculty member would be seen as contributing on the basis of his or her talents, and in the context of his or her appointment type (full or part time; tenure-based or fixed-term renewable). Each faculty member, regardless of that appointment type, would be expected to contribute to the unit's overall missions. Individuals would not necessarily all be expected to do the same work; rather, the unit as a whole would be responsible for fulfilling its multiple missions. Each individual would be respected, valued, evaluated, and rewarded for the particular contributions that he or she made to the collective responsibility of fulfilling those missions. This idea of focusing on unit responsibility for academic work has been suggested at times in the past—for example, in the work of the higher education scholar Jon Wergin (1994 and 2003; Wergin and Swingen 2000), but it has not yet become common in academe.

The vision we offer of faculty work that is collaborative and collegial is predicated on various assumptions. First is the assumption that each higher education institution has a responsibility for fulfilling its missions to society of teaching, research, and the application of knowledge to societal problems (with its institutional type determining its specific missions and the relative balance of attention it pays to these overall missions). A second and related assumption is that, in a complex world where fulfilling institutional missions requires a range of knowledge and multiple talents, groups of faculty members—rather than any single faculty member—must work together to advance these missions. Thus, achieving quality and excellence in twenty-first-century higher education requires the commitment, talents, and investment of every faculty employee, and the ability of faculty members to work collaboratively to achieve those goals. Creating vibrant academic workplaces requires effort, joint responsibility, collegiality, and collaboration among faculty members and administrative leaders. As we have suggested, conceptualizing academic work as this kind of collective effort requires rethinking faculty work. One part of this rethinking is to move from an individualistic understanding of academic work to a more collaborative perspective.

Another assumption is that the relationship between faculty member and employing institution is defined, as we have discussed above, by a reciprocal and mutually beneficial relationship. That is, faculty members are likely to bring different talents and have different employment arrangements (full or part time; permanent tenured positions or fixed-term appointments). However, regardless of the nature of the employment contract, each faculty member has responsibilities to the institution during the time of employment to do his or her best work and to participate in decision-making processes that contribute to the institution and to the unit's collective work to meet its responsibilities to the institution. At the same time, the institution is responsible for ensuring that the faculty employee is valued and respected and experiences the benefits of the essential elements of equity, academic freedom, flexibility, professional development, and collegiality. In a vision of academic work in the future, the nature of the appointment type does not define whether these elements should be present in a position. Rather, the nature of the reciprocal relationship requires these elements to be present in all positions, even as the relationship calls on each faculty member to be dedicated, as shown through conscientious work, to contributing his or her abilities and skills to the collective institutional and unit missions. This vision presupposes that, generally, those not in secure, permanent positions would enjoy fixed-term, renewable contract positions lasting at least one year. Very short-term positions would be used only occasionally and for particular reasons, but even they would include appropriate consideration and attention to the essential elements of faculty work.

An additional assumption in our vision of a more collaborative approach to faculty work in academic units is that the essential elements of faculty work would pervade the experience of each faculty member and would provide the framework within which groups of faculty with different employment arrangements could work collaboratively, productively, and respectfully. The presence of each element would support the satisfaction and morale of each faculty member as well as enforce the responsibility of each faculty member to contribute to the collective work of the unit. For example, equity across appointments ensures that individual faculty members may have different responsibilities but that each responsibility is seen as valuable to fulfilling the collective responsibility for unit and institutional work. Individual faculty members should each feel responsibility and should not feel marginalized based on their appointment type. Across a group of faculty members, specific responsibilities for teaching, research, advising, working in the community, and taking on leadership roles in the institution may vary—and for any individual faculty member, the relative weight of such responsibilities may vary across time.

The presence of academic freedom means that each faculty member is encouraged to use creativity in contributing to unit goals, and that each is expected to recognize and accept the responsibility of making significant contributions to the overall goals. The essential element of flexibility supports each individual's personal and professional needs, but enjoying flexibility also implies that faculty members need to help their colleagues have the flexibility that they also would like to exercise. For example, when one faculty member needs time away to care for a child who is new to the family, others need to meet that person's teaching or other responsibilities. Later, the faculty member who was supported may assume extra duties to help the unit when another colleague who is struggling with health issues needs a reduced load. The essential element of professional development implies that all faculty members, regardless of appointment type, should have opportunities to increase their skills and abilities. The accompanying responsibility is that faculty members of all appointment types should be willing to develop new abilities to contribute to the unit's collective missions, even when new responsibilities may not be their preferred areas of work. For example, if a department decides that offering online courses is in the best interests of fulfilling its teaching mission, faculty members should be willing to expand their teaching repertoire to include online teaching, even if that is not their preferred teaching mode.

Similarly, the essential element of collegiality involves benefits and responsibilities for each faculty member. Every faculty member, regardless of appointment type, should feel that he or she is welcomed and supported in the unit (for example, the academic department) and should experience this respect and valuing in tangible ways, such as having appropriate office space and being included in meetings and informal events. At the same time, benefiting from collegiality imposes the reciprocal responsibility of being willing to contribute at the level and extent appropriate for one's position to the many formal governance processes, informal meetings, and leadership roles that are necessary for units to achieve their collective missions.

In summary, meeting the expectations facing our universities and colleges in the twenty-first century involves shifting our understandings of the academic workplace and faculty work from an individualistic perspective toward a vision of collective unit responsibilities and collaborative work among colleagues. In this vision, faculty members in a range of appointment types would be likely to participate, and not every faculty member would be expected to do the same work. However, every faculty member would participate in a reciprocal relationship with the employing institution in which both the institution and the faculty employee would benefit and to which both would contribute. The result is likely to be both more satisfaction on the part of individual faculty members and the advancement of institutional work to achieve the missions of universities and colleges in service to the broader society. We can achieve much in academe when we envision faculty work as situated in units where individuals work together collaboratively, collegially, and collectively to meet shared unit and institutional goals. The framework of essential elements provides institutions with tangible and practical ideas for creating workplaces characterized by such collaboration and collegiality, and in which all faculty members would feel valued and respected for their part in helping achieve the overall missions and would understand their responsibilities in that process.

Moving toward the Vision

How can higher education institutions move toward this vision of academic work? It has been eight years since we first published these ideas, and time has only strengthened our belief in the value of the research that underlies them. Certainly other scholars are also calling for a more intentional, thoughtful response to the dramatic changes in faculty employment structures. In spite of the passage of time, the presence of empirical evidence, and multiple voices calling for change, why do most academic departments still operate with a strict hierarchy of tenure-track faculty members on top and fixed-term faculty members at the bottom? Why do many departments consist of isolated islands of individual faculty members or subsets of faculty rather than a unified system working toward common goals? Understanding aspects of American culture may help explain this resistance to change.

First, the dominant culture in American society emphasizes individual achievement, power, and material success. For many Americans, a primary life goal is to be the best, or at least to be a winner rather than a loser; as a result, some see much of life as a competition. These characteristics reflect what Geert Hofstede termed a "masculine" culture (2002). According to another intercultural scholar, "in America, one's sense of worth comes more from personal achievement than from relationships" (Nussbaum 2005, 51). For tenure-track faculty members who prioritize achievement, they are the winners, and those who work off the tenure track are the losers—or at least they are perceived as far less valuable to a department. With this perceived status differential, fixed-term faculty members have difficulty engaging with their tenure-track colleagues as equally important and respected members of a unified system. It is useful to note that women tend to be less achievement oriented than men, and that women often value relationships, cooperation, caring for the weak, and modesty over competition and winning (Hofstede 2002). Faculty members from a number of countries—including the Netherlands, Portugal, South Korea, and Thailand—also tend to hold what Hofstede called "feminine" values (2002). Thus, greater diversity in a unit, such as including in the faculty more women and people who grew up in more "feminine" cultures, may be a useful way to develop more collaborative environments.

In addition to holding "masculine," competitive cultural values, Americans are also highly individualistic. In fact, the United States is the most individualistic culture in the world, according to Hofstede's decades-long multinational research (2002). Americans esteem independent thinking and people who are not swayed by a crowd. Americans also tend to think in terms of "I" rather than "we," value plurality and diversity, and reward individual rather than group initiative. The nature of faculty work also supports this orientation toward the individual: faculty members tend to work independently rather than in collaboration with colleagues, as they teach, research, write, and mentor students.

Given Americans' cultural tendencies toward competitiveness and individualism, pursuing collaboration is countercultural and unlikely to happen without significant support and guidance. It will not occur simply because a few people are convinced of the arguments for it. Research on the nature of influence offers some ideas for moving forward in this kind of context. Joseph Grenny, David Maxfield, and Andrew Shimberg (2008) found that those who use a "critical mass" of influence strategies are up to ten times more successful in bringing about lasting, major change than people who do not use such a mass of strategies. The authors identified six specific strategies that can empower and encourage a person to change his or her behavior (see Table 4.1). The first two strategies focus on the individual level, the next two on the power of peers, and the final two on environmental factors. Each of these three levels includes one strategy to increase motivation and another to enhance one's ability to change. Brief descriptions of each of the strategies follow.

TABLE 4.1

How to Have Influence

Level	Strategies to increase motivation	Strategies to enhance the ability to change
Personal	Link behavior to mission and values	Invest in skill building
Social	Harness peer pressure	Create social support
Environmental	Align rewards and ensure accountability	Change the environment

Source: Grenny, Maxfield, and Shimberg 2008.

Link Behavior to Mission and Values

One way to influence change is to link the desired behaviors to a person's over-arching mission and values. Leaders who understand the power of healthy influence take the time to help people become personally motivated to try a new idea and develop a personal vision for what life could be like if they changed their behavior in a specific way. When tenure-track faculty members are encouraged to work collaboratively, they may perceive that this effort would primarily mean more work for them and would give undue status to fixed-term faculty. Pointing to models of high-functioning, collaborative departments that creatively use the strengths and experiences of each faculty member to achieve their goals can be a powerful way to help faculty members build a vision for change.

Invest in Skill Building

A way to influence change is investing in skill building. Influential leaders realize that if someone does not have the requisite intellectual or emotional skills to alter their behavior, no amount of motivational speeches or directives will bring change. Few people are willing to admit when they feel unprepared for change; they simply resist it in either overt or covert ways. What skills might faculty members not have? Working collaboratively will often involve discussing individuals' strengths, weaknesses, and preferences to determine how best to divide teaching, administrative, and advising responsibilities among department members. Individuals may benefit from coaching in how to make these discussions feel safe and affirming. It may also be worthwhile to provide training in group dynamics to help colleagues learn how to engage with one another as members of the same team rather than competitors in a situation where some win and others lose.

Harness Peer Pressure

Building faculty members' interpersonal skills and vision for collaboration makes change more likely, but if the power of peer pressure is not addressed, progress toward building a cohesive department will be minimal. Whether or not people recognize or admit it, they do things to win the approval of others. In terms of the faculty career, there are a multitude of unwritten rules about what work earns peers' praise or respect. Teaching senior-level courses is more valued than teaching freshman-level courses. Conducting research is more valued than teaching. Mentoring students, while generally perceived as good, will usually earn little notice from colleagues. Administrative work is a necessary evil and is best avoided when possible: it can require large amounts of time and almost never leads to accolades or even recognition from others. These are long-held unspoken norms, and if they are not openly discussed, faculty members will likely continue to follow them to receive affirmation from their peers. To promote behavioral change, department chairs and deans should talk frankly with faculty members about specific behaviors that they believe are blocking collaboration. They should bring in students, alumni, and employers to share their frustrations with departmental performance. Leaders can also be vulnerable and humble as they talk about how difficult some changes are for them and how wedded they still feel to unwritten rules that they too were enculturated to follow. Seeking counsel from chairs and other leaders who have successfully helped their departments become more collaborative can prove very useful as well.

Create Social Support

As a department begins to take steps toward a more collaborative work environment, faculty members will need support in trying new behaviors. This support may come through formal training at discrete points in time, but more likely it will come in real time as frustration is experienced. Champions of collaboration need to be available to talk through change and guide faculty members when they want to pull away and act autonomously. Leaders need to verbalize some of the hesitancy others may feel and to frequently encourage those who are trying risky new behaviors.

Align Rewards and Ensure Accountability

The final two components of the model address the power of the environment to influence change. On this level, influence can initially take the form of rewarding desired behavior and penalizing undesirable behavior. For example, when salary raises are determined, what measures are really used? When promotions are decided on or contracts are renegotiated, do evaluation criteria match the articulated priorities? Grenny, Maxfield, and Shimberg (2008) warn that using carrots and sticks is not a preferred first step in influencing change because it can dismantle a person's intrinsic motivation for altering his or her behavior. When used carefully and as a secondary approach to influencing change, however, using rewards and costs can prove to be a useful strategy.

Change the Environment

The final strategy identified in this research focuses on changing the environment to support the desired change. Leaders need to take a careful look at the environment in which faculty members function and identify ways to better align the environment with reality. Faculty members may believe that students, alumni, and employers are highly satisfied with their work. If that is not the case, leaders need to be sure that faculty members regularly see data demonstrating otherwise. Faculty members may believe that their peers feel a high level of personal satisfaction with their work and unit. This may not be the case if the department is characterized by very individualistic behavior and a strong hierarchy in which only a few members are perceived to be highly valued. Sharing survey results that reveal these feelings and perceptions may be a powerful way to encourage change.

In significant ways, American culture and academic culture work against a collaborative departmental climate. Empirical evidence of the benefits of collaboration, more time, or louder calls for change are not likely to lead to new faculty attitudes and behaviors. Leaders must do the hard but rewarding work of strategically creating an environment that supports collaboration. With mutual respect as a core value defining academic work, universities and colleges can value and celebrate the unique contributions of each faculty member, recognizing that difference is an asset rather than a weakness or problem. When the essential elements define the experience of each faculty member, regardless of appointment type, each colleague can apply his or her unique talents to a collegial, collaborative, and collective effort to ensure quality, excellence, and effectiveness as the institution advances its missions in service to societal needs and expectations.

REFERENCES

Alderfer, Clayton P. 1972. *Existence, Relatedness, and Growth: Human Needs in Organizational Settings*. New York: Free Press.

American Association of University Professors (AAUP). 1940. "Statement of Principles on Academic Freedom and Tenure." Washington: AAUP. Accessed December 8, 2015. http://www.aaup.org/report/1940-statement-principles-academic-freedom-and-tenure.

Austin, Ann E., and Roger G. Baldwin. 1991. *Faculty Collaboration: Enhancing the Quality of Scholarship and Teaching*. ASHE-ERIC Higher Education Report 7. Washington: George Washington University, School of Education and Human Development.

Bailyn, Lotte. 1993. *Breaking the Mold: Women, Men, and Time in the New Corporate World*. New York: Free Press.

Barnes, Laura B., Menna O. Agago, and William T. Coombs. 1998. "Effects of Job-Related Stress on Faculty Intention to Leave Academia." *Research in Higher Education* 39: 457–69.

Boice, Robert. 1992. *The New Faculty Member: Supporting and Fostering Professional Development*. San Francisco: Jossey-Bass.

Campbell, Alice, and Marci Koblenz. 1997. *A New Paradigm: The Work and Life Pyramid of Needs*. Deerfield, IL: Baxter Healthcare Corporation and MK Consultants.

Gappa, Judith M., Ann E. Austin, and Andrea G. Trice. 2007. *Rethinking Faculty Work: Higher Education's Strategic Imperative*. San Francisco: Jossey-Bass.

Gappa, Judith M., and David W. Leslie. 1993. *The Invisible Faculty: Improving the Status of Part-Timers in Higher Education*. San Francisco: Jossey-Bass.

Geiger, Roger. 1999. "The Ten Generations of American Higher Education." In *American Higher Education in the Twenty-First Century: Social, Political, and Economic Challenges*, edited by Philip Altbach, Patricia Gumport, and Robert Berdahl, 38–69. Baltimore, MD: Johns Hopkins University Press.

Grenny, Joseph, David Maxfield, and Andrew Shimberg. 2008. "How to Have Influence." *MIT Sloan Management Review*, fall. Accessed June 26, 2015. http://sloanreview.mit.edu/article/how-to-have-influence.

Healy, Cathy. n.d. "A Business Perspective on Workplace Flexibility: When Work Works, An Employer Strategy for the 21st Century." Accessed December 7, 2015. http://www.clalliance.com/EXPO/docs/BusinessPerspectiveonWorkplaceFlexibility-AnEmployerStrategyforthe21stCentury2003.pdf.

Herzberg, Frederick. 1966. *Work and the Nature of Man*. Cleveland: World.

Hofstede, Geert. 2002. *Culture's Consequences: Comparing Values, Behaviors, Institutions, and Organizations across Nations*. 2nd ed. Thousand Oaks, CA: Sage.

Kezar, Adrianna, and Cecile Sam. 2010. *Understanding the New Majority: Contingent Faculty in Higher Education*. ASHE Higher Education Report 36 (4). Hoboken, NJ: Jossey-Bass.

———. 2011. *Non-Tenure-Track Faculty in Higher Education: Theories and Tensions*. ASHE Higher Education Report 36 (5). San Francisco: Jossey-Bass.

Lindholm, Jennifer A., Alexander W. Astin, Linda J. Sax, and William S. Korn. 2002. *The American College Teacher: National Norms for the 2001–02 HERI Faculty Survey*. Los Angeles: University of California, Los Angeles, Higher Education Research Institute.

Maslow, Abraham H. 1970. *Motivation and Personality*. 2nd ed. New York: HarperCollins.

Nussbaum, Stan. 2005. *Why Are Americans Like That? A Visitor's Guide to American Cultural Values and Expectations*. Colorado Springs, CO: Enculturation.

Rice, R. Eugene, and Ann E. Austin. 1988. "High Faculty Morale: What Exemplary Colleges Do Right." *Change* 20 (2): 51–58.

Rice, R. Eugene, Mary Deane Sorcinelli, and Ann E. Austin. 2000. *Heeding New Voices: Academic Careers for a New Generation*. New Pathways Working Paper Series, No. 7. Washington: American Association for Higher Education.

Thelin, John. R. 2011. *A History of American Higher Education*. 2nd ed. Baltimore, MD: Johns Hopkins University Press.

Tierney, William G. 1993. *Building Communities of Difference: Higher Education in the Twenty-First Century*. Westport, CT: Bergin and Garvey.

Tierney, William G., and Estela M. Bensimon. 1996. *Promotion and Tenure: Community and Socialization in Academe*. Albany: State University of New York Press.

Wergin, Jon. 1994. *The Collaborative Department: How Five Campuses Are Inching towards Cultures of Collective Responsibility*. Washington: American Association for Higher Education.

———. 2003. *Departments That Work: Building and Sustaining Cultures of Excellence in Academic Programs*. Bolton, MA: Anker.

Wergin, Jon., and Judi N. Swingen. 2000. *Departmental Assessment: How Some Campuses Are Collectively Evaluating the Collective Work of Faculty*. Washington: American Association for Higher Education.

Whyte, William H., Jr. 1956. *The Organization Man*. New York: Simon and Schuster.

Williams, Joan. 2001. *Unbending Gender: Why Family and Work Conflict and What to Do about It*. New York: Oxford University Press.

5

The Anatomy and Physiology of Medical School Faculty Career Models

WILLIAM T. MALLON

The nation's MD-granting medical schools, many of which are affiliated with the largest research universities in the United States, have been in the vanguard of innovative pathways of faculty appointment and promotion for more than thirty years. These institutions have developed multiple career pathways that emphasize differentiated roles, permit flexibility, and reward contributions using a broadened definition of scholarship. While these advancements have been imperfectly developed and unevenly applied, they offer evidence that it is possible to evolve from a universal (and antiquated) one-size-fits-some approach of faculty appointment and career development to a system that recognizes and rewards variation in and diversity of faculty work.

This chapter reviews the historical drivers of faculty career innovation in medical school settings, explicates the faculty tracks that are common in most medical schools today, reviews a number of flexible policies that have emerged over the past three decades, and discusses the future of faculty models in academic medical centers.

A Primer on Medical School Faculty

To understand the drivers that prompted change in faculty appointment policies and practices, readers should be aware of four characteristics of medical school faculty. First, the majority of medical school faculty members are practicing physicians. Generally referred to as clinical faculty members, these physicians have responsibilities that include some combination of treating patients, conducting clinically oriented research, and instructing medical students and residents in clinical settings. A smaller set of medical school faculty members are appointed in basic science departments: they are typically research faculty members with a PhD and/or an MD who conduct basic research, instruct medical students in the basic sciences (for example, biochemistry, physiology, and pharmacology), and train graduate students.

Second, regardless of type, medical school faculty devote a small fraction of their time to traditional classroom teaching compared to the rest of the professoriate. Clinical faculty, by and large, are interacting with patients; their days can look like those of physicians in any health care setting: internists who diagnose ailments and illnesses; obstetricians who deliver babies; emergency medicine doctors who triage medical crises; and surgeons who resect tumors and repair aortas, to name only a few examples. Clinical faculty have university or medical school faculty appointments because they also instruct medical students or residents in the context of delivering care or conduct clinical or translational research. Research faculty in basic science departments may teach medical students or even undergraduates, but their classroom teaching loads are minimal. This nature of medical school faculty has not always been the case. In the first part of the twentieth century, medical school faculty focused primarily on education and research: "clinical practice was carried on as necessary for these elements of the primary mission, but was not, for the core faculty, an end in itself" (Barchi and Lowery 2000, 900).

Third, the size and composition of the medical school faculty has grown significantly over fifty years. In 2013, the 141 MD-granting medical schools employed 148,088 full-time faculty members: 128,308 (87 percent) in clinical departments, 18,347 (12 percent) in basic science departments, and 1,433 (1 percent) categorized as "other" (Association of American Medical Colleges 2014a). Since 1960, the number of full-time faculty in clinical departments has grown seventeenfold, while the number of basic science faculty has more than quadrupled (an increase comparable to all full-time faculty at four-year colleges and universities).

Fourth, the growth in medical school faculty during this time was not driven by instructional needs but by patient care. Beginning in the 1960s, with the enactment of the federal Medicare and Medicaid programs, medical school faculties began to receive professional service fees for what prior to this time would have been "charity" cases. With the opportunity to receive financial reimbursement for health care services, academic medical centers reacted in a perfectly rational way, by expanding the services they offered to patients with federal or private insurance. Thus, they greatly expanded their clinical faculties to take advantage of income-generating opportunities, which supported the educational and research missions of the institutions. In addition, academic medical centers developed highly specialized clinical care that required large numbers of expert faculty members. For example, organ transplantation services need not only transplant specialists, but robust expertise from faculty in general surgery, gastroenterology, hepatology, and laboratory science. The entire enterprise grew to support these specialized programs.

These factors led to the explosion in the number of medical school physician faculty. By the 1980s, many clinical faculty members were recruited with the expectation that the vast majority of their professional effort would be devoted to clinical care, with only limited time devoted to the teaching and research missions of the institution (Barchi and Lowery 2000). Today, nearly all clinical faculty members in US. medical schools are expected to generate income through their professional practice to cover their salaries and contribute to the revenue needs of the academic health system. Unlike most faculty members in the other divisions of the university, few clinical faculty members have "hard dollar" institutional support for their salaries. To a lesser extent, these circumstances hold true for basic science faculty as well. At many medical schools, research faculty are expected to cover, at a minimum, 50–75 percent of their salaries through external grant support.[1]

Driven by the economics and financing of the academic health system, medical schools altered their faculty appointment and career pathways in four important ways: (1) the introduction of differentiated faculty tracks, which led to a concomitant decline in traditional faculty appointments; (2) an expanded definition of scholarship and scholarly activity; (3) reduced financial guarantees with tenure and the use of variable compensation schemes; and (4) flexible approaches to traditional tenure-track faculty appointments.

Differentiated Faculty Tracks

One result of the need for clinical faculty members to generate professional service revenue was that few had the protected time to meet the requirements for traditional academic tenure and promotion, such as hypothesis-driven, peer-reviewed scholarship. Recognizing this reality, beginning in the 1970s and increasing in the 1980s, medical schools created a variety of faculty appointment arrangements with distinctive promotion criteria to accommodate the differentiated roles of their faculty members. By 1983, 55 percent of the 112 US medical schools with tenure systems had a clinical-educator track, defined as "a formal, full-time non-tenure-earning appointment track for M.D. faculty members who are primarily engaged in patient care and teaching" (Jones 1987, 444). By 1997, 73 percent of the schools had separate and distinct faculty tracks for full-time clinical faculty (Jones and Gold 1998). According to Frederick Lovejoy and Mary Clark, "the need to retain valuable teacher-clinicians was an overriding concern encouraging the creation of these tracks" (1995, 1079).

By 2011, each medical school had, on average, 3.6 career tracks for full-time faculty (ranging from 1 to 8), 60 percent of which were tenure-ineligible

(Coleman and Richard 2011). While there is variation across medical schools, five career tracks are most common (Coleman and Richard 2011, 935–36):

1. Tenure, or investigator, track: The faculty career pathway in medical schools that bears the most resemblance to a traditional faculty track in academe, the investigator track has conducting original, hypothesis-driven research as the main criterion for academic advancement. Both MDs and PhDs can be appointed to this track, although a much higher percentage of PhD faculty than of MD faculty are on it.

2. Clinical-educator track: As noted above, this track was designed for MD faculty who devote at least 50 percent and as much as 80–90 percent of their professional efforts to patient care, with a secondary focus on education—including medical student and resident education in clinical settings.

3. Clinical track: As academic health systems continued to expand in the 1990s, they increasingly hired physicians as clinical workhorses, with little or no expectation that they would make contributions in education or research. These faculty members typically devote 90–100 percent of their professional efforts to patient care activities. This track is always non-tenure-track and often has a modified title (for example, "clinical assistant professor"). In other divisions of the university, these faculty members would be called adjuncts or professors of practice.

4. Research track: Comparable to the clinical track, this career pathway is for faculty who spend almost all of their professional effort on grant-funded research, typically in support of and directed by a tenured or tenure-track principal investigator. The track is typically tenure-ineligible, is dependent on grant funding, and gives short notice of nonreappointment.

5. Educator track: The newest faculty career pathway to emerge at medical schools, this track is for faculty who are either PhDs or MDs and who devote more than 50 percent of their professional efforts to medical, graduate, or resident education. This track typically carries an expectation of original research in medical education and scholarly output such as educational resources (curricular content, case studies, simulations, educational texts, and so on). Michelle Coleman and George Richard (2011) found that 40 percent of the educator tracks were eligible for tenure.

The growth of these various differentiated and mostly tenure-ineligible tracks has had a profound impact on the appointment trends at US medical schools (see figure 5.1). In 1966, of those full-time MD clinical faculty with known appointment tracks, 73 percent were tenured or on the tenure track. By 1991, the percentage of tenured or tenure-eligible physician faculty members had dipped below 50 percent, and in 2013, it was only 26 percent—12 percent

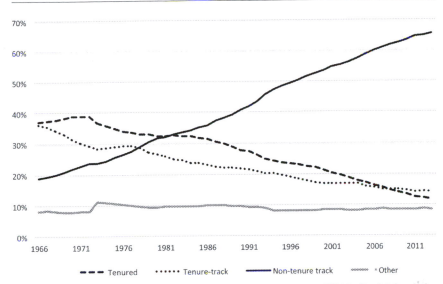

FIGURE 5.1 Full-Time MD Faculty in Clinical Departments at US Medical Schools by Appointment Type, 1966–2013

Source: Association of American Medical Colleges 2014b.

Note: The data represent faculty members who were active as of December 31 of each year. Faculty members whose appointment track was unknown in the Association of American Medical Colleges' Faculty Roster, a national database of all full-time faculty members appointed at US medical schools, are excluded. In the 1960s, more than 50 percent of faculty track data were missing from the database; since 1980, fewer than 10 percent have been missing.

of full-time MD clinical faculty were tenured and 14 percent were on the tenure track (Association of American Medical Colleges 2014b).

The use of tenured and tenure-track appointments has also declined for basic science faculty, albeit much less significantly (see figure 5.2). In 1966, of those full-time basic science PhD faculty with known faculty tracks, 53 percent were tenured and 38 percent were on the tenure track. Only 6 percent were non-tenure track. In 2013, the percentage of basic science PhD faculty with tenure had only dipped slightly, to 49 percent. But the percentage on the tenure track had fallen to 20 percent, and the percentage in tenure-ineligible tracks had increased to 27 percent. Given these trends, it seems only a matter of time before the percentage of tenured basic science PhD faculty will start to wane.

Growth in the Clinical Educator Track

Of the various types of faculty appointment tracks in US medical schools, the clinical educator track arguably represents the most novel approach to accommodating the changing nature of faculty work life. A substantial body of literature describes these tracks at institutions, including Stanford University

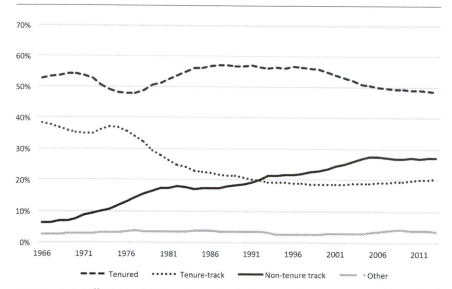

FIGURE 5.2 Full-Time PhD Faculty in Basic Science Departments at US Medical Schools by Appointment Type, 1966–2013

Source: Association of American Medical Colleges 2014b.

Note: The data represent faculty members who were active as of December 31 of each year. Faculty members whose appointment track was unknown in the Association of American Medical Colleges' Faculty Roster, a national database of all full-time faculty members appointed at US medical schools, are excluded. In the 1960s, more than 50 percent of faculty track data were missing from the database; since 1980, fewer than 10 percent have been missing.

(Jacobs and Tower 1992), Harvard (Lovejoy and Clark 1995), the University of Kentucky (Nora et al. 2000), the University of California (Howell and Bertakis 2004), the University of Chicago (Feder and Madara 2008), and the University of Pennsylvania (Pati et al. 2013). These case studies and descriptions cite two primary drivers for the emergence of the clinical educator track, which are discussed next.

DISSONANCE BETWEEN TWO STANDARDS OF PROFESSIONAL EXPECTATIONS. As noted above, the number of full-time faculty members skyrocketed once the clinical enterprise at academic medical centers became a viable and profitable business line and helped underwrite the institutions' educational and research missions. With so many faculty members hired for patient care and, to a lesser extent, education, the traditional appointment and tenure system that defined faculty excellence in terms of scholarship and education proved too inflexible (Barzansky and Kenagy 2010; Feder and Madara 2008; Pati et al. 2013). Many clinical faculty members were under great pressure to meet clinical productivity standards—expectations that made it difficult if not impossible to simultaneously meet academic productivity standards. Something had to give.

Medical schools and their parent universities were willing to experiment and innovate in faculty tracks because, frankly, they had no choice—to insist on a single traditional track for appointment and promotion would have meant cadres of physician-educators had no viable pathway for career advancement (Feder and Madara 2008; Lovejoy and Clark 1995). The driver of this change was not necessarily that physician-educators had more direct power over university decision making than, say, non-tenure-track faculty members in other schools or programs in academe. Rather, an active and robust physician-educator workforce was needed to ensure that the clinical enterprise of the academic medical center was viable and could grow. If medical schools and teaching hospitals did not create career tracks for such faculty members, then they ran the risk of not retaining these individuals and not being competitive in the health care delivery marketplace. A multiple-track system allowed medical schools to appoint and promote faculty members with different career foci and recognized that a one-size-fits-all approach was neither realistic nor wise.

MITIGATION OF FINANCIAL RISK. A second driver of the creation of these non-tenure-track appointments was to minimize financial risk to the institution. By design, tenure is intended to provide a degree of economic security to the individual professor (American Association of University Professors 1940). But an individual's economic security can be an institution's economic risk, especially when tenured faculty members are highly paid specialist physicians as opposed to faculty members in, say, the humanities or social sciences.[2] In the 1970s and 1980s, universities and their medical schools recognized that the financial risk associated with tenuring clinical faculty members was becoming too great. For example, Stanford University added a clinical educator track in part because of "the fact that the university could not reasonably be expected to assume financial liability for the career-life tenures of a large number of faculty needed to meet the clinical requirements of the school of medicine" (Jacobs and Tower 1992, 627).

The Challenges of Multiple Faculty Tracks

The creation of differentiated faculty tracks has not been without challenges. The first concern is that clinical-educator faculty do not advance in academic rank because of a lack of traditional scholarship (Levinson and Rubenstein 2000). Over time, this concern about lack of career progression has been proved valid but nuanced. Studies conducted at individual medical schools have demonstrated that faculty members in non-tenure tracks who have gone up for promotion have been at least as successful as tenure-track faculty. In 1995, Lovejoy and Clark found that 74 percent of clinical-educator faculty were promoted in the five-year period following the establishment of a clinical-educator track at Harvard Medical School. In a study of faculty promotions at the five University of California medical schools in 1999–2001, Lydia Howell and Klea Bertakis (2004) found that alternative tracks had promotion rates of more than 90 percent, compared to an average promotion rate in the tenure track of 82 percent.

Going up for promotion is the critical factor. A significant percentage of non-tenure-track clinical faculty do not make it that far. For MD assistant professors in clinical departments at US medical schools who started in a non-tenure track between 1983 and 2003, only 29 percent were promoted to associate professor within ten years, compared to ten-year promotion rates of about 46 percent for MD tenure-track assistant professors (see figure 5.3). A large percentage of MD clinician faculty who do not achieve promotion leave their institutions before they even try: more than four in ten first-time MD assistant professors in clinical departments leave their institutions within ten years (Association of American Medical Colleges 2014b). These trends suggest that the primary challenge may be the inability to retain physicians in clinical careers in academic medical centers. The challenge for clinical-educators to produce sufficient scholarship to be eligible for promotion may be an important, but secondary, deficiency. The reasons for attrition among these faculty members are complex. Physician burnout in both academic and nonacademic settings is increasing, given the changes in the delivery and financing of health care (Shanafelt et al. 2012). Layered on top of this reality is the fact that non-tenure-track clinical faculty typically have less protected time for scholarship than tenure-track clinicians and may find it impossible to meet the expectations for career progression (Bunton, Corrice, and Mallon 2010).

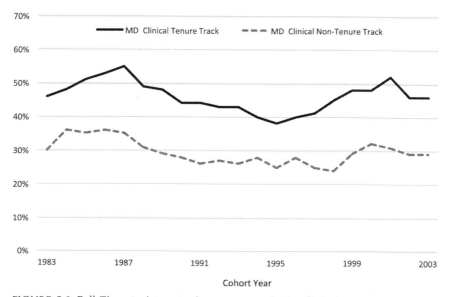

FIGURE 5.3 Full-Time Assistant Professor MD Faculty in Clinical Departments at US Medical Schools Promoted to Associate Professor within Ten Years, 1983–2003

Source: Sloane 2014.

A second challenge cited in the literature is that multiple tracks create a "caste system in which some faculty are perceived as more valuable or important than others" (Howell and Bertakis 2004, 250). It was this concern about creating a sense of elitism that led the Johns Hopkins University School of Medicine to reaffirm its single-track system in the early 2000s (Thomas et al. 2004). Interestingly, Patricia Thomas and colleagues report that a single-track appointment system did not eliminate the perception of elitism or second-class status among different types of faculty. Unfortunately, those feelings of superiority and inferiority are baked into the culture of academe, in which educator-focused faculty receive tacit or explicit cues about their standing relative to research-oriented faculty (Metzger 1987).

At some universities and medical schools, the inequities among faculty types are not just perceptional—there are, in fact, real differences in terms of faculty rights and perquisites. Faculty on some clinical non-tenure tracks at the University of California medical schools, for example, are prohibited from membership in their institution's academic senate and are not eligible for state-funded sabbatical leave (University of California, San Francisco 2005). Of course, not all universities and medical schools have codified such differences. But whether or not non-tenure-track faculty members are limited in their access to formal faculty perquisites, they often find that their status differs from that of their tenure-track colleagues.

A third potential drawback to non-tenure tracks at US medical schools is a lack of acceptance of and credibility for alternate tracks by both appointed faculty and the faculty at large (Lovejoy and Clark 1995). While this concern may have been prevalent during the 1980s when these tracks were being created, tested, and implemented, evidence indicates that alternate tracks are now prevalent and that faculty on these tracks are, generally speaking, as satisfied as their tenure-track counterparts. Multiple studies have shown similar or even higher rates of global work satisfaction by clinical-educator, non-tenure-track faculty compared to tenure-track faculty (Howell et al. 2010; Thomas et al. 2004). A case study of the medical school at the University of Chicago concluded: "The growing body of experience . . . is eroding faculty concerns and facilitating the appointment and retention of academic faculty at our institution" (Feder and Madara 2008, 85).

Non-tenure research tracks at US medical schools have been studied less than clinical educator tracks; therefore, we must be more careful in drawing conclusions about the acceptance and credibility of and satisfaction with non-tenure research tracks. Physician faculty, even if ineligible for tenure, exist in a professional and societal milieu that affords them great respect and credibility by dint of their MD degree. Academic tenure is arguably less important for professional self-identity of MD faculty than those in other disciplinary traditions. Medical school PhD faculty, in contrast, are closer to the dominant academic culture that places higher premium on tenure as an indicator of professional status. Generally speaking, PhD faculty on non-tenure research tracks do not produce independent research, the coin of the realm in academic biomedical science. Rather, they often work under the direction of, and sponsored by, a tenure-track PhD scientist. Their salary support comes almost entirely from extramural grant funding. If the grants dry up, their faculty appointment ends. Howell and colleagues (2010) highlighted some of the disadvantages of this track, including perceptions of second-class status, ineligibility for some faculty perquisites, insufficient voice in departmental and institutional governance, disadvantages when applying for grant funding, and inequities in resources and space.

Other drawbacks and barriers in the non-tenure track in US medical schools have been cited in the literature, including inconsistent or unclear promotion criteria; lack of institutional support to reward all types of scholarship; unreasonable time expectations for promotion; and perceived disparities in promotion by gender, race, and ethnicity (Beasley et al. 1997; Ruiz et al. 2009). Yet these barriers are not unique to non-tenure track positions in academic medicine: they are also prevalent among tenure-track faculty members in medical schools and academe in general.

Broadened Definitions of Scholarship

In addition to the creation of multiple faculty tracks, a second major alteration in faculty appointment and promotion pathways in US medical schools is the continuing expansion of the definition of scholarship for both faculty members who are eligible for tenure and those who are not, accompanied by changes in the structural elements that allow that expanded definition to be operationalized in the promotion process (Bunton and Mallon 2007). Twenty years ago, Lovejoy and Clark observed that "increasingly, medical school promotion for the teacher-clinician is based on faculty contributions within the context of [the] expanded view of scholarship [as defined by Ernest Boyer], in particular using the 'scholarship of teaching and integration' as the essential criterion, with some schools using the 'scholarship of application'" (1995, 1080). The literature includes examples of a broadened definition of scholarship at an institutional level to support the career advancement of a variety of faculty types (for example, see Nora et al. 2000) and the increased use of educator tracks as a viable career pathway at medical schools (for example, see Klingensmith and Anderson 2006).

Medical schools have dramatically increased their use of tools to support expanded definitions of scholarship in the promotion process. In 1990, only five medical schools used education portfolios in the academic promotion process; in 2003, seventy-six did (Simpson et al. 2004). National education organizations in academic medicine defined expectations for medical educators (Pangaro et al. 2003), outlined the institutional resources and infrastructure required to support educational scholarship (Fincher et al. 2000), and articulated common standards for evaluating the evidence of educational contributions for promotion (Simpson et al. 2006). In the past ten years, a number of peer-reviewed educational resources have been created to assist both medical educators in preparing for promotion and members of promotion committees in assessing the performance of education-focused faculty members (for example, see Baldwin, Chandran, and Gusic 2012; Gusic et al. 2013; Simpson, Marcdante, and Fenzel 2007; Tewksbury et al. 2009).

A key component in the successful expansion of scholarship in the promotion process has been a national mechanism called MedEdPORTAL, which allows medical school faculty members to credibly demonstrate the quality of their educational scholarship. While research faculty have long been able to demonstrate quality and impact via peer-reviewed journal publications, education-minded faculty in medical schools did not have a comparable venue to earn peer-reviewed publication and the concomitant recognition, reputation, and visibility that publication affords. Created in 2005, MedEdPORTAL was designed as a rigorous peer-reviewed publication process to recognize and disseminate works of educational scholarship (Association of American Medical Colleges 2014c).

Limitations of the Financial Guarantee of Tenure

The third major change in faculty appointments at US medical schools is the redefinition of the financial guarantee of tenure. While the percentage of tenured faculty members has declined over the past thirty years at US medical schools, the number of tenured faculty members has increased because of the growth in faculty appointments (Bunton and Mallon 2007). Greater numbers of tenured and tenure-track faculty members bring financial risk to the institution, however. As noted above, one of the reasons medical schools created nontenure clinical faculty tracks was to lower the financial risk of employing highly paid physician faculty members in a volatile health care environment. For the same reason, in the past twenty to thirty years medical schools have revised their definitions of what portion of faculty salaries are guaranteed by tenure.

Legal experts and historians note that the link between tenure and salary is tenuous (Lee 2014; White 2000). Salary reductions are not violations of academic freedom or tenure due process; moreover, courts have found the American Association of University Professors' phrase "sufficient degree of economic security" (1940) to be too vague to be legally enforceable (Lee 2014). As a case in point, Northwestern University's Feinberg School of Medicine successfully defended its policy of reducing a tenured faculty member's salary to zero (*Daniel Kirschenbaum v. Northwestern University* 1999).

As table 5.1 indicates, medical schools clarified or redefined their policies on salary guarantee of tenure in the early 2000s. Many of the schools defined tenure to carry no financial guarantee or narrowly defined the guarantee as one of a base salary (such as the amount of state funding per full-time-equivalent faculty member) or linked the guaranteed portion to an internal or external standard (for example, the average salary of tenured university faculty members). These policy clarifications have allowed medical schools to cut the compensation of tenured faculty members for performance reasons. In the recent era of stagnation of federal funding for biomedical research and volatility in the

TABLE 5.1

Relationship between Tenure and Financial Guarantee for Faculty at US Medical Schools, 2005

	Clinical faculty No. of schools (%)	Basic science faculty No. of schools (%)
Tenure has a specific financial guarantee	56 (50%)	62 (52%)
Total institutional salary	3 (5)	8 (13)
State-funded base salary	16 (29)	18 (29)
Base salary, otherwise defined	9 (34)	18 (29)
Fixed dollar amount	4 (7)	5 (8)
Amount referenced to an internal standard	10 (18)	10 (16)
Amount referenced to an external standard	3 (5)	3 (5)
No response	1 (2)	0 (0)
Subtotal for respondents in above category	56 (100)	62 (100)
Financial guarantee is not clearly defined	10 (9)	12 (10)
Other	4 (4)	3 (3)
No financial guarantee	43 (38)	42 (35)
Total for all respondents	113 (100)	119 (100)

Source: Bunton and Mallon 2007. Reprinted with permission.

Note: Percentages do not include medical schools without tenure systems. Percentages may not add to 100 because of rounding.

health care industry, several medical schools have reduced salaries of tenured and non-tenured faculty alike (Mallon 2014).

One might assume that the redefinition of salary guarantees afforded by tenure would be a controversial move, but medical schools have encountered little if any resistance to such redefinitions. Two factors may explain why. First, it may be unlikely that anyone—from individual professors to the American Association of University Professors (AAUP)—could mount a credible argument that tenure guarantees the full salary of highly compensated physician faculty members. The AAUP's statement on "Tenure in the Medical School" (1999) acknowledged as much. Second, with much higher percentages of non-tenure-track faculty than tenured faculty, some institutions have viewed tenure guarantees as institutionalizing inequities among faculty members. For example, faculty members at the University of Vermont College of Medicine voted 315–0 to reduce the salary guarantee of tenure for PhD faculty. About 80 percent of them were on the non-tenure track and had no such guarantees; a smaller percentage of MD faculty members on the tenure track had minimal guarantees. Thus, the faculty as a whole questioned the equity of tenured PhD faculty members' having such different salary guarantees (Morin 2014).

Concurrent with the clarifications of the salary guarantee associated with tenure, medical schools began to institute variable compensation schemes for both clinical and basic science faculty. Sometimes referred to as XYZ plans, these schemes included a fixed base component; a variable or supplement component, allowing for compensation to vary based on market factors; and a bonus or incentive component, which rewarded faculty for achieving productivity goals (Jones and Gold 2001). Once popular for clinical faculty, such plans spread to basic science faculty, incentivizing and rewarding them for securing external research funds (Mallon and Korn 2004).

Flexibility in the Tenure Track

The fourth innovation in faculty appointment and career pathways in US medical schools is the use of considerable flexibility in tenure-track policies. While the percentage of tenure-track faculty members has markedly declined over the past thirty years, the number of medical schools that offer tenure has not changed: 94 percent of schools offer tenure as an option to basic science faculty, and 88 percent offer it as an option to clinical faculty (Bunton and Corrice 2011). At tenure-granting medical schools, four major changes have occurred over the last several decades: the lengthening of the probationary period for tenure-track faculty, the introduction of flexible ("flex") tracks, tenure-clock stopping, and part-time tenure appointments.

Perhaps the most dramatic change in tenure policies at US medical schools has been the lengthening of tenure probationary periods (see table 5.2). In 1983,

TABLE 5.2

Probationary Period Lengths for Basic Science and Clinical Faculty in US Medical Schools, 1983–2008

	Percentage of institutions						
	1983	*1994*	*1997*	*1999*	*2002*	*2005*	*2008*
Basic science faculty							
7 years or fewer	74	73	66	62	63	58	55
8 years or more	26	27	34	38	37	42	45
Clinical faculty							
7 years or fewer	74	69	59	58	53	54	50
8 years or more	26	31	41	42	47	46	50

Source: Bunton and Corrice 2011. Reprinted with permission.

Note: The number of medical schools included in the calculation of these percentages varies by year because of variability in response rate, data classification, and number of accredited institutions.

only one-quarter of medical schools had probationary periods exceeding the seven years recommended by AAUP guidelines. By 2008 (the most recent year for which data are available), 45 percent of schools did for tenure-track basic science faculty, and 50 percent did for tenure-track clinical faculty.

A second innovation in faculty appointments is the use of flexible tracks. Available at only a handful of institutions, this track type is akin to the undeclared major for a first-year undergraduate student. Under such a system, a new first-time faculty member does not need to choose a tenure-eligible or tenure-ineligible track when he or she is hired (Bunton and Mallon 2007). Rather, the undeclared track allows a faculty member time to decide whether he or she wants to pursue a career of hypothesis-driven original investigation or one with a greater focus on educational scholarship and clinical care. These undeclared tracks have been created for two main reasons (Bunton and Mallon 2007). First, the parent universities at some medical schools do not allow the probationary period to be formally extended, and the undeclared track gives a new investigator or clinician additional time to establish his or her lab or practice before starting the seven-year tenure clock. Second, the undeclared track keeps open the possibility that some clinical-scientists and researchers will ultimately choose a tenure-track appointment, whereas they might select a non-tenure track appointment if forced to choose when they are hired.

A third flexible program instituted widely at medical schools is the stopping of the tenure clock. Under such policies, tenure-track faculty members put their probationary period on hold—typically for one year but sometimes longer. Nearly 80 percent of medical schools with tenure systems offered tenure-clock-stopping policies in 2008 (the most recent data available), typically for reasons of child care, caring for an ill family member, or personal medical disability (Bunton and Corrice 2011). Yet having such a policy on paper does not mean having it in practice. Sarah Bunton and April Corrice (2011) reported that 75 percent of medical schools with such policies in 2008 had five or fewer faculty members use the policies in each of the previous two academic years.

A fourth innovation in tenure policies at medical schools is the use of part-time tenure-track positions. In concept, part-time tenure-track appointments allow faculty members to balance an academic career with other demands on their time. Susan Pollart and colleagues (2014) found that men and women cite different reasons for part-time employment at medical schools. Men often work part time to accommodate work at another practice site or in another professional position, while women do so for child-care reasons. As of 2008, 45 percent of medical schools allowed tenure-track faculty members to work less than full time during their nine- or twelve-month appointment while remaining on the track (Association of American Medical Colleges 2008). Of those institutions that had such policy provisions, 65 percent had no time cap for part-time tenure-track appointments.

The Future of Appointment, Tenure, and Career Pathways in Medical Schools

Despite significant experimentation and innovation in faculty career pathways, medical schools continue to face new challenges. First, biomedical research increasingly relies on teams of researchers from a variety of fields, and universities have created interdisciplinary research centers and institutes as a way to catalyze and coordinate these teams (Mallon 2006). However, the promotion and tenure process at medical schools traditionally has focused on the individual contributions of principal investigators rather than contributions to team-based research (Bunton and Mallon 2007). There are indications that schools are beginning to confront the need to recognize and reward faculty members for contributions to these new ways of conducting research: in a 2012 survey, 29 percent of medical schools indicated that they had revised their tenure and promotion guidelines in the previous four years to include emphasis on interdisciplinary team science, and another 16 percent of schools indicated that such policy changes were under active consideration (Association of American Medical Colleges 2012).

A second area of continued evolution relates to the definition of what it means to be a faculty member in a medical school. As academic medical centers have morphed into large health care delivery systems, thousands of physicians have been awarded full-time faculty appointments with little or no expectation of having a meaningful role in the institution's research or education missions (Barzansky and Kenagy 2010). Medical schools will need to clarify the fundamental features of what it means to be part of a full-time faculty in academic medicine (Block, Sonnino, and Bellini 2014) and clearly differentiate the duties, obligations, responsibilities, and rewards of a faculty role from those of the role of a full-time physician who happens to be employed by an academic health system.

What could the rest of academe learn from the evolution of faculty appointment, promotion, and career progression at US medical schools? Let me offer three main messages:

- Multiple career pathways with differentiated goals and expectations yet successful outcomes, in fact, can be implemented in higher education. However, a change in policy is necessary but not sufficient—a change in organizational culture is also needed. The experience of medical schools suggests that it can take years if not decades for the culture at the department and institutional levels to embrace a change in policy. An unanswered question for universities is whether they can accelerate not only the implementation but also the *acceptance* of alternative faculty career pathways.
- Career tracks that truly value, recognize, and reward education—not just research—require an infrastructure through which educators can credibly document and demonstrate their contributions to educational scholarship. In medical education, national disciplinary organizations made significant contributions to defining the expectations of rigorous education scholarship. Associations and societies in other disciplinary associations may have a similar role to play in other areas of the academy. A corollary is that faculty members need a rigorous, peer-reviewed mechanism to substantiate their educational scholarly contributions that is comparable to the peer-reviewed journal process in research. Medical educators have such a rigorous peer-reviewed mechanism; educators in other areas of higher education may need one as well.
- Higher education, including academic medicine, needs to take a holistic approach to the life cycle of faculty career development—recruitment, selection, development, evaluation, and transition—for all types of faculty needed to meet institutional missions. Simply expanding faculty career tracks will not create a more sustainable faculty workforce. Higher education institutions also must improve the processes by which they recruit faculty members, support their career development, offer more regular and

useful performance feedback, allow career focus to change and evolve over time, and improve the ways that faculty members transition through the various stages of their careers.

NOTES

1. For example, at the University of Pittsburgh, "the target for the School of Medicine is to obtain an overall average of 75% support of faculty salaries from research grants" (University of Pittsburgh 2013).

2. For example, the average salary for an associate professor at a doctoral university in 2013–14 was $90,447 (American Association of University Professors 2014); the average salary for an associate professor in a clinical department at a medical school in 2013–14 was $299,800 (Association of American Medical Colleges 2015).

REFERENCES

American Association of University Professors (AAUP). 1940. "Statement of Principles on Academic Freedom and Tenure." Washington: AAUP. Accessed December 8, 2015. http://www.aaup.org/report/1940-statement-principles-academic-freedom-and-tenure.

———. 1999. "Tenure in the Medical School." *Academe* 82 (1): 40–45.

———. 2014. *Losing Focus: The Annual Report on the Economic Status of the Profession, 2013–14.* Washington: AAUP.

Association of American Medical Colleges (AAMC). 2008. *Faculty Personnel Policies Survey.* Washington: AAMC.

———. 2012. *Faculty Personnel Policies Survey Report.* Washington: AAMC.

———. 2014a. *AAMC Data Book: Medical Schools and Teaching Hospitals by the Numbers 2014.* Washington: AAMC.

———. 2014b. *Current State of Faculty: A Snapshot of Data and Trends.* Washington: AAMC.

———. 2014c. "MedEdPORTAL Mission and Vision." AAMC. Accessed December 31, 2014. https://www.mededportal.org/about/missionandvision.

———. 2015. *Report on Medical School Faculty Salaries 2013–14.* Washington: AAMC.

Baldwin, Constance, Latha Chandran, and Maryellen Gusic. 2012. "Educator Evaluation Guidelines." *MedEdPORTAL.* Accessed December 9, 2015. https://www.mededportal.org/publication/9072.

Barchi, Robert L., and Barbara J. Lowery. 2000. "Scholarship in the Medical Faculty from the University Perspective: Retaining Academic Values." *Academic Medicine* 75: 899–905.

Barzansky, Barbara, and Gretchen Kenagy. 2010. "The Full-Time Clinical Faculty: What Goes Around Comes Around." *Academic Medicine* 85:260–65.

Beasley, Brent W., Scott M. Wright, Joseph Cofrancesco, Stewart F. Babbott, Patricia A. Thomas, and Eric B. Bass. 1997. "Promotion Criteria for Clinician-Educators in the United States and Canada: A Survey of Promotion Committee Chairpersons." *JAMA* 278:723–28.

Block, Steven M., Roberta E. Sonnino, and Lisa Bellini. 2014. "Defining 'Faculty' in Academic Medicine: Responding to the Challenges of a Changing Environment." *Academic Medicine* 90:279–82.

Bunton, Sarah A., and April M. Corrice. 2011. "Evolving Workplace Flexibility for U.S. Medical School Tenure-Track Faculty." *Academic Medicine* 86:481–85.

——— and William T. Mallon. 2010. "Clinical Faculty Satisfaction with the Academic Medicine Workplace." Washington: Association of American Medical Colleges.

Bunton, Sarah A., and William T. Mallon. 2007. "The Continued Evolution of Faculty Appointment and Tenure Policies at U.S. Medical Schools." *Academic Medicine* 82:281–89.

Coleman, Michelle M., and George V. Richard. 2011. "Faculty Career Tracks at U.S. Medical Schools." *Academic Medicine* 86:932–37.

Daniel S. Kirschenbaum v. Northwestern University. Appel. Ct. Ill (3rd Div. 1999). http://www .state.il.us/court/opinions/appellatecourt/2000/1stdistrict/april/html/1983059.htm.

Feder, Martin E., and James L. Madara. 2008. "Evidence-Based Appointment and Promotion of Academic Faculty at the University of Chicago." *Academic Medicine* 83:85–95.

Fincher, Ruth-Marie E., Deborah E. Simpson, Stewart P. Mennin, Gary C. Rosenfeld, Arthur Rothman, Martha C. McGrew, Penelope A. Hansen, Paul E. Mazmanian, and Jeffrey M. Turnbull. 2000. "Scholarship in Teaching: An Imperative for the 21st Century." *Academic Medicine* 75:887–94.

Gusic, Maryellen, Jonathan Amiel, Latha Chandran, Ruth-Marie Fincher, Brian Mavis, Patricia O'Sullivan, and Jamie Padmore. 2013. "Using the AAMC Toolbox for Evaluating Educators: You Be the Judge!" *MedEdPORTAL.* Accessed December 9, 2015. https:// www.mededportal.org/publication/9313.

Howell, Lydia P., and Klea D. Bertakis. 2004. "Clinical Faculty Tracks and Academic Success at the University of California Medical Schools." *Academic Medicine* 79:250–57.

Howell, Lydia. P., Chao-Yin Chen, Jesse P. Joad, Ralph Green, Edward J. Callahan, and Ann C. Bonham. 2010. "Issues and Challenges of Non-Tenure-Track Research Faculty: The UC Davis School of Medicine Experience." *Academic Medicine* 85:1041–47.

Jacobs, Michael B., and Donald Tower. 1992. "Enhancing the Training of Internal Medicine Residents at Stanford by Establishing a Model Group Practice and Raising Its Clinical Educators' Status." *Academic Medicine* 67:623–30.

Jones, Robert F. 1987. "Clinician-Educator Faculty Tracks in U.S. Medical Schools." *Journal of Medical Education* 62:444–47.

———. 2001. "The Present and Future of Appointment, Tenure, and Compensation Policies for Medical School Clinical Faculty." *Academic Medicine* 76:993–1004.

Jones, Robert F., and Jennifer S. Gold. 1998. "Faculty Appointment and Tenure Policies in Medical Schools: A 1997 Status Report." *Academic Medicine* 73:212–19.

Klingensmith, M. E., and K. D. Anderson. 2006. "Educational Scholarship as a Route to Academic Promotion: A Depiction of Surgical Education Scholars." *American Journal of Surgery* 191:533–37.

Lee, Barbara. 2014. "Compensation and Tenure: Flexibility in a Traditional Environment." Paper presented at the annual meeting of the Association of American Medical Colleges, Chicago, IL, November 10.

Levinson, Wendy, and Arthur Rubenstein. 2000. "Integrating Clinician-Educators into Academic Medical Centers: Challenges and Potential Solutions." *Academic Medicine* 75:906–12.

Lovejoy, Frederick H., and Mary B. Clark. 1995. "A Promotion Ladder for Teachers at Harvard Medical School: Experience and Challenges." *Academic Medicine* 70:1079–86.

Mallon, William T. 2006. "The Benefits and Challenges of Research Centers and Institutes in Academic Medicine: Findings from Six Universities and Their Medical Schools." *Academic Medicine* 81:502–12.

———. 2014. "Toward a 21st-Century Model of Financial Sustainability in U.S. Medical Schools: Circumstances and Strategies." Unpublished report to the dean and vice president for health affairs, Geisel School of Medicine, Dartmouth College.

Mallon, William T., and David Korn. 2004. "Education: Bonus Pay for Research Faculty." *Science* 303:476–77.

Metzger, Walter. 1987. "The Academic Profession in the United States." In *The Academic Profession: National, Disciplinary, and Institutional Settings*, edited by Burton R. Clark, 123–208. Berkeley: University of California Press.

Morin, Frederick. 2014. Public comments made at the annual meeting of the Association of American Medical Colleges, Chicago, IL, November 11.

Nora, Lora M., Claire Pomeroy, Thomas E. Curry, Nancy S. Hill, Phillip A. Tibbs, and Emery A. Wilson. 2000. "Revising Appointment, Promotion, and Tenure Procedures to Incorporate an Expanded Definition of Scholarship: The University of Kentucky College of Medicine Experience." *Academic Medicine* 75:913–24.

Pangaro, Louis, Jay Bachicha, Amy Brodkey, Heidi Chumley-Jones, Ruth-Marie Fincher, Douglas Gelb, Bruce Morgenstern, and Ajit K. Sachdeva. 2003. "Expectations of and for Clerkship Directors: A Collaborative Statement from the Alliance for Clinical Education." *Teaching and Learning in Medicine* 15:217–22.

Pati, Susmita, Josef Reum, Emily Conant, Lucy W. Tuton, Patricia Scott, Stephanie Abbuhl, and Jeane A. Grisso. 2013. "Tradition Meets Innovation: Transforming Academic Medical Culture at the University of Pennsylvania's Perelman School of Medicine." *Academic Medicine* 88:461–64.

Pollart, Susan M., Valerie Dandar, Linda Brubaker, Linda Chaudron, Leslie A. Morrison, Shannon Fox, Elza Mylona, and Sarah A. Bunton. 2014. "Characteristics, Satisfaction, and Engagement of Part-Time Faculty at U.S. Medical Schools." *Academic Medicine* 90:355–64.

Ruiz, Jorge. G., Christopher S. Candler, Syeda S. Qadri, and Bernard A. Roos. 2009. "E-Learning as Evidence of Educational Scholarship: A Survey of Chairs of Promotion and Tenure Committees at U.S. Medical Schools." *Academic Medicine* 84:47–57.

Shanafelt, Tait D., Sonja Boone, Litjen Tan, Lotte N. Dyrbye, Wayne Sotile, Daniel Satele, Colin P. West, Jeff Sloan, and Michael R. Oreskovich. 2012. "Burnout and Satisfaction with Work-Life Balance among US Physicians Relative to the General US Population." *Archives of Internal Medicine* 172:1377–85.

Simpson, Deborah, Ruth-Marie E. Fincher, Janet P. Hafler, David M. Irby, Boyd F. Richards, Gary C. Rosenfeld, and Thomas R. Viggiano. 2006. "Advancing Educators and Education: Defining the Components and Evidence of Educational Scholarship: Summary Report and Findings from the AAMC Group on Educational Affairs Consensus Conference on Educational Scholarship." Washington: Association of American Medical Colleges.

Simpson, Deborah, Janet Hafler, Diane Brown, and LuAnn Wilkerson. 2004. "Documentation Systems for Educators Seeking Academic Promotion in U.S. Medical Schools." *Academic Medicine* 79:783–90.

Simpson, Deborah, Karen Marcdante, and Julie Fenzel. 2007. "The Educator's Portfolio and Curriculum Vitae—Workshop and Resource Guide." *MedEdPORTAL*. Accessed December 9, 2015. https://www.mededportal.org/publication/677.

Sloane, Rae Anne. 2014. "10-Year Promotion Rates for Full-Time Faculty by Degree, Department Type, and Tenure Status." Unpublished manuscript. Washington: Association of American Medical Colleges.

Tewksbury, Linda, Cynthia Christy, Robin English, Joseph Gigante, Antionette Spoto-Cannons, Nasreen Talib, and Janice Hanson. 2009. "Scholarship of Application: When Service Is Scholarship—A Workshop for Medical Educators." *MedEdPORTAL*. Accessed December 9, 2015. http://dx.doi.org/10.15766/mep_2374–8265.7734.

Thomas, Patricia. A., Marie Diener-West, Marcia I. Canto, Don R. Martin, Wendy S. Post, and Michael B. Streiff. 2004. "Results of an Academic Promotion and Career Path

Survey of Faculty at the Johns Hopkins University School of Medicine." *Academic Medicine* 79:258–64.

University of California, San Francisco (UCSF). 2005. *A Faculty Handbook for Success: Advancement and Promotion at UCSF*. San Francisco: UCSF. Accessed December 9, 2015. http://senate.ucsf.edu/facultyhandbook/FacultyHandbook-UCSF.pdf.

University of Pittsburgh. 2013. "Faculty Performance and Evaluation Update, School of Medicine." Accessed December 9, 2015. http://www.medfaculty.pitt.edu/documents/ Performance_Plan_and_ Evaluation_Update_SOM2.pdf.

White, Lawrence. 2000. "Academic Tenure: Its Historical and Legal Meanings in the United States and Its Relationship to the Compensation of Medical School Faculty Members." *Saint Louis Law Review Journal* 44:51–80.

6

Students Speak about Faculty

What Students Need, What They Want, and What Helps Them Succeed

ARLEEN ARNSPARGER

JOANNA DRIVALAS

He's great. He'll talk to you like you're equal; he won't talk down to you like you don't know anything. You ask questions. He'll walk by you to see if you're all right. He's real hands-on with you. He's there for you no matter what, and he says it. "If you need me for anything, not just for this class or anyone else's class, I'll try to help you out as much as I can." I love that. —Community college student

Student voices are a valuable source of information about future faculty roles.[1] In fifteen years of conducting focus groups with college students throughout the country, the first author of this chapter has observed thematic consistencies regarding what students want from the faculty at their colleges. Increasingly, however, the faculty practices unfolding in many higher education settings run counter to both what students say they want and need and to what research identifies as effective practice. Current faculty models—including adjunct and, in some cases, tenure-track appointments—in many colleges and universities make it difficult for faculty to provide what students need and are seeking.

By using student voices as a guide, colleges and universities have the opportunity to redefine faculty roles in several important ways both inside and outside the classroom. Students offer a clear picture of the faculty practices and behaviors they believe have a positive impact on their collegiate experiences. In this chapter, we focus on two major areas consistently identified by students as important to their success: the value of faculty serving as advisors and mentors and the need for expert faculty who are skillful in teaching course content. We will explore these two areas through the perspective of the student voice and conclude with recommendations for a new faculty model that addresses these needs. But first we review research on student success and show its alignment with student voices.

Student Voices Align with Research

During focus group discussions, students reveal specific experiences that they say help them achieve their academic goals. They describe best teaching practices and their own academic behaviors, interactions with faculty, collaboration with peers, participation in extracurricular activities, and connections with programs and services that they believe support their learning. Though higher education is not in the business of making students happy, it is important to note that as students describe what works for them (in terms of their own actions and those of college faculty and staff), they are, in fact, echoing the research-based components of effective student engagement.

Both the National Survey of Student Engagement (NSSE) and the Center for Community College Student Engagement (CCCSE) measure undergraduate student engagement as the time and energy students invest in meaningful educational practices. Both organizations collect data from students about their college experiences and report the themes through publications and presentations. NSSE measures student engagement at four-year institutions in the following areas: academic challenge, active and collaborative learning, faculty-student interactions, enriching educational experiences (for example, service learning and study abroad) and supportive campus environment. CCCSE measures student engagement in community and technical colleges in active and collaborative learning, student effort, academic challenge, student-faculty interaction, and support for learners. Both CCCSE and NSSE also look at experiences specific to entering undergraduate students and identify high-impact practices that incorporate high-intensity student engagement.

The connection between student engagement and student success is well documented (Shapiro et al. 2014). Learning, persistence, and college completion are consistently associated with students' active engagement with faculty, staff, other students, and their subject matter. In separate studies analyzing NSSE and CCCSE data, researchers have confirmed the relationship between specific measures of student engagement and increased student learning, persistence, and completion (Blaich and Seifert 2009; McClenney and Marti 2006; Price and Tovar 2014).

When students describe the experiences that make a difference for them, they are giving voice to the learning paradigm described by Robert Barr and John Tagg. Barr and Tagg describe the need for a shift to a learning paradigm in which "the college's purpose is not to transfer knowledge but to create environments and experiences that bring students to discover and construct knowledge for themselves, to make students members of communities of learners that make discoveries and solve problems" (1995, 15). Their article compares the standard, accepted practices of college faculty, the instruction paradigm (in which the primary function is to provide instruction to students and focus on knowledge and content transfer, with students as passive receivers), to a new model, the learning paradigm (which instead is targeted at making students active agents in the learning process). The instruction paradigm is one of transfer: knowledge, as it is known by the so-called great knowers, is imparted to the students who have come to receive it. Success is measured by the quality of entering students, the faculty, and their lectures. This paradigm employs end-of-course assessments in traditional college settings: the teacher at the front of the classroom, who is siloed in his or her department and separate from the rest of the university. In the learning paradigm, however, traditional structures—such as teachers lecturing behind a lectern, endless note taking from PowerPoint slides, and individually completed assignments—are altered in service of the goal of learning. For example, faculty members focus on practices that enhance students' engagement, such as active and collaborative learning. Learning is encouraged inside and outside the classroom, and classroom learning is connected to students' outside experiences. The learning paradigm values student learning above all else and measures success by the quality of student learning and the success of diverse student populations on campus. It uses holistic approaches to grading and evaluating success to create learning environments and experiences that differ from the traditional classroom. Degrees are awarded based on a demonstration of knowledge and skill, not just seat time.

While Barr and Tagg advocate the use of a learning paradigm that functions in a manner quite different from the current model, we suggest that elements of the learning paradigm can and should be used to frame a new faculty model. Outdated practices embedded in faculty culture that are no longer conducive to student learning can be replaced by learning-centric methods aimed at improving the outcomes of college students.

Components of Barr and Tagg's learning paradigm have been reinforced and expanded by higher education leaders and organizations, including Vincent Tinto (1994 and 2012), in his principles of effective action to improve student retention; the American Association of Colleges and Universities in its discussion of high-impact practices; and NSSE and CCCSE, which also highlight high-impact educational practices (Center for Community College Student Engagement 2002–14; Kuh et al. 2005; National Survey of Student Engagement n.d. and 2015).

If higher education leaders promote environments in which learning is the focus and students are "co-producers" of their own learning, as Barr and Tagg (1995, 14) suggest, such a revamped faculty model would enable faculty to fulfill roles that fully support student learning both inside and outside the classroom.

Advising and Mentoring

From the student perspective, faculty members are the go-to people for information and guidance. Students expect faculty to play a substantial role as both advisors and mentors. NSSE and CCCSE focus group data show that students believe that the instructors who have helped them most have done so by advising them on selecting a major and identifying a career path, connecting them to campus resources, remaining available for support and counsel beyond class hours, and frequently reaching out, either in person or electronically, to help them stay on track with their studies. A new faculty model must explore the potential of having both full- and part-time faculty members play an increased role in advising.

While important to students throughout their academic careers, mentoring and advising should have different shapes and focuses at different phases. Freshmen and transfer students will need guidance in areas such as academic planning and selecting a major, while seniors will need help looking for jobs and graduate programs and navigating the graduation process. However, mentorship that helps students persist year to year will be useful to all students, regardless of how many credits they have earned. Faculty advising and mentoring are valuable to students as they transition into, persist through, and transition out of a collegiate institution.

Expectations

Entering students immediately want to connect with those who will be teaching their classes. They are nervous as they begin college and have questions for faculty. They want guidance about how to successfully navigate college courses (Center for Community College Student Engagement 2009–10; McClenney and Arnsparger 2012). One student asked: "What will my teachers expect from me?" The uncertainty so plainly stated by this student demonstrates not only a desire to know the answer to the question but also a need to know where to find that answer. Is this student used to knowing his or her teacher's expectations? Does a disconnect exist between how students understand expectations in the K–12 system compared to the postsecondary one? It is unclear whether this student is specifically concerned with knowing teachers' expectations regarding level of class participation, degree of previous knowledge, or sophistication of writing, for instance. The student may, more simply, care about the clarity with which the teacher presents his or her expectations to the class. For example, "[I don't] know what to expect in my classes, if I'm gonna get a really strict, harsh teacher or a very caring teacher." Here, the student has constructed expectations more specifically. The dichotomy drawn between "really strict, harsh" and "very caring" indicates that the student believes that classroom expectations are connected to the disposition of the teacher. Even the choice of terms—strict and harsh versus caring—is interesting, since the student seems to consider them opposites. The assumptions which students carry into the classroom regarding expectations have the potential to become troublesome if teachers do not explicitly address them. If students interpret demonstrating care as synonymous with not being strict, the consequences could be that students do not take teachers' leadership seriously. Furthermore, if students believe that a teacher who does not actively show "caring" in the ways that they expect it to be demonstrated is therefore "harsh," then they might shut down and lose opportunities for learning. It is up to faculty, then, to be explicit in their expectations and therefore set the culture of their classroom.

Including Faculty Members Early in Orientation

In collecting data about students' perspectives on college and actual college experiences, the first author of this chapter frequently hears students complain that faculty members are not participating in college orientation nor advising new students at the time when students hope to learn about faculty expectations. In many institutions, students have no opportunity prior to the start of classes to meet faculty members, ask them questions about faculty expectations, learn about how college classes are conducted, or discuss possible career directions. In many institutions, neither full- nor part-time faculty members are expected to interact with students before classes begin. Faculty are rarely formally included in early college experiences, such as orientation, registration, and academic advising or career planning, and no incentives are offered to encourage their participation. This lack of early connection to students runs counter to students' need for faculty to play an important role in helping them more confidently transition to college and in supporting them as they move toward graduation.

Structured Pathways for Learning

In addition to being pivotal to college transition through their advising and mentoring role, faculty also help students succeed and complete college by creating a coherent academic pathway and providing important information on majors and an understanding of future options that provide the motivation to finish college. The national focus on increasing on-time college completion has led to an emphasis on creating coherent academic and career pathways for all students (Center for Community College Student Engagement 2014b; Complete College America 2012). For students to benefit from the pathway design, they need to understand how their courses and college experiences fit together into a bigger picture that will lead them to their academic goal. If faculty members are not available or supported enough to provide this sort of guidance, or if they do not themselves understand the bigger picture, how will students be sure that they have a coherent academic plan with aligned classes? Additionally, if faculty members are not collaborating with advising staff members to ensure an integrated approach both inside and outside the classroom, then students are not receiving all the direction they need to develop an academic plan. Faculty members can help create coherent pathways that lead to student success if they are appointed to advising assignments or work in partnership with academic advisors, and if they integrate advising components into class assignments.

One student noted: "I started researching the career I'm looking at . . . and I discovered it was completely different from the job I thought it was. I wouldn't have known that if I didn't have [this] assigned to me. They gave us, in assignment form, the research we should have been dong on our own to find out the things we need to know about our future." The student suggests how faculty can serve as advisors on choice of major and career planning. Choosing a major and preparing for a career are not simple tasks, and for many students, identifying a job of interest is not synonymous with knowing how to prepare for it—either in a practical or an academic way. By intentionally integrating this task as an assignment into the syllabus, this student's professor created an opportunity for students to ask questions they did not know they had and to do the research necessary to answer them. Having this experience in a first-year major course would help ensure that students are on the track that is best for them and their goals, and could prevent regret later in their academic careers. Understanding the requirements and expectations of a potential career is important to becoming a competitive future candidate in the job market. In many fields, such as business, the arts, and education, faculty members have unique insights and experiences that can help prepare students for their postacademic careers.

Academic and Career Advising

Students view faculty members as their primary college contacts for academic and career advising. When both full- and part-time faculty are knowledgeable about their programs, departments, and the intersections between programs and career options, students benefit. One student said: "One of the things that came up during the first session of class was that [the teacher] led a group discussion and explained exactly what the program was about and made very clear to everybody in the class—this is in a group setting—that this is what you can expect to get out of this program. [He] ran that through a PowerPoint presentation and gave a pretty clear and concise view of what you were gonna be able to do if you completed the program." This quote demonstrates the specificity with which faculty members can and should be able to articulate the demands of their classes and programs. By hearing the expectations on the first day of class, the students now have each other as support as well, since they have all been exposed to the same information at the same time. This information also makes it possible for students to reevaluate their choices. If a student enrolls in a gatekeeper course making incorrect assumptions about the program of study (in terms of either its expectations or what it prepares students for after graduation), an explanation and overview such as the one this student was given on the first day would correct the student's assumptions and give him or her plenty of time to make other plans as needed.

Faculty members who are disconnected from academic information are not able to provide the continuing guidance that students need. In particular, part-time faculty members who are not collaborating with their full-time colleagues on curriculum design and have little interaction with them may have difficulty seeing how their courses fit into structured pathways for students. They do not know what their students have learned before enrolling in the classes they are teaching, and they have no knowledge of what their students' curricular next steps will be. Working independently, part-time faculty members might not be familiar with sequenced learning outcomes related to their courses, or with the alignment of those outcomes with other course or program outcomes. A lack of participation in governance and curriculum development might also be to blame. Such gaps in part-time faculty members' knowledge about college offerings make it difficult for them to help students see connections between college courses and their professional goals. It also decreases the contribution that part-timers can make by drawing on their own field experiences to make connections with college curriculum. If part-time faculty members do have the appropriate institutional and curricular knowledge, they might be limited in their mentoring efforts, compared to full-time faculty members, because of the strain on their limited time and the absence of designated office space.

Simply helping students plan a course of study or understand the expectations of the classes is not enough to ensure that students are able to persist through their programs. During the past twenty years, more than thirty-one million students have started college but never earned a degree (Shapiro et al. 2014). Data from both four- and two-year institutions consistently show that despite students' goals and intentions when they begin college, many students drop out (Planty et al. 2009).

Fostering a Sense of Belonging

When a student drops out of school, college faculty and staff members often attribute his or her decision to leave to extenuating personal circumstances, such as work or family responsibilities. However, during focus group discussions students typically point to their lack of connection at the school. When the first author of this chapter asks students in focus groups about what keeps them in school, they frequently name a member of the faculty or staff who reached out to them, encouraged them, and gave them the extra attention and support that they needed to succeed. Acts of mentorship like this throughout their collegiate tenure allow students to connect to the campus community and persist through to graduation. Students say that faculty act as mentors and show them they care by calling them by name, providing targeted feedback on their performance, and expressing concern and offering support when they are struggling or distracted by personal issues. Students begin to think of faculty as "colleagues" who have "their doors always open" to them and "take time to listen." These associations help facilitate mentoring relationships between faculty and students.

Students feel more at ease when faculty members intentionally acknowledge them and their experiences, as shown when students cite listening and other forms of visible and personal investment. Students benefit from faculty members who go beyond the teaching role to establish connections during class and make themselves available beyond class hours. Is it realistic to expect faculty members whose role and compensation are limited to credit hours taught to offer the personal contact students need? A new faculty model will need to address the question of how to ensure that all faculty members, whether full or part time, make student connections paramount in a learning environment in which they engage with, advise, and mentor students to help them achieve their academic goals.

Teaching and Learning

Students expect college faculty members to know and impart knowledge to them, as described in the instruction paradigm (Barr and Tagg 1995). However, without specific practices and considerations, the likelihood that students will acquire the knowledge is reduced. Expertise in a field is not equal to or synonymous with the ability to use and share that expertise for the instruction of students. Students look to their teachers to help them learn the skills and content they need for their academic and professional careers, and to help them transition into an unfamiliar learning environment. In this section, the authors of the chapter use student voices to identify the important aspects of teaching for faculty members to employ.

Engaging Pedagogies

Engaging students beyond the traditional lecture-style class is important to learning. Students cite as helpful professors who "[go] more in-depth with it" by "doing it hands-on with me." The use of small breakout groups and in-class practice, establishing clear goals, and other evidence-based practices help students take control of their learning. Learning from other students and constructing knowledge together can be just as valuable as the learning that occurs from a book or a professor. When teachers promote new teaching models, they engage the group and depend on the students' ownership to create new opportunities for learning. Students recognize that lecture-only teaching is limited, claiming that "talk[ing] about [the course content] is okay, I'll kind of get it," and craving something more to prove their understanding. Active lessons signal to students that professors are invested in classroom practices: "everybody interacts with the professor, asks questions, has discussions about the subjects we are going to see," which leads to a situation in which "everybody's interested and everybody's active and the teacher is treating us like it's not just another lecture."

Students describe the need to actively participate in class to promote learning. As Barr and Tagg (1995) note, good teaching requires letting go of some control and allowing students to take ownership. Approaches such as problem-based and project-based teaching and learning give students the opportunity to engage with the concepts and theories in a practical way.

High Expectations

Students also identify the best teachers as those who have high expectations. They are grateful for faculty members who reach out to them to provide the support they need to meet expectations. They seek faculty members who know how to teach—how to engage diverse twenty-first-century learners who are comfortable with technology, learn best by understanding how their courses relate to their personal and professional lives, and thrive in a hands-on environment. They respond to faculty members who are up to date on their content knowledge and passionate about what they teach. For example, one student said of a professor: "She had a reputation of just being really tough, and her classes were really tough, it was a lot of work. But it's five credits; it's what you signed up for when you went into it. Having that base of knowledge that I have after making it through her class, it's just indispensable." By embracing high expectations, students recognize the value of classes that challenge them. Through understanding the expectations of the faculty member described above, the student internalized the value of foundational knowledge in a more critical way than he or she perhaps would have done otherwise. High expectations, coupled with expertise, allowed this faculty member to challenge students in a meaningful way, thus facilitating opportunities for learning.

Challenge and Support

While students acknowledge that they want their instructors to set high expectations, they also recognize that they might not yet have the skills needed to meet those expectations. Knowing that their professors will "help you get back up" if you "fall below [expectations]" builds a safety net for students and allows them to take risks in the classroom. Students appreciate instructors who offer encouragement and support and teach them the skills needed to succeed in the course: "He walked us through [the work], and I would even go up to him after class every time I had problems or any type of question, and he was just there."

This student demonstrates the confidence needed to meet high expectations. While students may have entered the collegiate environment already equipped with the skills to advocate on their own behalf, the teacher supports those actions to advance student learning. Going through tough material step by step, while helpful, may not be enough on its own, and invested teachers recognize that students may still need extra help.

Contextualized Learning

Students also consistently give high marks to faculty members who connect course content with other aspects of students' lives. Understanding the value of course content and how it relates to their greater aspirations, including career goals, is important to students. Students also crave opportunities to use what they are learning and speak favorably about the opportunities to apply their newly acquired knowledge that faculty members provide: "I'm actually participating this week in the Cardinal Cravings Store; we get to run the store. We're split into five different groups in our business class and we use our own marketing strategies; it's a very hands-on project." This student and his or her classmates were given the chance to bring their learning to life and test their marketing skills in a useful and realistic manner. When students have to independently apply what has been taught in the classroom to a real-life situation, they learn how to assess and evaluate the practices they have studied. By working in groups, these students also experienced many of the team-focused elements of successful business and marketing plans.

Student success can be facilitated when faculty members focus both on setting ground rules and high expectations and on teaching skills, but adjuncts often struggle to be strong teachers. First, they are hired for their specific content knowledge, not their expertise in teaching. Second, they are unaware of departmental learning goals and expectations, so it is often hard for them to set up a challenging environment. Because student evaluations are used in decisions about rehiring faculty members, adjuncts are also fearful of having high expectations of students. Part-time faculty contracts cover a limited number of class hours per week, not additional hours to dedicate to students outside of class. If adjuncts make extra time available to students, they are doing so voluntarily and without compensation. In addition, the lack of office space for part-time instructors often leaves these faculty members searching for locations to have private conversations with students. The lack of time for students is not limited to part-time faculty members. Full-time faculty members frequently have committee assignments and other responsibilities that are given a higher priority than time spent with students outside of class. A new faculty model will require that colleges revisit these structural impediments and current priorities to shift to student-centered learning environments, as the learning paradigm describes (Barr and Tagg 1995).

Designing Faculty Models That Best Serve Students

To meet the learning needs of students, as articulated by the focus group excerpts in this chapter and as defined by Barr and Tagg (1995), faculty practices and expectations need to shift. Changes need to occur on both the institutional and individual levels. Colleges and universities must adjust reward systems for faculty and provide opportunities for pedagogical development. Through orientations, professional development seminars, and collaborative meetings, institutions could offer faculty the tools necessary to build intentionally structured approaches to teaching and learning. Institutions must also offer incentives and adequate office or working space for full- and part-time faculty members to interact with students. Multiyear faculty contracts and the elimination of last-minute hiring would bring more stability to faculty assignments, making it possible for students to identify who will be teaching the classes they are considering and allowing time for faculty members to adequately prepare for their teaching assignments and develop their expertise. Individual faculty members would need to be willing to make the effort to experiment with new classroom techniques. Institutions and individuals would also need to understand and accept a paradigmatic shift, replacing old values with a new system of measuring quality.

A challenge to all of this is the strong reliance on part-time faculty members. In some colleges and universities, welcome efforts are under way to create more full-time positions. Simply hiring more full-time faculty members alone is inadequate, however. It is unrealistic to expect a significant shift to occur quickly, particularly in institutions where part-time faculty members teach a majority of the courses offered. Yet where possible, more hiring of full-time faculty members should be emphasized.

In addition to creating more full-time faculty positions, colleges and universities can take other steps to strengthen the roles of both full- and part-time faculty members to meet student needs more effectively. Institutional leaders can reallocate existing resources to support practices that build collaboration between full- and part-time faculty members. They can provide incentives for faculty members to participate in designing models that will enable them to fully engage students in effective learning environments that go beyond the classroom.

In this chapter we have focused on two major areas consistently identified by students: the importance of having faculty members serve as advisors and mentors, and the need for faculty members who are experts not only in course content but also in how to effectively engage students. In these two areas, we imagine a shift in faculty roles designed to provide what works best for students, based on what we have learned from research and student voices. We next offer targeted recommendations for the new faculty model in two areas.

ADVISING AND MENTORING

- Faculty roles in the advising and mentoring of college students should be increased and present throughout students' tenure. Freshmen and transfer students need support from faculty as they choose their major and create academic plans. Seniors need advice on jobs and graduation programs, and help navigating the graduation process. All students need faculty members to support their persistence from year to year.

- Students expect faculty expectations to reflect care and consideration. Faculty members need to clearly articulate expectations throughout mentoring and advising processes that demonstrate the investment they have in the students.

- Faculty members should make early connections with students through orientation for freshmen and transfer students. Since the learning process begins for new college students the moment they arrive on campus, the faculty role should begin before the first day of class. Students expect to learn about classroom operations and expectations from faculty members, so they must be made available to students before classes begin. At this time, faculty members should also capitalize on their visibility and advise students on ways in which they can take advantage of opportunities to work with faculty members and other students to ensure their learning. Part-time faculty members should be paid to participate in aspects of student orientation and initial advising sessions.

- Faculty members should advise students on courses of study and career alignment. Ensuring that full- and part-time faculty members are informed about institutional opportunities and curricular alignment would facilitate the advising process and ensure that students receive accurate information from experts in the field. Ideally, first-year major courses should offer opportunities for faculty members to assess students' career aspirations and determine if they are aligned with the students' programs of study. Time will need to be built in to full- and part-time faculty members' schedules to facilitate this process.

- To increase the quality of faculty members' academic and career advising to students, they should be permitted and expected to participate in curricular design. Barriers to faculty involvement, including separation from governance and lack of information and time, must be addressed at the institutional level.

- Students expect the faculty to connect them to the campus. Since students cite a lack of connections as reasons for dropping out, faculty members have the opportunity to encourage students and build relationships through listening to students, responding to their needs, and sharing elements of their own academic and career experiences, where appropriate.

TEACHING AND LEARNING

- Faculty members should be experts in their field, prepared to impart their knowledge to students through intentional pedagogical practices mastered through professional development and other learning opportunities. While faculty members must be hired based on their expertise, a demonstration of content mastery is not sufficient to ensure that students will learn from them. Intentionally incorporating effective teaching practices and pedagogical strategies into courses gives faculty members an opportunity to engage students in learning. Institutions should support discipline-based professional development for faculty members so that they can be informed about the best practices for teaching in their field. Professional development should be aligned with institutional goals and promote teaching strategies that research, practice, and student voices show are most effective. Both full- and part-time faculty members should collaborate regularly with colleagues by sharing their content and pedagogical expertise through on-campus sessions, online training, or structured faculty inquiry groups (Carnegie Foundation for the Advancement of Teaching n.d.). Faculty members should have access to funds to support their attendance at conferences and workshops, conduct their own research, and refresh their professional knowledge through sabbaticals that include work in their discipline or occupational field. Future faculty models should reflect an understanding of the fact that students benefit from faculty members who have knowledge, skills, and technological savvy to connect with students in multiple ways and engage them in creative approaches to learning, both inside and outside the classroom.
- Faculty members should learn and develop the use of evidence-based teaching practices in their classrooms. Institutions must offer compensated opportunities for part- and full-time faculty members to improve their teaching skills. Faculty members must do their part and be willing to change their practices and develop new approaches to student learning. Evidence-based teaching practices such as facilitating group work and interaction, creating opportunities for hands-on practice in real-life simulations, and interrupting lectures for student-led discussion must be prioritized. Institutions and faculty members should plan to assess the new practices and develop strategies for improvement.
- Faculty members should hold their students to high academic expectations. If faculty members demonstrate and maintain such expectations—and offer support and encouragement for underprepared students struggling to meet them—students will respond positively and award greater value to the course and the material. Faculty members should

expect to put in tutoring hours and therefore should expect to be compensated for and have a designated space to perform such work.

- Faculty members should use their experiences in the field of study and their interests to motivate and encourage students. Abstract concepts become real-world applications when faculty members demonstrate the concrete ways in which the material is valuable and necessary to given courses of study and future careers. Students crave the energy and excitement that faculty members have about their work and feel more connected to the subject when these connections are made.

Learning from Student Voices

Student voices make a critical contribution to creating learning environments that support increased student success. Students are clear about what works for them. The needs and perspectives they express are aligned with and bring to life what research and institutional practice show leads to improved student engagement, persistence, and completion.

Students can teach us much about college-level learning. Students look to faculty members as advisors and mentors. They turn to faculty members to help them identify and create their academic and career paths and show them how each course relates to their interests and goals. Students seek faculty members who believe they can succeed, yet who understand that they have to learn new skills to master college-level work. They want faculty members who challenge them in their course work and help them develop the skills to meet rigorous expectations. Students say that they benefit from faculty members who employ varied approaches to connect them to the content and skills they need to learn, from practices inside the classroom to experiences beyond it.

Student voices can be a powerful co-creator of learning to help guide higher education leaders in redesigning faculty roles. Students are the experts about their own experiences, and they can help us understand how to best support their learning. In most colleges and universities, student voices are not often considered when making institution-level decisions. Nonetheless, their insights prompt questions for higher education leaders to consider, including how to think about new faculty models.

NOTE

1. All student quotes in this chapter come from focus groups conducted by the Center for Community College Student Engagement (n.d.; see also 2002–14 and 2009–10) as part of the Initiative on Student Success and, specifically, the Starting Right Focus Groups.

REFERENCES

Barr, Robert B., and John Tagg. 1995. "From Teaching to Learning—A New Paradigm for Undergraduate Education." *Change* 27 (6): 12–26.

Blaich, Charles F., and Tricia A. Seifert. 2009. "Validation of NSSE with Liberal Arts Outcomes: Findings from the Wabash National Study of Liberal Arts Education." Paper presented at the NSSE Tenth Anniversary Symposium, Indianapolis, IN, October.

Carnegie Foundation for the Advancement of Teaching. n.d. "Faculty Inquiry Toolkit." Accessed December 10, 2015. http://specctoolkit.carnegiefoundation.org/category/faculty-inquiry-groups-fig/.

Center for Community College Student Engagement. n.d. Home page. Accessed December 10, 2015. http://www.ccsse.org/center/.

———. 2002–14. Initiative on Student Success. Austin: Center for Community College Student Engagement, The University of Texas at Austin.

———. 2005–15. Community College Faculty Survey of Student Engagement. Austin: Center for Community College Student Engagement, The University of Texas at Austin.

———. 2009–10. Starting Right Focus Groups. Austin: Center for Community College Student Engagement, The University of Texas at Austin.

———. 2013. *A Matter of Degrees, Engaging Practices, Engaging Students.* Austin: Center for Community College Student Engagement, The University of Texas at Austin.

———. 2014a. *Contingent Commitments: Bringing Part-Time Faculty into Focus.* Austin: Center for Community College Student Engagement, The University of Texas at Austin.

———. 2014b. *A Matter of Degrees, Practices to Pathways.* Austin: Center for Community College Student Engagement, The University of Texas at Austin.

Complete College America. 2012. *Guided Pathways to Success: Boosting College Completion.* Washington: Complete College America.

Kuh, George D., Jillian Kinzie, John H. Schuh, Elizabeth J. Whitt, and Associates. 2005. *Student Success in College: Creating Conditions That Matter.* San Francisco: Jossey-Bass.

McClenney, Kay M., and Arleen Arnsparger. 2012. *Students Speak, Are We Listening? Starting Right in the Community College.* Austin: Center for Community College Student Engagement, The University of Texas at Austin.

McClenney, Kay, and C. Nathan Marti. 2006. *Exploring Relationships between Student Engagement and Student Outcomes in Community Colleges (Report on Validation Research Working Paper).* Austin, TX: Community College Survey of Student Engagement.

National Survey of Student Engagement. n.d. Faculty Survey of Student Engagement. Bloomington: Indiana University.

———. 2015. Home page. Bloomington: Indiana University. Accessed December 9, 2015. http://www.nsse.iub.edu/.

Planty, Michael, William Hussar, Thomas Snyder, Grace Kena, Angelina Kewal Ramani, Jana Kemp, Kevin Bianco, and Rachel Dinkes. 2009. *The Condition of Education 2009.* Washington, DC: National Center for Education Statistics. Accessed December 10, 2015. http://nces.ed.gov/pubs2009/2009081.pdf.

Price, Derek V., and Esau Tovar. 2014. "Student Engagement and Institutional Graduation Rates: Identifying High-Impact Educational Practices for Community Colleges." *Community College Journal of Research and Practice* 38 (9): 766–82.

Shapiro, Doug, Afet Dundar, Xin Yuan, Autumn T. Harrell, Justin C. Wild, and Mary B. Ziskin. 2014. "Some College, No Degree: A National View of Students with Some College Enrollment, but No Completion." Herndon, VA: National Student

Clearinghouse Research Center. Accessed December 9, 2015. http://nscresearchcenter
.org/signaturereport7.

Tinto, Vincent. 1994. *Leaving College: Rethinking the Causes and Cures of Student Attrition.*
Chicago: University of Chicago Press.

———. 2012. *Completing College: Rethinking Institutional Action.* Chicago: University of
Chicago Press.

7

Faculty as Learners

The New Faculty Role through the Lens of Faculty Development

MALCOLM BROWN

Higher education is frequently castigated for being impervious to change. Certainly nobody would mistake the tempo of change at a college or university for that at a Silicon Valley start-up. Nevertheless, changes are afoot in higher education with respect to its teaching and learning mission, and this is clearly visible with respect to faculty roles in teaching and learning and to the development and engagement support they receive. The thesis of this chapter is that new practices in faculty development and engagement both reflect and influence the rapid evolution of the role of the faculty member as an instructor.

To appreciate this, we only need to think back to a time fifteen or twenty years ago and consider the teaching styles and classroom designs that were then predominant at most institutions. Back then, very few people were thinking about active learning classroom designs, hybrid course models, or an overall learning-centered foundation for campus instructional practice. Significantly, the first great wave of the online university, unleashed by the dot-com boom, was quickly losing both money and momentum.

Back then, with the Web beginning to hit its stride and learning management system (LMS) applications arriving at almost every campus, the spotlight was on technology. Faculty workshops were often called "teaching with technology," implying that technology was the key ingredient to improved teaching: just add technology and stir. The possibilities of the Internet were catching the collective imagination, resulting in a preoccupation with technology.

This approach to faculty development reflected the reality that the traditional roles for higher education faculty were fully in place. These roles focused on the tenure-track professor, who was a scholar first and a teacher second. The adjunct professor was in the minority, both in terms of the size of this group in the instructor population and with respect to professional status. The tenure-track professor held dominion over his or her courses; teaching and the conduct of a course was anything but a "team sport."[1] Hence faculty development programs were not in a position to do much beyond proffering suggestions at individual workshops where attendance was optional. The idea of teaching as a lifelong craft was remote.

But today the landscape is different. Faculty roles are undergoing significant changes, along with campus programs associated with those roles. Perhaps most conspicuous is the new emphasis on pedagogical practice. The higher education teaching and learning community has rallied around the theme of active learning. We are implementing new classroom designs and are flipping our courses to take advantage of them. In publications like the EDUCAUSE Learning Initiative's (ELI's) *7 Things You Should Know About* and the *NMC Horizon Report*,[2] developments like the flipped class model are mentioned in the same category as wearable technology and the Internet of Things. While this is not to suggest that higher education has been utterly transformed, it is clear that it is evolving, and at a pace that is unprecedented in its history.

Younger faculty members, having grown up with these models, are increasingly looking to teach the way they were taught. In general, faculty readiness to explore new course models and pedagogical techniques is greater than is sometimes commonly thought. A study commissioned by the Bill and Melinda Gates Foundation about postsecondary faculty practices summarizes its findings this way: "We look at faculty through a new lens which shows that 40% of faculty have already adopted, or are ready to adopt, new techniques which benefit students" (McGoldrick, Watts, and Economou 2015). Yet there is still disparity between the numbers of faculty members who describe themselves as ready to adopt and the numbers of those who have actually adopted such techniques, which means that faculty development is appropriately seen as a strategic priority for nearly every college and university.

While this shift toward the learning-centered approach is plainly visible with respect to undergraduate and graduate education, it is also informing—and perhaps transforming—the practice of faculty development. Perhaps the shift can best be characterized as one from viewing faculty members as users of applications to seeing them as adult learners developing a craft. Once the perspective shifts in this way, then all the insights and new approaches for undergraduate education become highly relevant to faculty development. Nor is it an accident that these changes are happening in tandem: the overall cultural shift to a learning-centered approach has implications for faculty as instructors and for the programs in place to support them in that role.

The term *user* comes to us from information technology (IT) shops, dating back to at least the 1960s. It focuses on the use and operation of a computer, abstracted from the person's work environment and the practices of that environment. It positions technology in the foreground. Implied in this perspective is that the user, once proficient in the operation of the computer and its applications, will be able to successfully use the computer in the context of his or her work. However, this approach raises an important question: does proficiency with information technology guarantee an improvement in the quality of the work? Clearly the answer is no, and that is what is lacking in this approach. In the domain of teaching and learning, proficient users are not necessarily better teachers.

In the past, faculty development was often characterized by this user paradigm. The role of the faculty member was that of the course ringmaster, in sole control of nearly all aspects of the course. One videotaped faculty members, gave them the tapes, and assumed that they would figure out what to change. As we will see, such an approach all too often falls short of producing transformative outcomes and new practices. Once information technology arrived on the scene, one conducted workshops and training sessions on how to program, use the Web, and especially how to use the LMS. One evaluated the success of faculty development efforts by means of attendance numbers at workshops and faculty satisfaction surveys.

But that is now somewhat old school. Technology workshops typically attract early adopters, resulting in a limited scope and impact. I suggest that this approach to faculty development and engagement is being supplanted in a way very similar to the way that the transmission model of education is being supplanted by the learning-centric model.

This development is of particular importance in light of the fact that faculty development remains a key issue for teaching and learning in higher education. Technologies may come and go, but faculty development seems to endure as a programmatic cornerstone for professionals concerned about advancing postsecondary learning.

A set of indicators support this claim. The ELI has conducted an annual survey of the teaching and learning community for the past five years to identify the community's key themes and opportunities. The survey canvasses all players in higher education teaching and learning, including faculty members, instructional designers, instructional technologists, librarians, and staff members at teaching and learning centers. In 2014, faculty development ranked third in the list of issues in teaching and learning, and in 2015 it ranked first (EDUCAUSE 2015). Another indicator is the EDUCAUSE "Top Ten IT Issues," another annual survey focused on information technology in higher education. Here faculty development, when it has appeared as one of the top ten, has consistently ranked among the top five (Grajek et al. 2015). Finally, for the past three years the *NMC Horizon Report* has called attention to the challenge of faculty training and overall digital literacy (Johnson et al. 2015). All of these indicate that the community continues to attach significant institutional importance to faculty teaching practice and the efforts to develop that practice.

Another contextual factor is the fairly radical shift away from the preponderance of tenured faculty positions. In 1969 roughly 75 percent of faculty were tenured, but in 2009, 75 percent were nontenured faculty (Kezar and Maxey 2013). In addition, conducting a course is a much more complicated business today than it was in 1969. Course models are increasingly complex, as are the technologies needed to conduct courses. We are seeing a shift toward what Herbert Simon anticipated in the quotation mentioned above: a team approach, with staff members such as instructional designers and technologists forming teams to work with faculty members in the design of a course.

From Menus to Curricula

How might this shift in thinking manifest itself? One way is conceiving of faculty development efforts as a matrix of ongoing development experiences, organized thematically into a curriculum that enables participants to perceive progress and the cumulative acquisition of expertise. An illustration of the importance of this point is an article that appeared in the journal *BioScience* (Ebert-May et al. 2011). The article reported on a study focused on faculty members who participated in one of two national teaching development programs. The purpose of both programs were nearly identical: "The overarching goals for faculty in both workshops were to increase knowledge about the principles of active learning . . . to collaboratively develop active, inquiry-based instructional materials; and to gain experience and confidence in implementing active-learning pedagogies" (ibid., 551).

A year after participating in one of these programs, faculty members were surveyed about their implementation of active-learning strategies (hence, the results were self-reported) and were rated by an independent observer on whether or not their actual classroom practices reflected an active learning approach. The variance in the results is astonishing. In the survey, 89 percent of the faculty reported that they "had implemented reforms in the prior academic year that stemmed from their participation in PD [professional development] activities" (Ebert-May et al. 2011, 554). In contrast, "the majority of faculty (75%) used lecture-based, teacher-centered pedagogy, showing a clear disconnect between faculty's perceptions of their teaching and their actual practices" (ibid., 550).

This discovery led the article's authors to this conclusion: "We posit that true understanding and implementation of learner-centered teaching cannot be taught without direct practice and feedback on that practice, which parallels how students learn" (Ebert-May et al. 2011, 557). But this study also suggests that the development of a craft such as teaching in a learner-centered way cannot be done by a one-time immersion in a workshop or institute, even if the institute has national visibility. This raises what we can call the *last-mile problem*: how to provide development experiences that result in adoption—that is, actual changes in practice. Such experiences as workshops may be powerful ways to initiate such development, but without ongoing feedback (based on observed practice), reinforcement, and supplemental experiences (such as faculty learning communities), they may fall short with respect to the last-mile problem. A craft cannot be mastered via a single experience, however immersive it might be.

Another study (Steinert et al. 2006) suggests that a more sophisticated and comprehensive approach to faculty development is more effective. The authors of this article surveyed faculty development studies in three databases (Medline, ERIC, and EMBASE) from 1980 to 2002, in an attempt to understand the characteristics of effective faculty development efforts. Their conclusion is that it is a matrix of development experiences that contribute to effectiveness and actual adoption, which they summarize as follows: "Key features of effective faculty development contributing to effectiveness included the use of experiential learning, provision of feedback, effective peer and colleague relationships, well-designed interventions following principles of teaching and learning, and the use of a diversity of educational methods within single interventions" (Steinert et al. 2006, 497).

This study also has intriguing implications for what constitutes effective faculty development practice, ones that address the last-mile problem. Some of these are:

- "Develop more programs that extend over time, to allow for cumulative learning, practice, and growth";
- "Develop programs that stimulate reflection and learning among participants, raising their awareness of themselves as teachers"; and
- "Continue to develop and utilize performance-based measures of change. The use of these methods, which do exist, is an essential and natural next step." (Steinert et al. 2006, 522)

Such studies provide useful clues about what the new practice of faculty development needs to look like. One key element is an emphasis on observed outcomes as opposed to attendance counts and satisfaction surveys: "the question has changed from 'What do you do?' to 'What difference do you make?'" (Dobbin, Diaz, and Brown 2014, 2). The second key element is the delivery of curricula—thematically structured series of ongoing learning experiences—that sustain and nurture development over time as opposed to reliance on isolated workshops. A third is thinking of the faculty as a community of adult learners and designing their professional development on that basis.

This shift from workshops to curricula is also evident in recent work on ways to evaluate development programs. As an example, Sue Hines (2014) at Saint Mary's University of Minnesota has been developing a comprehensive system for this kind of program evaluation that espouses a comprehensive four-phase approach. The second phase is what she calls "program conceptualization" (Hines 2014), quoting the insight that "quality evaluation can occur only if it is built on a well-conceptualized curriculum" (Killion 2007). This entails moving away from thinking of faculty development experiences as a menu of disconnected events. Curricula enable you to clearly articulate what you are trying to accomplish with your faculty development efforts, and thus they lay the groundwork for effective program evaluation. Hines's approach also moves explicitly away from reliance on participation and attendee satisfaction data and toward broader measures entailing adoption, such as measurable impacts on teaching, student learning, and the institution.

Tool Sets

Sometimes a shift in your conceptual paradigm can transform something from being irrelevant to being relevant. The shift in perspective enables you to recognize resources that were not apparent before the shift. One such shift, relevant to faculty development, is to view teaching as a craft. Development of a craft, such as playing a musical instrument, is an ongoing—even lifelong—endeavor. Learners of a craft need development experiences over time that are appropriate to their current level of practice. For staff members conducting faculty development programs, the challenge is how to provide this kind of tailored experience that is appropriate to each faculty member.

A successful salesperson will keep notes on his or her key clients to maintain a dialogue that is relevant to the client's current situation. Recognizing this, staff members at Harvard University have adopted a customer relationship management (CRM) application as a way of tracking their faculty clients. This enables them to track what a faculty member is doing, what kinds of active learning engagements he or she is using, and what training he or she has received. This approach is especially important in contexts where faculty development is delivered by several semi-autonomous campus units, as it enables cross-organizational coordination. While Harvard has been a pioneer of this approach, conversations at the 2015 conference of the NorthEast Regional Computing Program make it clear that other campuses are taking a similar approach.

A well-designed curriculum provides learners with ways to get assistance when they need it and ways for them to collect and reflect on their work. Recognizing this, Azusa Pacific University is using a pair of applications to support its faculty development efforts. The university has repurposed the help desk application Zendesk to create a second support channel, through which faculty can receive on-the-spot assistance with their curricular work. Faculty members at the campus also use the application Digital Measures—a sort of e-portfolio, in which faculty members can articulate professional goals and track activities leading toward realizing them (Dobbin, Diaz, and Brown 2014, 4).

Peer-to-Peer Engagement and Learning Communities

Another dimension of the new learning-centered approach is the value seen in the peer-to-peer engagement of learners and the role of learner communities.

An example of this is the California State University digital ambassadors program (California State University 2012; Google Faculty Institute n.d.). One of the motivations for the program is to put educational innovations (in this case, peer-to-peer learning) into practice. The program appoints faculty members to be digital ambassadors, who encourage the exploration of new and improved pedagogical practices. This can include organizing workshops, setting up meeting points on social media networks, organizing campus conferences, and even distributing small grants to enable innovations and curricular experimentation.

Indiana University (IU) provides a good example of the potential of faculty learning communities (FLCs) (Hammersmith 2015). Building on increased faculty interest in new active-learning classroom designs, staff members at IU helped organize a self-directed faculty community to explore the implications of these new designs. The goal of this FLC was to adopt a "reflective and critical approach" to assessing the "effectiveness of active learning spaces and the teaching and learning they are designed to foster" (ibid.) The original research conducted by this group (which was approved by an institutional review board) has enabled the participants to disseminate their research and make recommendations to the IU Teaching and Learning Spaces Committee (the university's classroom governance body). These recommendations included expanding the number of active-learning classrooms, making improvements to existing classrooms (such as movable furnishings), and expanding the ways to collect and share teaching strategies that take fuller advantage of the new learning environments. In this way, the faculty development effort becomes a participatory experience, with the learners taking the lead and constructing knowledge (Indiana University Bloomington 2015).

Personalization

The personalization of learning is currently one of the key topics of discussion in the teaching and learning community. A more personalized learning experience has greater relevance to the learner and hence fosters his or her engagement with the subject. In the past, it was difficult to sustain faculty engagement in development activities, especially when the activities themselves were fairly generic. But if the context shifts to that of thinking of the faculty as a lifelong learner of a craft, then personalization is highly relevant. Thus, we are seeing this concept being applied in faculty engagement contexts. A key component of the personalization of faculty development is the recognition that faculty learners are adult learners and so share most of the characteristics of the typical adult learner. This means that they are very busy professionally and need flexible scheduling options, more tailored learning opportunities, and multiple access points to their learning.

For example, microcredentials are another recent innovation in both undergraduate and adult learning, and the teaching and learning community is actively exploring badging. The idea is to motivate learners by enabling them to complete smaller, incremental steps in the learning process, thereby working to retain engagement and reinforce the motivation to completion. The social dimension (the display of the badges) also contributes to the overall effect.

An example of an institution that is trying this approach is Granite State College, in New Hampshire. Its microcredentialing program enables the staff to better track faculty members' acquisition of competencies, resulting in stronger, more demonstrable outcomes. But the college's badging program is not deployed in a vacuum. Its faculty development program now consists of self-paced tutorials; customized modules for specific schools; and shorter, more frequent instructor-led modules. Instructional designers work with faculty members on course design and mentors assess live courses. The goal of this development plan is to deliver experiences that are more flexible, available, and customizable.

One dimension of personalization is placement, situating the learner in a context that is neither too advanced nor too elementary. The University of Central Florida (UCF) has developed a way to assess a faculty member's prior experience with online teaching, which enables the university to place faculty members in learning experiences that are appropriate to their past experiences. The standard preparatory course at UCF for online teaching is IDL6543, an award-winning flagship program that spans eleven weeks. But online teaching is no longer as novel as it once was, and faculty members have begun to arrive at UCF with prior online experience. In light of this, UCF created the Online Faculty Readiness Assessment (OFRA), a web-based, evidence-based instrument. Faculty members who complete the OFRA instrument can essentially test out of some of the modules of the IDL6543 course (Cavanagh 2014; McQuiggan et al. 2013).

Scaling

Personalized approaches are important, and in some contexts so is scaling faculty training. One illustration of this is Southern New Hampshire University, whose online program has been growing by leaps and bounds. In 2006, there were 25 full-time-equivalent faculty members associated with the university's online program; by 2014 there were 800. In 2014 there were 35,000 online students; by the end of 2015 the number was expected to be 60,000. The growth of the faculty has been equally dramatic: as of spring 2014, the university had added 1,600 faculty members (mostly adjuncts) in the past year and had plans to add an additional 2,000 in the coming year.

At such a scale, how do you preserve a more personalized and learner-centered approach that is effective? The university has all faculty members attend an online course, with a cohort size of no larger than twenty-five. It also emphasizes pedagogy more strongly than technology, with the goal of ensuring that new faculty members feel prepared to teach online. One indication of the success of the university's approach is that in November 2013, some 44 percent of the faculty agreed that they were prepared to teach online, but by January 2014 that percentage had grown to 72 percent. This suggests that a learner-centered approach to faculty development and delivering the curriculum at scale are not inherently incompatible. This tailoring and the prioritization of pedagogy over technology illustrate ways of retaining elements of the new style of faculty development, even in a scaled-up context.

Implications

In this chapter, I have identified some of the key dimensions that characterize the new practice of faculty development. Let us now take a look at some of the implications these new practices have for staff who plan and conduct faculty development.

Teaching as an Evolving Craft

The shift to viewing teaching as a craft is perhaps the most important dimension of the new practice, since it implies that both faculty and staff members who conduct faculty development will need to significantly rethink their practices. For staff members, it means providing continuous and evolving learning experiences that enable faculty members to continuously improve their skills. This also entails keeping abreast of new practices and associated technologies, as well as implementing effective program evaluations. For faculty members, this shift in perspective entails continuously developing expertise in how people learn and evolving pedagogical designs that reflect that expertise. In fact, we could view this as a cooperative venture of staff and faculty members, who jointly develop a common understanding of teaching practice.

Thematic Curricular Organization

This entails moving away from menus of workshops and toward thematic curricula. All learners are encouraged by feeling a sense of progress, and the curriculum map enables faculty to know where they are in their learning. Progress and refinement are essential components of a craft. Hence, embedding faculty development in a context of curricular organization reinforces and promotes the notion of teaching as a craft, which entails continuous development and a deepening of one's understanding of how people learn. Curricular organization also enables staff members to selectively emphasize specific themes, which can directly address institutional priorities. Finally, the thematic coherence of curricula provides a much better basis for program evaluation, since the cornerstone of curricular design are a set of clearly stated learning outcomes or objectives.

Faculty Development as an Adult Learning Context

Adult learners have unique challenges, such as busy schedules and professional and family responsibilities. Postsecondary faculty members have an additional, very significant challenge: the tradition of prioritizing research excellence over teaching excellence, especially at four-year institutions. These challenges can be addressed in part by development programs that are flexible and can be tailored to addess items such as academic discipline and previous teaching experience. Another tactic is to design development programs that are ongoing and offer faculty members opportunities that are incremental, aiming to make changes that are gradual and evolutionary rather than sweeping and revolutionary.

Outcomes Assessment

This means no longer asking "What did you think of the training?" but instead "What observable and measurable impact has our faculty development program had on teaching practices, student learning, and the achievement of institutional strategic goals?" This change highlights not only the importance of faculty development assessment in general, but also the focus on tangible (and hence measurable) outcomes. One way to accomplish this is suggested by the article from *BioScience* discussed above (Ebert-May et al. 2011): observing faculty members' classroom performance to see if they have adopted new practices. A second approach is measuring student outcomes and levels of engagement. This kind of assessment is vital if the rate of actual adoption is to be determined, but of course it brings with it a host of challenges. For example, it is resource intensive. More important, some faculty members may resist the idea of being observed and evaluated. One way to address these challenges is to leverage the faculty grant programs that many institutions conduct to encourage and enable faculty innovation in teaching. Typically these programs award small or medium-size grants to faculty members who have innovative ideas for their curriculum. Funds to enable outcomes assessment can be built into these grants, and a condition for the grant can be observation or some other agreed-on means of outcome assessment.

These developments in faculty development reflect and have an impact on the faculty member's role in the design and conduct of a course. At the outset

I called attention to the tradition in which the faculty member was in full control of all aspects of his or her course. Nor did faculty members question or in any way interfere with the way their colleagues taught. This has produced what George Mehaffy calls a "cottage industry model" (Mehaffy 2012), in which "each course is designed, delivered, and assessed by an individual faculty member" (McQuiggan et al. 2013, 30). Mehaffy goes on to point out that frequently there were as many versions of a course as there were faculty members teaching it. It is obvious that the new dimensions of faculty development, such as learning communities, cannot succeed in that situation.

As I noted at the outset, new practices in faculty development reflect a new thinking about the faculty role of instructor, while at the same time they shape that role. One dimension of this is the faculty member's acquisition of knowledge and expertise about how students learn. It is becoming increasingly important to ground decisions about pedagogy and educational technology in such expertise, as options for course design and technology increase and diversify. This, incidentally, is parallel to an overall trend in the postsecondary teaching and learning support community, which is deemphasizing technology in favor of pedagogy and best instructional practices.

Another dimension is the increasing importance of collaboration in all areas of faculty development and in faculty instructional practice. As discussed above, tenure-track faculty members have been "lone rangers" with respect to teaching, but that is changing. Expertise from colleagues and support staff members (such as instructional designers and instructional technologists) is becoming a key element in course design, especially if the faculty member is seeking to strike out in new pedagogical directions. In addition, communities of practice and other collective bodies enable collaborative discovery about what works in addition to providing an increasing number of options and information about what is being done elsewhere in the academy. Instruction, as Simon anticipated, is indeed shifting from being a solo to a team sport.

Obviously, the tempo of these changes can be retarded or accelerated by the institutional culture and context. The increasing use of non-tenure-track faculty members to deliver instruction may be a factor, as these faculty members are focused on teaching instead of research. But the key factor is clearly how an institution rewards faculty progress and accomplishment in these areas. Higher education is clearly at a crossroads, with the pressures it is facing with respect to student outcomes. This is clearly a unique opportunity to make faculty accomplishment in teaching a more pronounced element in promotion decisions.

Perhaps the most important insight arising from recent work on faculty development is that we are all learners. Faculty roles are shifting, as is the nature of the work of those who support the roles. In both cases, increased expertise on how people learn and on pedagogically informed course designs is required. Given that we find ourselves at a transformative moment in higher education, this is a promising development, as it is a way to respond to the challenges and opportunities we face.

NOTES

1. I am thinking here of a comment attributed by staff members at Carnegie Mellon University to Herbert Simon: "Improvement in postsecondary education will require converting teaching from a 'solo sport' to a community-based research activity."
2. The ELI *7 Things* series is a free monthly publication (EDUCAUSE Learning Initiative 2015). The *Horizon Report*, published annually as a joint project of the New Media Consortium and the ELI, describes six key developments in education technology, seen form the context of the key trends and challenges current in higher education (see, for example, Johnson et al. 2015).

REFERENCES

California State University. 2012. "Innovative Digital Applications: The CSU Digital Ambassador Program." Accessed December 11, 2015. http://teachingcommons.cdl.edu/ngss/digital/.

Cavanagh, Thomas. 2014. "Assessing an Instructor's Prior Online Experience." Paper presented at the EDUCAUSE Learning Initiative 2014 Online Spring Focus Session, April 1. Accessed December 11, 2015. http://www.educause.edu/events/online-spring-focus-session-faculty-engagement-and-development/2014/how-evaluate-faculty-development.

Dobbin, Gregory, Veronica Diaz, and Malcolm Brown. 2014. "Faculty Engagement and Development—Effective and Innovative Practice: A Report on the ELI Spring 2014 Focus Session." EDUCAUSE. Accessed December 11, 2015. https://net.educause.edu/ir/library/pdf/ELI3032.pdf.

Ebert-May, Diane, Terry Derting, Janet Hodder, Jennifer Momsen, Tammy Long, and Sarah Jardeleza. 2011. "What We Say Is Not What We Do: Effective Evaluation of Faculty Professional Development Programs." *BioScience* 61 (7): 550–58.

EDUCAUSE. 2015. "Key Issues in Teaching and Learning." Accessed December 10, 2015. http://www.educause.edu/eli/initiatives/content-anchors.

EDUCAUSE Learning Initiative. 2015. "*7 Things You Should Know About . . . .*" Accessed December 10, 2015. http://www.educause.edu/eli/publications?filters=sm_cck_field_super_facet%3A%22EDUCAUSE%20Library%20Items%22%20tid%3A33152%20tid%3A33438.

Google Faculty Institute. n.d. "Digital Ambassadors." Accessed December 11, 2015. https://sites.google.com/site/facultyinstitute/resource-portal/digital-learning-ambassador.

Grajek, Susan, and the 2014–2015 EDUCAUSE IT Issues Panel. 2015. "Top 10 IT Issues, 2015: Inflection Point." Accessed December 10 2015. http://www.educause.edu/ero/article/top-10-it-issues-2015-inflection-point.

Hammersmith, Leslie. 2015. "Advancing Scholarship on Active Learning Spaces through Faculty Learning Communities." Paper presented at the ELI Annual Meeting, Anaheim, CA, February 9. Accessed December 11, 2015. http://www.educause.edu/eli/events/eli-annual-meeting/2015/advancing-scholarship-active-learning-spaces-through-faculty-learning-communities.

Hines, Sue. 2014. "How to Evaluate Faculty Development." Paper presented at the EDUCAUSE Learning Initiative 2014 Online Spring Focus Session, April 1. Accessed December 11, 2015. http://www.educause.edu/events/online-spring-focus-session-faculty-engagement-and-development/2014/how-evaluate-faculty-development.

Indiana University Bloomington. 2015. "Faculty Learning Communities." Accessed December 11, 2015. http://citl.indiana.edu/programs/flc/index.php.

Johnson, Larry, Samantha Adams Becker, Victoria Estrada, and Alex Freeman. 2015. *NMC Horizon Report: 2015 Higher Education Edition*. Austin, TX: New Media Consortium. Accessed December 10, 2015. http://www.nmc.org/publication/nmc-horizon-report-2015-higher-education-edition/.

Kezar, Adrianna, and Daniel Maxey. 2013. "The Changing Academic Workforce." *Trusteeship Magazine* 21 (3): 15–21.

Killion, Joellen. 2007. *Assessing Impact: Evaluating Professional Development*. Thousand Oaks, CA: Corwin.

McGoldrick, Brent, John S. Watts, and Kate Economou. 2015. "U.S. Postsecondary Faculty in 2015: Diversity in People, Goals and Methods, but Focused on Students." FTI Consulting. Accessed December 10, 2015. http://postsecondary.gatesfoundation.org/wp-content/uploads/2015/02/US-Postsecondary-Faculty-in-2015.pdf.

McQuiggan, Carol, Lisa Byrnes, Melissa Hicks, and Amy Roche. 2013. "Faculty Online Readiness Tool 2.0." Paper presented at 19th annual Sloan Consortium International Conference on Online Learning, Lake Buena Vista, FL, November 21. Accessed December 11, 2015. http://olc.onlinelearningconsortium.org/conference/2013/aln/faculty-online-readiness-tool-20.

Mehaffy, George. 2012. "Challenge and Change." *EDUCAUSE Review* 47 (5): 25–42.

Steinert, Yvonne, Karen Mann, Angel Centeno, Diana Dolmans, John Spencer, Mark Gelula, and David Prideaux. 2006. "A Systematic Review of Faculty Development Initiatives Designed to Improve Teaching Effectiveness in Medical Education." *Medical Teacher* 28 (6): 497–526.

8

More Than a Zero-Sum Game

Shared Work Agreements

KERRYANN O'MEARA

LAUREN DeCROSTA

Consider the following three scenarios:

> After a faculty member is appointed on the tenure track, he or she sits down with the department chair and is given a choice between two pathways that lead to tenure: one that emphasizes research and one that emphasizes teaching and the development of new curricular programs. Although some research is required in the teaching model and some teaching in the research model, both are considered equally legitimate and have the same reward: tenure. Both pathways fulfill critical campus missions and strategic goals.

> Two recently tenured faculty members who have young children decide to forgo their sabbaticals in lieu of a new contract they negotiate with their institution to go part-time for two years as tenured associate professors.

> A dashboard is created that shows the campus service, teaching, and research contributions of all faculty members in a college. Faculty members can easily see what the average, high, and low contributions are and assess how their contributions measure up. A series of organizing practices are then put in place in each department to ensure equity in contributions. The practices include required rotating key campus service roles, using banking systems, and providng rewards for above-average contributions in all three areas via merit pay.

Each of these reforms involves a change in organizational practices to balance faculty and institutional needs and goals. Each requires the faculty member and the institution to compromise on some benefit, norm, or expectation to succeed. Each also goes against the assumption that every faculty member should be an ideal worker, available to work twenty-four hours a day and excel in every area of work simultaneously. At the same time, such reforms acknowledge the financial constraints and organizational goals of higher education institutions. These reforms assume something more than a zero-sum game—both institutions and individuals can win, as long as they enter into agreements in which there is trust and flexibility.

In this chapter, we consider reform in organizational practices to allow faculty and institutions greater flexibility to achieve individual and institutional goals. Following the model of efforts in industry and government, many colleges have put work-life policies in place to allow faculty members to balance work and family care. In an effort to respond to shifting individual and institutional needs, many universities have created new differentiated workload options. Last but not least, equity-minded institutions have initiated new ways of thinking about faculty workload that ensure greater fairness and acknowledge campus service and teaching contributions, especially in the case of women, people of color, and non-tenure-track faculty members—all of whom may have been burdened with invisible and uncredited institutional housekeeping. Although it is too early to know the long-term benefits of many of these new initiatives, research on such programs implemented in industry (Schawbel 2015) and in higher education (Clegg and Esping 2005; Lester and Sallee 2009) suggests that institutions investing in such programs are likely to benefit from improved recruitment, retention, and morale of faculty; cost savings from not having to replace faculty members; and greater faculty agency and productivity in meeting institutional goals. Such initiatives also take advantage of a hidden resource to achieve faculty and institutional goals: flexibility (O'Meara 2015).

New Work Agreements: Differentiated Workloads, Integrated Teaching-Research Models, and Banking Systems

It is well known that most full-time tenure-track faculty in four-year universities struggle to balance teaching, research, and service roles effectively to earn tenure. Relatedly, institutions struggle to accomplish all parts of their missions well. In fact, Alexander Astin and Mitchell Chang (1995) found that few colleges or universities are able to create a work environment that is highly student-centered, offering rich opportunities for student learning and engagement, and also highly research productive, with faculty publishing prolifically at the top of their fields. In 2002, James Fairweather conducted a study to investigate what percentage of faculty are "simultaneously productive in both teaching and research" (30). The data for his study came from a nationally representative sample of 25,780 full-time and part-time faculty members from 817 institutions of higher education used in the 1992–93 National Survey of Postsecondary Faculty. Fairweather found that only "22% of all faculty in 4-year institutions simultaneously attained high productivity in teaching and research" (ibid., 43). He defined *high research productivity* as authoring more refereed publications than the median for the field of study and institution and/or serving as the "principal investigator on a funded research project" that was "above the median in both total research dollars and conference presentations" or in the top quartile of funding or number of conference presentations (ibid., 35). In many cases, these two activities of research and teaching alone can seem like a zero-sum game for faculty. Ranking systems like that used by U.S. News & World Report evaluate and reward faculty members for contributions to disciplines (O'Meara and Meekins 2012). Effective teaching also requires significant time and attention but is not recognized in ranking systems or prioritized in many academic reward systems. Faculty often feel pulled in different directions, wanting to do both well, but not having enough time. As a result, few institutions are able to produce teaching and research outcomes even moderately well (Astin and Chang 1995). Those institutions that are able to achieve teaching and research goals have found a way to merge such activities, so that more than one task is being accomplished at a time; or allow different groups of faculty members to make contributions to these missions or contribute to all missions, but at different times in their careers. Given many non-tenure-track faculty members are hired to teach but have PhDs and want to continue to learn and contribute to scholarship as well, the issue of finding ways to balance faculty roles and meet institutional needs affects both the tenure and non-tenure-track faculty (Kezar 2012). In this chapter we provide examples of several institutions that have taken steps to create new, flexible work agreements to balance faculty roles.

Customizing Careers and Equitable Divisions of Labor: The Stanford University School of Medicine Banking System

For many years, scholars have observed that increasing demands by institutions and decreasing staff have resulted in an overloaded plate for full-time tenure-track faculty (Gappa, Austin, and Trice 2007; Rice, Sorcinelli, and Austin 2000; Trower 2012). Working fifty to sixty hours or more per week, and not feeling that they are performing adequately in any one area, can contribute to burnout and stress among faculty members (Kreuter 2013). In addition to juggling their professional and personal lives, faculty members at Stanford University School of Medicine also noted that their careers as medical faculty members required them to balance their teaching, research, and campus service work with clinical care.

The Stanford University School of Medicine created the Academic Biomedical Career Customization (ABCC) program as a solution to problems of flexibility and control in workload. The program's creators—Hannah Valantine, senior associate dean for diversity and faculty development, and Christy Sandborg, vice president of medical affairs at Lucile Packard Children's Hospital—explain that they adapted Deloitte's Mass Career Customization flexibility model to provide medical school faculty members with the ability to individualize their career trajectory and tempo (Valantine and Sandborg 2013). By customizing their careers, medical faculty members can plan for themselves the type of work they want to take on and the time period in which they intend to complete it. Valantine and Sandborg describe how faculty members work in teams with their department chairs and professional career-life coaches to develop each of the five dimensions of their three-to-five-year plans. These five dimensions are "pace (anticipated time to promotion); workload (disaggregated into clinical, research, teaching, and administration); role as an individual contributor or leader; schedule predictability; and work-life integration" (ibid., 3). These teams reconvene regularly to confirm the plan is still acceptable to the faculty member, make any necessary alterations, and evaluate the individual's responsibility for it.

In addition, the ABCC program has a time-banking system that allows professors to earn credits for completed work, which they can redeem for assistance with other tasks at work or home. Valantine and Sandborg (2013) explain how this system allows faculty members to take on responsibility when they can and rewards them with benefits to solve work-life and work-work conflicts when needed. For example, Lauren Rikleen notes "the banking system allows hours spent on mentoring students and participating on committees to be converted into support mechanisms such as grant writing assistance, meal deliveries, and housecleaning" (2013, 1). Lindsey Trimble O'Connor suggests that the system provides professors with flexibility in managing work-life conflicts by offering faculty the opportunity "to accelerate their careers when possible and decelerate when family and personal responsibilities are greatest" (2013, 10).

This system might be especially beneficial to women because, as Jennifer Raymond, an associate professor of neurobiology and associate dean for faculty career flexibility at Stanford University Medical School, notes, "women in academic medicine also experience more work-work conflict than men," and women faculty members often are responsible for more teaching and service work than their male counterparts—which could be detrimental to their ability to conduct and publish research, typically required for promotion (paraphrased by Trimble O'Connor 2013, 1). The flexibility offered by the time-banking system and career customization model assists faculty members in managing their time and workload. The ABCC program was awarded the Alfred P. Sloan Award for Excellence in Faculty Career Flexibility. Rikleen (2013) reports that initial evaluations of the program are positive, and the intent is to scale it up beyond its first fifty participants to the rest of the medical school faculty after the conclusion of the second pilot phase.

Flexible Allocation of Talent: Kansas State University

In 1988, several female professors at Kansas State University (KSU) expressed their desire to have "more explicit standards" for evaluating their performance (Clegg and Esping 2005, 167). They were concerned that they and their male counterparts were being evaluated based on different standards and that their potential for promotion and tenure might be negatively affected by the lack of explicit standards. Also, faculty members who were exceptional at teaching were not being rewarded as often or through as clear a process as were faculty members with achievements in research. Responding to these concerns, the university began to develop a new policy in 1990 under which faculty members would meet with their department chair at the beginning of every academic year to develop "individualized agreements" that would both make the best use of each faculty member's strengths and ensure that department work needs were met (ibid., 177). Rather than stipulate departmental standards for time allotted to research, teaching, and service, the faculty member and the department chair would develop mutually agreed-on performance standards that would be "specific and unique to the individual" and serve as the basis of the individualized assignment (ibid., 170). In other words, every faculty member would meet with his or her department head to set his or her own personal goals and ensure that those goals corresponded to the needs of the department. During these annual meetings, the faculty member and the department chair would also jointly evaluate whether or not the professional goals stipulated during the previous year's meeting and in the faculty member's work plan had been met. If the faculty member did not achieve previous goals, he or she and the department chair would together create a plan for remedying any problems (Clegg and Esping 2005). In addition, responding to faculty complaints about the lack of credit for teaching, KSU's provost and college deans encouraged all departments to review their practices for evaluating teaching and to make the scholarship of teaching an integral component of faculty evaluations. Victoria Clegg and Gretchen Esping (2005) note that KSU established the University Chair for Distinguished Teaching Scholars, which recognized the importance of teaching. The faculty members who were awarded this honor would be appointed to a half-time position for one academic year and would permanently retain the title of University Distinguished Teaching Scholar.

In evaluating the effectiveness of the individual faculty assignments, Clegg and Esping interviewed all college deans, department heads, and the university provost individually during forty-minute taped sessions. In addition, Clegg and

Esping also requested faculty members in all departments to participate in an anonymous online survey (with both close- and open-ended questions). The authors found that "nearly 90 percent of all department evaluation documents [were revised to] mention flexibility in the allocation of time and talent, one way or another," and a few departments had even amended their evaluation materials so that faculty members could receive credit for research on teaching in their fields (2005, 173). Overall, they found that faculty members were generally supportive of the individualized arrangements. Furthermore, the term *scholarship* had been broadened and was commonly used on campus to include research, teaching, and service components, a change that Clegg and Esping attributed to the campuswide discussions about flexible or individualized work arrangements.

There was a consensus that teaching had come to be viewed with greater appreciation and given more weight as a component of scholarship, but these results were not universal. As of 2005, some departments had not fully embraced the changes or institutionalized them as a permanent part of KSU (Clegg and Esping 2005). The lack of universal implementation, according to Clegg and Esping, was the result of different department members' degree of buying into the benefits of implementing flexible workload arrangements and of changes in department leadership. However, the program has continued, and the *University Handbook* states: "Institutional excellence is enhanced by both faculty specialization and versatility in the kind of work done within and across departments and units. Faculty members will have individual responsibility profiles. . . . When included as part of a faculty member's appointment, each of the responsibility areas below is considered in decisions for reappointment, tenure and promotion as well as in annual merit evaluations" (Kansas State University Office of the Provost and Senior Vice President 2015, 1).

Overall, Clegg and Esping (2005) observe that implementation of individualized agreements requires regular, ongoing communication and collaboration between faculty members and departmental administrators. Also, the individualized agreements must be honored in all parts of the faculty members' reward system, from annual merit reviews to promotion and tenure—as is noted in the KSU *University Handbook*. Some might wonder if individualized agreements emphasizing engaged scholarship or the scholarship of teaching hurt faculty mobility, as this work does not generally bring as much prestige as traditional research does. This could be true, but it is hard to know because there is no national database of faculty members who have left one position for another or felt unable to leave because of the emphasis of their work resulting from such policies. However, given that a relatively small percentage of tenure-track faculty members move from one institution to another, a better question may be whether these policies add to faculty satisfaction and productivity and the ability of the department to meet collective goals.

Ideal, but Not the Ideal Worker: Part-Time
Tenure Track and Phased Retirement

Research has shown that both Generation X and millennial academic mothers and fathers are more interested than ever before in balancing work and life goals. Many such faculty members are looking for ways to take specific periods of time away from work, or to work part-time for a period while children are young or other family members need care (Lester and Sallee 2009). Also, as baby boomer faculty members continue to retire, Colleen Flaherty (2013) found that many do not want to leave their posts completely and still have much to give to their institutions, but are left with all-or-nothing options before retirement. Thus, a good number of Gen X and millennial full-time faculty members are looking for careers that are not full time. It is important to note that we did not say they want to teach a class here and there or become adjunct faculty members. Rather, they want to maintain their identity and status as career faculty members—just not serve at a full-time pace. Over the past twenty years, many higher education institutions and state systems have put work-life policies and programs in place to support academic parents who want to switch to part-time status and faculty members looking for phased retirement. Fueled and supported by such catalysts as the National Science Foundation's Increasing the Participation and Advancement of Women in Academic Science and Engineering Careers (ADVANCE) program, Alfred P. Sloan Foundation, American Association of University Professors, and American Council on Education, institutions have implemented part-time tenure-track positions and phased-retirement programs and policies.

In responding to the frequent difficulties that faculty members, especially women early in their careers, have faced in requesting and receiving parental leave, Robert Drago and Joan Williams (2000) proposed the creation of half-time tenure-track positions. They observed:

> Raising a child takes 20 years, not one semester. American women, who still do the vast majority of child care, will not achieve equality in academia so long as the ideal academic is defined as someone who takes no time off for child-rearing. . . . It is possible that delayed childbearing could resolve this problem. However, the numbers do not fit this strategy. As of 1995, the mean age for receipt of a PhD was 34, placing the tenure year at age 40. Asking women to delay having children until such a late age seems unfair and unkind, and involves health and infertility risks. Fathers receive no such requests, nor do they face comparable dangers. The tenure clock precludes gender equality in academics, as [Arlie] Hochschild showed 25 years ago. Hochschild suggested that universities permit faculty to work part-time. We go further to argue that the solution is to redefine the ideal worker in academia, by offering

proportional pay, benefits, and advancement for part-time work. This idea boils down to a part-time tenure track. (2000, 47)

A part-time tenure track includes reducing the productivity requirements for faculty members and/or lengthening the time allowed for those working part time to meet stipulated productivity requirements. Today, "there are more than 8,000 individuals working in the United States on PTTT [part-time tenure-track] appointments" (Herbers 2014, 14). In these half-time tenure-track arrangements, the faculty member's tenure clock runs at half speed. In other words, if the faculty member requested half-time status for two years, her or his tenure clock would be extended for one year. The University of California (UC), Berkeley, Family Friendly Edge provides one example of how a half-time tenure-track option could work. This program, which was initially funded by the Alfred P. Sloan Foundation, allows faculty members to sign a memorandum of understanding with the university to change from full-time to part-time status (temporarily or permanently) to accommodate family needs. However, the eight-year limitation of service still applies for assistant professors (University of California 2003). In addition, the UC 2006 "Policy on Appointment and Promotion: Professor Series" notes that "teaching and service expectations for part-time appointees shall be pro-rated in accordance with the percentage of time of the appointment" (n.d.). The policy on research is less clear, but it does indicate that "if an appointee only receives part of a full-time salary, equity demands some effort to arrange an appointment with partial responsibilities" (ibid.). Although the university has made the part-time tenure-track option available to professors since 1985, Mary Ann Mason and Angelica Stacy note that only two professors had taken advantage of it prior to 2003 (n.d.) Joan Herbers offers one possible explanation for that underuse: she argues that a part-time tenure track appears to clash with the cultural norms in academe, according to which "ideal workers do not work part-time" (2014, 14). Likewise, studies of other institutions that have created part-time tenure-track options have found them underused because of fear that an academic on such a track will not be considered serious about his or her career and will lose career momentum and the inability to sustain a 50 percent pay cut, even for a year, because of high cost of living (Lester and Sallee 2009). Although the first barrier can be addressed by trying to create more family friendly campuses, the second is less under institutional control as more families require two salaries to meet costs.

Phased retirement might be viewed as another kind of part-time tenure-track arrangement. As Mary Beckman (2003) notes, many mandatory retirement policies for university faculty were abolished in 1994. Laurie Fendrich explains the consequences of this change: "The average age for all tenured professors nationwide is now approaching 55 and creeping upward; the number of professors 65 and older more than doubled between 2000 and 2011. In spite of those numbers. . . . three-quarters of professors between 49 and 67 say they will either delay retirement past age 65 or—gasp!—never retire at all" (2014). The increasing number of faculty members delaying retirement has affected the diversity of faculty members at many universities. Fendrich cites Cornell University, the University of Virginia, the University of Texas at Austin, Duke University, and the University of North Carolina (UNC) at Chapel Hill as institutions of higher education at which more than 25 percent of faculty members are above the age of sixty. In responding to the change in demographics and in an effort to negotiate the amount of time faculty members stay on staff, many universities have begun offering gradual retirement or phased-retirement plans. According to Christopher Phelps (2010), phased retirement involves reducing professors' teaching loads and prorating their salaries in return for their tenure commitment waiver at a future date and time. Phelps suggests that such a plan allows faculty members to test-drive retirement. Furthermore, Roger Baldwin and Michael Zeig (2013) suggest phased-retirement plans are also beneficial to institutions: "colleges and universities should think of late-career professors [faculty who have served for at least twenty years and who are fifty-five or older] as distinctive assets that can be utilized in diverse ways to the benefit of their institution and its various stakeholders—students, junior colleagues, alumni and administrators" (2013). One mutually beneficial aspect of phased retirement, according to Phelps (2010), is a university's ability to call on professors' expertise to teach on a per course basis: this arrangement provides professors with an opportunity to gradually transition into retirement while simultaneously helping universities meet needs. Baldwin and Zeig (2013) highlight additional advantages of phased retirement, including mentorship opportunities for new faculty members and community involvement, either through consulting partnerships or enrichment courses.

UNC offers its faculty members a phased-retirement plan designed to help ease their transition into retirement. The UNC program "provides an opportunity for eligible full-time tenured faculty members to make an orderly transition to retirement through half-time (or equivalent) service for a predetermined period in return for half-time compensation" (University of North Carolina n.d.). It is voluntary and can be employed after a full-time tenured faculty member (eligible to receive retirement benefits and with at least five years of service at UNC) enters into a written agreement with the employing institution. Any faculty members with such agreements will receive "fifty percent (50%) of the full-time salary they received immediately prior to phased retirement," which will be paid out over a period of twelve months during each year (and for up to five years) of phased retirement (ibid.). Faculty members are also entitled to 50 percent of their paid sick leave and vacation time. Under this program, faculty members "can work no more than .75 FTE and . . . no more than 30 hours in any given semester" (ibid.). Additionally, the faculty member has the same "professorial rank and the full range of responsibilities, rights, and general benefits associated with it, except for tenured status" (ibid.).

In a case study of workplace flexibility, Ken Giglio (n.d.) notes that 524 faculty members at UNC have taken advantage of the phased-retirement program since its full-scale implementation in 2001, and participants in the program generally report being satisfied with it. Given the increase in full-time non-tenure-track faculty in higher education, it is likely we will see more phased-retirement and part-time options offered to non-tenure-track faculty. Activists organizing contracts and representing non-tenure-track faculty might consider ways to negotiate parallel programs in new faculty contracts and agreements.

Balancing Teaching and Research: The College of New Jersey

Faculty members at the College of New Jersey reported that the majority of their workdays were spent teaching and completing campus service activities, and that any research they conducted was primarily done on their own time. To reward them for the amount of time they spent teaching and mentoring undergraduate students while simultaneously increasing the amount of time available for research, the College of New Jersey overhauled its curriculum in 2003 to focus on undergraduate research and what Jeffrey Osborn, the dean of the School of Science, calls the "scholar-teacher" model (quoted in Flaherty 2014). Flaherty explains how this new model, which was pilot tested during the 2004–5 academic year, reduced the average number of courses that faculty members taught from four to three, to give them six additional working hours per week to devote to research. In this new arrangement, faculty members were asked to involve undergraduate students in their research to the greatest extent possible. To encourage greater collaboration with professors on research initiatives, undergraduate students could enroll in four courses per semester (instead of five); each course would be worth one more credit than was the case under the previous model (Flaherty 2014). Thus, each course would be more intensive and allow students more time to engage in collaborative research. In addition to offering support for faculty research objectives, this new curriculum benefited students, according to Flaherty, because the rigorous nature of the courses helps prepare students for graduate studies. Faculty then had one less course to prepare for, and more of their teaching time was supporting their research.

To further assist faculty members in focusing on research, the university permits them to apply for support in the form of what are known as scholarly activity course releases, which allow them to devote more of their work hours to research (Flaherty 2014). In addition to course releases, professors can request workload credit (determined on a departmental basis) for organizing and facilitating independent research group sessions. Flaherty provides an example of professors in the humanities who have led such sessions and received a course release (one per year) in return. This new curricular model also has a summer component: an eight-week mentored summer session, during which under-graduate students work with professors on research-related activities; profes-sors receive a stipend for their work on campus over the summer (Flaherty 2014). The College of New Jersey encourages professors and students to present the collaborative research they conducted at conferences and at the Celebra-tion of Student Achievement every spring.

Faculty rewards have also been revised to reflect this new "scholar-teacher" model: Flaherty notes that the College of New Jersey has incorporated "heavy involvement in undergraduate research" into its tenure and promotion guidelines (2014). Amanda Norvell, an associate professor of biology and presi-dent of the Faculty Senate at the College of New Jersey, contends that the new model also encourages faculty recruitment and retention: "I think faculty see that the college supports faculty and students working meaningfully together. It really puts the money behind it and gives credit where credit is due" (quoted in ibid.).

Conclusion

In reflecting on the vignettes at the beginning of this chapter and the real reforms described above, we ask: what is needed to implement these new work agreements? First, institutions and individuals need to get out of the mind-set that there is only one career track and one way of working that is ideal, legiti-mate, and satisfying. Careers need to be customized, and there is no one-size-fits-all model. However, the diversity of faculty members' interests and talents can benefit institutional missions and goals if targeted appropriately. Second, individual faculty members and institutions need to enter into a trust relation-ship that assumes there is not a zero-sum game. That is, faculty members and institutions need to be willing to compromise in ways that allow both parties to win, and to trust that both will live up to their part of the bargain. For example, if faculty members enter an alternative career track, but its standards are not used by department committees in making tenure or promotion decisions, the agreement will not work. Likewise, if a faculty member agrees to work part time for one institution but then simultaneously collects full-time pay from another institution, the program will not work and will be eliminated. Third, institutions need to recognize that they have a valuable resource that can be used to attract and retain talent: flexibility. Dan Pink describes "the ingredients of genuine motivation as . . . autonomy, mastery, and purpose" (2009, 46). He notes that organizations need to think about motivating people not with money but with other things they want in their lives, such as flexibility in time and tasks. Many institutions may not be able to recruit faculty stars away from other institutions with larger labs, higher salaries, and other financial resources. Yet if they create flexible policies such as those described in this chapter and enter into shared agreements with faculty members, they will have the kinds of resources that motivation research shows us are most valuable to today's workers. We suggest that the above-mentioned reforms in organizing practices and work structures may result in greater satisfaction for faculty members and their institutions by allowing both parties to achieve their goals.

REFERENCES

Astin, Alexander W., and Mitchell J. Chang. 1995. "Colleges That Emphasize Research and Teaching: Can You Have Your Cake and Eat It Too?" *Change* 27 (5): 44–49.

Baldwin, Roger G., and Michael J. Zeig. 2013. "The Potential of Late-Career Professors." *Inside Higher Ed*, May 10. Accessed December 12, 2015. https://www.insidehighered.com/advice/2013/05/10/tapping-potential-late-career-professors-essay.

Beckman, Mary. 2003. "The Not-So-Retired Scientist." *Chronicle of Higher Education*, March 25. Accessed December 12, 2015. http://chronicle.com/article/The-Not-So-Retired-Scientist/45130.

Clegg, Victoria, and Gretchen R. Esping. 2005. "Optimism with Our Eyes Wide Open: Reconsidering Scholarship at Kansas State University." In *Faculty Priorities Reconsidered: Rewarding Multiple Forms of Scholarship*, edited by KerryAnn O'Meara and Eugene Rice, 164–86. San Francisco: Jossey-Bass.

Drago, Robert, and Joan C. Williams. 2000. "A Half-Time Tenure Track Proposal." *Change* 32 (6): 46–51.

Fairweather, James S. 2002. "The Mythologies of Faculty Productivity: Implications for Institutional Policy and Decision Making." *Journal of Higher Education* 73 (1): 26–48.

Flaherty, Colleen. 2013. "Not a Retirement Club." *Inside Higher Ed*, October 7. Accessed December 12, 2015. https://m.insidehighered.com/news/2013/10/07/emeritus-colleges-allow-professors-stay-engaged.

———. 2014. "Faculty Work, Student Success." *Inside Higher Ed*, October 16. Accessed December 12, 2015. https://www.insidehighered.com/news/2014/10/16/how-college-new-jersey-rethought-faculty-work-student-success-mind.

Fendrich, Laurie. 2014. "The Forever Professors." *Chronicle of Higher Education*, November 14. Accessed December 12, 2015. http://chronicle.com/article/Retire-Already-/149965/.

Gappa, Judith M., Ann E. Austin, and Andrea G. Trice. 2007. *Rethinking Faculty Work: Higher Education's Strategic Imperative*. San Francisco: Jossey-Bass.

Giglio, Ken. n.d. "Workplace Flexibility Case Study: The University of North Carolina and Phased Retirement." Accessed December 12, 2015. https://workfamily.sas.upenn.edu/sites/workfamily.sas.upenn.edu/files/imported/pdfs/UNC.pdf.

Herbers, Joan M. 2014. *Part-Time on the Tenure Track*. ASHE Higher Education Report 40 (5). San Francisco: Jossey-Bass.

Kansas State University Office of the Provost and Senior Vice President. 2015. "University Handbook Section C: Faculty Identity, Employment, Tenure." Accessed December 12, 2015. http://www.k-state.edu/academicpersonnel/fhbook/fhsecc.html.

Kezar, Adrianna. 2012. "Needed Policies, Practices, and Values: Creating a Culture to Support and Professionalize Non-Tenure Track Faculty." In *Embracing Non-Tenure Track Faculty: Changing Campuses for the New Faculty Majority*, edited by Adrianna Kezar, 2–27. New York: Routledge.

Kreuter, Nate. 2013. "The Math Doesn't Work." *Inside Higher Ed*, April 22. Accessed December 11, 2015. https://www.insidehighered.com/advice/2013/04/22/essay-hours-faculty-members-work-each-day.

Lester, Jaime, and Margaret Sallee, eds. 2009. *Establishing the Family-Friendly Campus: Models for Effective Practice*. Sterling, VA: Stylus.

Mason, Mary Ann, and Angelica Stacy. n.d. "UC Faculty Family Friendly Edge proposal (DOC)." Accessed December 12, 2015. http://ucfamilyedge.berkeley.edu/reportsandpresentations.html.

O'Meara, KerryAnn. 2015. "Flexible Workplace Agreements: Enabling Higher Education's Strategic Advantage." TIAA-CREF Working Paper. Washington: TIAA-CREF Institute. Accessed December 12, 2015. https://www.tiaa-crefinstitute.org/public/pdf/flexible_workplace_agreements.pdf.

O'Meara, KerryAnn, and Matthew Meekins. 2012. *Inside Rankings: Limitations and Possibilities*. Working Paper Series, Issue No. 1. Boston, MA: New England Resource Center for Higher Education.

Phelps, Christopher. 2010. "We Need to See Retirement as a Hiring Issue." *Chronicle of Higher Education*, April 25. Accessed December 12, 2015. http://chronicle.com/article/We-Need-to-See-Retirement-as-a/65187/.

Pink, Dan. 2009. *Drive: The Surprising Truth about What Motivates Us*. New York: Penguin.

Rice, R. Eugene, Mary Deane Sorcinelli, and Ann E. Austin. 2000. "Heeding New Voices: Academic Careers for a New Generation." Paper presented at the American Association for Higher Education's Forum on Faculty Roles and Rewards, Washington, January.

Rikleen, Lauren Stiller. 2013. "Stanford Medical School's Plan to Attract More Female Leaders." *Harvard Business Review*, August 19. Accessed December 11, 2015. https://www.hbr.org/2013/08/how-stanford-medical-school-ho.

Schawbel, Dan. 2015. "Why Companies Are Investing More in Workplace Flexibility Programs in 2015." Recruiting Intelligence. ERE Media. Accessed February 13, 2016. http://www.eremedia.com/ere/why-companies-are-investing-more-in-workplace-flexibility-programs-in-2015.

Trimble, Lindsey B. 2013. "School of Medicine Initiative Helps Faculty Achieve Balance." Stanford University Clayman Institute for Gender Research. January 21. Accessed December 11, 2015. http://gender.stanford.edu/news/2013/school-medicine-initiative-helps-faculty-achieve-balance.

Trimble O'Connor, Lindsey. 2013. "New Program Uses 'Banking' to Take Aim at Work-Work and Work-Life Conflict." *Uprising* 3. Accessed December 11, 2015. http://gender.stanford.edu/sites/default/files/UpRising2013.pdf.

Trower, Cathy Ann. 2012. *Success on the Tenure Track: Five Keys to Faculty Job Satisfaction*. Baltimore, MD: John Hopkins University Press.

University of California. n.d. "Appoint and Promotion—Professor Series." Accessed December 12, 2015. http://ucop.edu/academic-personnel-programs/_files/apm/apm-220.pdf.

———. 2003. "The UC Faculty Family Friendly Edge: Existing Elements of the Family Friendly Package for UC Ladder-Rank Faculty." Berkeley: University of California. Accessed December 12, 2015. http://ucfamilyedge.berkeley.edu/initiatives.html.

University of North Carolina. n.d. "Summary: University of North Carolina Phased Retirement Program." Accessed February 13, 2016. http://academicpersonnel.unc.edu/files/2014/10/PRP-Summary.pdf.

Valantine, Hannah, and Christy I. Sandborg. 2013. "Changing the Culture of Academic Medicine to Eliminate the Gender Leadership Gap: 50/50 by 2020." *Academic Medicine*, October. Accessed December 11, 2015. www.ncbi.nlm.nih.gov/pmc/articles/PMC3785938.

9

A New Paradigm for Faculty Work and Evaluation

RICHARD ALAN GILLMAN

NANCY HENSEL

DAVID A. SALOMON

A universitywide commitment to student learning is the most productive way to address contemporary concerns about the value of higher education in an environment of increasing costs and limited employment opportunities for graduates. To facilitate the shift from a primarily individualistic approach to a community-based approach to faculty work, a new model for faculty work and evaluation is needed—one that places student learning at the center. A grant from the Teagle Foundation, "Preparing 21st Century Students through New Visions for Faculty Evaluation," provided an opportunity for members of the New American Colleges and Universities (NAC&U) to study changes in faculty work as a result of technology, dual-career families, new student-centered pedagogies, and increased expectations for faculty involvement in community service.

We propose an approach to the faculty reward system that recognizes the totality of faculty work and an approach to managing the faculty workload that will more effectively support student learning. A new management approach for departments that provides more departmental autonomy is needed to support these changes in faculty workload and evaluation.

Our work has led us to three conclusions:

1. Academic departments need the flexibility to support differential work by its members.
2. The faculty workload needs to be defined in ways beyond the number of credits hours taught, to include all aspects of faculty work.
3. Faculty evaluation must recognize that the expanding definitions of teaching, scholarship, and service necessitate a more flexible and holistic approach to evaluation.

Many authors have called for changes in the way faculty work is perceived and how departments are organized. Ernest Boyer (1996) called for a broader understanding of faculty scholarship, and Debra Humphreys wrote that "just as in the business community, today's challenging environment in and for the higher education sector demands more collaborative leadership" (2013, 4). Jon Wergin (2002) and John Saltmarsh, Kevin Kecskes, and Steven Jones (2005) anticipated Humphrey's work, calling for a new way of thinking about the basic academic work unit by shifting the perspective from my work to our work and calling this new model an engaged or collaborative department. Consistent with this, Mark Hower (2012) has found that faculty members themselves are not firmly wedded to autonomous models for their work but rather appreciate and desire a blend between autonomy and community. Judith Shapiro describes this desire for a blended approach to the academic community in detail in an essay on shared education. Among other things, she wrote that building this community "requires that faculty members see their individual courses not as private property but as part of a common project that engages them with their colleagues" (2014, 23).

NAC&U has a history of anticipatory responses to change in higher education to fully meet the diverse needs of students. Founded to promote the integration of the liberal arts, professional studies, and civic engagement, NAC&U has studied the relationship between faculty members and their institutions to support and improve student learning. Linda McMillin and William Berberet (2002) suggest that NAC&U campuses subscribe to Alexander Astin's (1993) proposal of measuring institutional excellence by student-learning outcomes rather than institutional resources. In addition, NAC&U campuses have long embraced Boyer's (1990) ideas about defining the work of faculty in ways that realistically reflect the full range of academic and civic social mandates. To fully implement differentiated faculty workload and evaluation, one must begin at the departmental level. We suggest an approach that we call the holistic department.

The Holistic Department

A holistic department is an organic whole rather than a collection of talented specialists. It is committed to shared governance and transparency of faculty work and evaluation, while maintaining the flexibility to support differential work by its members. Its focus is on the work of the department rather than on the work of individual faculty members. It is committed to a culture that supports faculty members' mentoring each other as well as its students, and it has a deep sense of shared obligations to students, its members, and the institution. The institution can rely on a holistic department to advance the goals and objectives of the institution rather than prioritizing the objectives of individual faculty members.

To illustrate these ideas, one can imagine a department in which the faculty members have collectively agreed that, in a given year, one member's service requirement is somewhat less than that of everyone else so that he or she can complete a major research project, while a second faculty member, who has just completed a project, may take on extra service activities. In the same year, a particular faculty member may be responsible for completing critical assessment work, another for implementing significant pedagogical change, and a senior member for teaching an extra course. All faculty members are assured that their contributions to the work of the department will be equally valued in the annual evaluation system.

In the traditional model of a department, if faculty members are encouraged to pursue their individual objectives and rewarded for doing so, ensuring that student-learning objectives are appropriate to the mission of the institution and the department and that the curriculum is designed to help students meet these objectives can easily receive a lower priority. In contrast, in a holistic department, student learning receives increased visibility as an institutional, and hence departmental, priority. Alignment of the curriculum is more likely to occur as members of the department discuss student-learning goals. Assessment of student learning becomes a natural task for the faculty as the department is rewarded for its achievements in this core function. Assessment of student learning, along with most activities involving program development and substantial pedagogical change, cannot be conducted as the work of individual faculty members; rather, it must be seen as the work of the entire unit. The holistic department attends to this work while also recognizing and rewarding the individual faculty members who make significant contributions to it in any given year.

As in a traditional department, the holistic department is committed to a culture that supports critical inquiry by the faculty. However, the scholarly work of individual faculty members, while still valued, is subordinate to the collective scholarly production of the department. James Fairweather suggests that "viewing faculty productivity as an aggregate across faculty members permits department chairs and department committees to combine the efforts of their individual members to achieve acceptable levels of productivity" (1997, 23). A holistic department's scholarly productivity is measured as a whole rather than on an individual basis. Thus, a holistic department is able to establish scholarly goals for the department that are reasonably balanced against its other responsibilities. It can then distribute the work required to reach these goals among its faculty members. This permits greater variation among the work of the faculty in terms both of scholarly productivity and of teaching activities and service to the department in a given academic year.

The holistic department supports and rewards faculty members for doing differentiated work to meet institutional and departmental goals, including those expectations that extend well beyond the traditional definitions of teaching and scholarship or even of service. Faculty work plans are negotiated and then made public to all members of the department to build the sense of community, trust, and transparency that are essential to a high-functioning collective of scholars and teachers. The department makes an effort to respond to changes in stages of the life cycle and career paths of faculty members, as well as their special needs. The department recruits new faculty members to support the curriculum and help meet goals such as service learning, undergraduate research, expert use of technology, assessment, and other related tasks critical to a department that puts student learning first. Thus, a mathematics department recruits not just an algebraic topologist, but rather one that might also be able to teach effective online courses and has experience in developing curricula via current best practices.

Creating a Holistic Department

The move to a holistic department requires several fundamental paradigm shifts that affect the institution, the department, and individual faculty members. At the macro level, colleges and universities need to develop new ways to interact with departmental-level units to become less centralized and allow more departmental autonomy. Institutions need to develop policies and procedures that enable these units to function with increased independence and flexibility. New measures of accountability need to extend beyond the balance sheet and recognize the diverse ways that a particular unit is able to contribute to the institutional whole. Institutional policies need to reward departments as collectives, as well as the individuals within the unit, as a way of recognizing the collective work of the unit.

For example, the timetables for faculty evaluation and compensation and the development of annual work plans need to be aligned with each other and the academic calendar. In one model, work plans for the following academic year are developed in the spring semester, in tandem with the schedule of course offerings for the year. Thus, by May, each faculty member has an approved work plan for the following year, and the department also has an agenda of items that it would like to accomplish. It follows that the evaluation of work from the previous year would occur in June, and adjustments in compensation would follow in August.

Institutions need to find ways to reward departments that achieve their goals, as well as continuing to reward individual faculty members. Departmental rewards may range from simple public recognition of work well done to bonuses added to the departmental budget. Institutions also need to develop the infrastructure required to identify and correct problems within departments that consistently fail to meet their stated objectives for scholarship, course offerings, supporting institutional initiatives, and community service.

Among other changes, program and departmental review procedures need to be developed to reflect the new model. Program review criteria need to put increased emphasis on the contribution that the unit makes to the institutional mission and strategic goals beyond, perhaps, the support of its majors. These criteria also need to place greater attention on the professional development activities of the faculty members—what are they doing to adapt to a changing workplace and profession? These changes may cause a corresponding shift in attention to the scholarly production of individual faculty members, because there needs to be continued attention to the primary work of an academic unit, which is the learning and teaching process.

As a department works through this process of identifying its essential and elective work assignments and distributing these among its faculty members, an immediate consequence is that this work becomes transparent. Gone is an environment in which much of the faculty work is invisible and hence both underappreciated and unlimited in scope. This transparency enables the department to provide a richer context to any request for additional resources. It also provides institutions with more robust opportunities to determine the contribution of the department to the larger mission of the institution. For example, a larger department may choose to have more faculty members serve on university committees, intentionally relieving small departments of this task. Transparency of the department work will make this contribution visible to other departments, while possibly justifying why a given department is not engaged in some other activity.

Leadership in a Holistic Department

Critically, department chairpersons must shift from a managerial perspective to a leadership perspective. Often the work of a chairperson is perceived as unrewarding, largely because of the routine, often clerical, work that he or she must accomplish. This work includes activities such as course scheduling, addressing student complaints, managing the departmental budget, updating its website, and meeting with prospective students. In the worst case, a chairperson has no particular skill or interest in accomplishing these tasks. However, in a holistic department, this type of work might be delegated to members of the department who have more appropriate skills and interest in completing the work. The significant difference is that the efforts of the faculty member doing this essential work would be recognized, both by colleagues in the department and by the institution, and he or she would be rewarded for high-quality work.

In a holistic department, the chairperson needs to have and use a wide range of leadership skills, not just administrative ones (or the ability to delegate administrative tasks). First and foremost, a holistic department chairperson needs to be able to facilitate discussions among faculty members about how to prioritize and accomplish tasks and about the equity of differentiated workloads. Needless to say, these discussions might be quite contentious.

A holistic department chair needs to demonstrate strong leadership skills as he or she helps the department implement its strategic priorities. The chairperson will need to guide the faculty away from activities that detract from departmental priorities while still allowing for individual growth and for new ideas to develop. As a leader, the chairperson needs to be articulate in describing the work of the department to the administration and demonstrating how it adds value to the institutional mission; this will be an ongoing, rather than a periodic, activity. Chairpersons need to work closely with deans to ensure that the department's strategic goals and work are aligned with the goals of the institution.

Changes at the institutional and chairperson levels mean that the department, not the individual faculty member, has primary responsibly for the work to be completed. As a unit, the department establishes what its work priorities are, both those that it is required to complete (for example, teach courses) and those that it has the flexibility to make high priorities and/or distribute among the faculty in nonuniform ways (such as commitments to scholarship and service). For example, a department may identify which of AAC&U's high-impact learning practices its members have the skill and capacity to implement. It may decide that it is essential in a given year that a faculty member be assigned the task of retooling to implement pedagogy new to the department (such as flipped classrooms).

Departmental Accountability

With transparency comes accountability. When a faculty member is intentionally given time by his or her colleagues to produce a creative or scholarly piece of work, there is a clear expectation that the work will be produced and that he or she will be rewarded—or not, if the work is not produced. The same principle applies to other work: if a faculty member agrees to redesign the department's website, he or she will or will not be rewarded, according to the quality of that product. In the same way, a department can be held accountable for its collective work. By sharing with the administration and department members its intended work for the year—assessment efforts, pedagogical or scholarly retooling, and myriad other tasks—the department enables the institution to accurately assess its contribution to institutional goals and objectives and provide appropriate rewards.

Work models in which faculty members are treated as interchangeable game pieces must be replaced with a system that maximizes the flexibility given to the departmental unit to distribute both teaching and nonteaching responsibilities. In particular, policies mandating that each faculty member must carry a standard teaching load (for example, eighteen, twenty-one, or twenty-four credits) per year (with the exception of release time given by a dean) must be replaced by policies that set departmental teaching expectations and leave the distribution of teaching loads up to the department. The department will also have the responsibility for assigning nonteaching activities, within broad university guidelines and resources. Nonteaching activities such as scholarly leaves and service for national organizations can be assigned credits. This approach also provides additional flexibility for accommodating personal leaves, such as parental ones. (The sidebar "An Ideal Holistic Department" illustrates how this might work in practice.)

Annual faculty activity reports, with their retrospective perspective, need to give way to forward-looking annual work plans. As mentioned above in regard to their timing in the academic year, these work plans need to be created transparently within the department, which requires both greater trust among faculty members and a deeper understanding of their collective work. Evaluation and reward structures need to be expanded in response to the work plan model to include departmental as well as individual perspectives. Fundamental to the ability of departments to manage work flexibility within the department is the holistic evaluation of faculty work.

Learning-Centered Faculty Evaluation

Previous chapters in this book have outlined the ways in which faculty work has expanded in recent years because of an increased emphasis on experiential learning and the use of technology. As a result of these changes, we recognized that faculty evaluation must change to adequately reflect the expanded parameters of faculty work. The traditional faculty workload is most often based on the number of credit hours taught, but faculty evaluation includes scholarship and service as well as teaching. Each of these areas has evolved and is no longer clearly distinguishable as a separate category. The expanding faculty workload has affected the role of academic departments, as faculty members try to juggle multiple responsibilities. With support and encouragement from the NAC&U, we are developing the concept of a holistic department, an approach to departmental management that provides flexibility in determining workload. We are also developing a new approach to faculty evaluation to address the convergence of teaching, scholarship, and service that we call the learning-centered paradigm.

Faculty members in a university community have a diverse range of individual and collective responsibilities that have broadened and deepened in recent years. In addition to these increased responsibilities, the traditional categories for faculty work no longer apply as clearly as they did in the past. Given changes in the faculty workload, a radical revision of faculty evaluation is

An Ideal Holistic Department

As Dr. Green drove to her office, she thought about the previous week's department meeting on departmental goals and the upcoming discussion about the coming year's workload that would be the topic for this morning's meeting. Still in her first year at the university, she was a little nervous about presenting her work plan. She liked her colleagues in the department and the way in which the department managed its work. When she arrived at the university, she and the chairperson had discussed her goals for the coming year and then shared them with the department. Her colleagues had been supportive and encouraging. They offered to review the syllabus she would be using in her courses and to help her design an appropriate assessment of student-learning outcomes. This morning she was going to present her plan for the following year to use her faculty workload credits toward completing a book based on her dissertation; a publisher was interested in the project, so she was hopeful that it would be published. As the meeting began, each member shared his or her work plan. Dr. Smith's wife was expecting a baby in December. He hoped that he would be able to arrange for parental leave toward the end of the semester. Dr. Bennett had recently attended a workshop on undergraduate research, and she was anxious to put her plan into action. She wanted to use her faculty workload credits to support extra time working with students at the local historical society. Dr. Jones was finishing up a major project and looking forward to spending more time teaching. Dr. Brown, a senior member of the department, had been asked by the university president to head up the self-study process for the regional accreditation in two years. The self study was an unexpected activity, but after some discussion department members felt that they would be able to include it in the departmental work plan. The university was interested in engaging more faculty members and students in undergraduate research, so department members approved Dr. Bennett's plan and asked her to do a workshop for the department at the end of the semester. Dr. Jones offered to take over Dr. Smith's classes during his parental leave. The department also suggested that Dr. Smith might work from home updating the department's guide for internships while Dr. Jones taught his spring course. The department reviewed Dr. Green's book proposal and timeline. While approving her plan, they asked her to revise what they thought was an overly ambitious timeline. She appreciated their advice and was pleased with the outcome of the meeting. She knew that in the following year she would need to report on her progress and that her evaluation would be based in part on whether or not she had met her goals. The following week the department chairperson circulated the department's work plan.

That evening Dr. Green had dinner with a colleague who taught at a university across town. She shared the results of the department meeting, and her colleague was amazed. "You mean," the colleague asked, "that your department could adjust how many courses each professor teaches and that you will be evaluated on your progress on your book?"

"Yes," Dr. Green replied. "Several years ago the university adopted the concept of the holistic department to provide flexibility to support differential faculty work. We are evaluated on all of our work. Some years we may do more teaching than someone else in the department, and other years we may have a special project that the department wants to support. They see my book, for example, as possibly leading to the development of a new course that they would like to offer. What I really like about this approach is that the focus is on student learning, but they see that faculty learning, such as the undergraduate research project I told you about or my book, as increasing opportunities for students. I haven't been here long enough to know everything about how this approach works, but I like the way the campus has a mission and yearly goals and how we can all contribute to those goals. It makes our work more rewarding when we can work collaboratively in our department, with other departments, and with the institution as a whole. I'm preparing my evaluation of my work for this year. My workload consisted of eighteen hours of teaching, but it also included work credit hours. These are work activities other than teaching. This year, because I am new, my work credit hours were used to develop my courses and identify specific pedagogical activities for each course. The department will look for those pedagogical activities in my syllabus. When students evaluate my teaching, they also evaluate their own learning. I've found their comments about what and how they learned in my classes very helpful, and I may revise some of my approaches next year."

needed. If the traditional criteria and methods for evaluation no longer capture the complexity of faculty work, how should the evaluation process change? Our thinking is rooted in the following important principles:

- Faculty work is too complex to be neatly categorized into the three broad categories of teaching, scholarship, and service.
- All faculty work should be recognized and valued in the evaluation process.
- The evaluation process should encourage faculty work that is supportive of student learning and faculty professional development.

- Faculty members alone cannot be held responsible for student learning; students who benefit the most from their education are those who actively engage in the learning process and assume responsibility for their own learning.

Evaluation in Support of Student and Faculty Learning

A new integrated approach to faculty evaluation is needed that looks at faculty work holistically, allows flexibility among areas of faculty work, and recognizes the diversity of faculty work by valuing it in the evaluation process. Such an approach would no longer look at the percentage of time spent on scholarship, teaching, and service but instead would look at a faculty member's accomplishments and productivity as a whole. This is a fundamental change in faculty evaluation, one that puts the emphasis on learning—student learning and faculty learning. It allows faculty members to be productive and contribute to the mission of the institution in ways that are most compatible with their skills and knowledge. In this approach, faculty members are encouraged to continue their own learning and research, be innovative in their work and take risks as they expand its boundaries, and engage in professional community service. The approach recognizes that faculty learning should be a model for student learning. Adopting this approach to faculty work and evaluation necessitates other changes in the operation of the university.

The new model embraces difference and aims to be inclusive. Faculty evaluation of teaching must progress beyond classroom observation and simple evaluation of syllabi and assignments; it must look at the use of evidence-based practices that support student learning. Carl Wieman (2015) suggests that an evaluation system for science, technology, engineering, and math courses might be based on the high-impact learning strategies identified by George Kuh (2008). Such evaluation should consider important areas such as undergraduate research, digital scholarship, experiential learning, inter- and crossdisciplinary teaching and research, cooperative learning, field labs, and service learning. In many ways, teaching, scholarship, and service converge in experiential learning that encourages student and faculty collaboration. Whether such learning takes place in the biology laboratory or at the local historical society, it is rooted in hands-on interaction with tangible materials, which produces a type of functional knowledge so often lacking from current and more traditional classroom learning.

A learning-centered approach to faculty evaluation should be less about the sum of the parts and more of an assessment of the whole based on the interaction and quality of the parts. It should embrace collaborative student and faculty work, a type of social learning that has developed through centuries of pedagogical innovation and exploration. Very, very few faculty members currently have the interest, talent, or time to excel in all areas of faculty work. Fairweather (1997) found that only 10–13 percent of faculty members are highly productive in research and teaching. He also found that only about 7 percent of faculty members in four-year institutions who are highly productive in research use collaborative teaching practices. The holistic department provides opportunities for faculty members to engage in the activities for which they do have interest and talent. More generally, the intent of a holistic department is not to pigeonhole faculty members for life, but rather to enable them to bring their desires for personal growth to the community for support and thoughtful opportunities to pursue them.

Student Self-Evaluation of Learning

The increased availability of student-learning experiences through technology, internships, competency-based education and project-based learning suggests that expectations for students have changed as well. As students participate in a variety of learning opportunities, they need to assume more responsibility for their own learning and see the professor as a facilitator of learning rather than as a transmitter or dispenser of knowledge.

Thus, faculty evaluation should embrace diversity in the classroom, accounting for the myriad approaches to student learning. This new evaluation embraces the theory that everyone involved in the educational enterprise is responsible, albeit in different ways, for learning. The notion that responsibility for learning is shared among the agents involved—especially between the professoriate and the student body—increases the likelihood that student learning will flourish. Students can be asked to evaluate their contribution to their own learning, what strategies were most effective for them as they tried to meet established student-learning outcomes, and how actively they engaged in the learning process. They might also be asked what they learned about their personal learning process and how they might apply this knowledge in future classes.

This new approach to faculty evaluation allows flexibility in the work that faculty members do each year. It also suggests a longitudinal approach to evaluation in recognition that faculty work will change each year. Fundamental to a holistic evaluation of faculty is the ability of departments to manage work flexibility within the department and reflect that flexibility in evaluation.

Implementation of the Holistic Department and Learning-Centered Evaluation

To implement the holistic department and the corresponding revision of faculty evaluation, it is vital that the institution ready itself in several ways. One prerequisite for this change is a common belief among the faculty and administration that faculty work conditions need to be reexamined. Beginning with this assumption, faculty and staff members and administrators should reexamine

the institutional mission in light of current trends in and the changing landscape of higher education and should use that mission to describe the breadth
and depth of faculty work. In addition the faculty must be open to innovation
and invention at the level of faculty evaluation so that the full breadth and
depth of faculty work is included.

We suggest the following actions for implementing holistic faculty
evaluation and departments (for more details, see Hensel, Hunnicutt, and
Salomon 2015):

1. Administrators consider the impact of developing holistic departments on
   current policies and procedures and determine how they can be changed.
   A holistic department is an integral part of a holistic approach to faculty
   evaluation. For a holistic department to function effectively, administrators
   must adapt campus policies to allow for the necessary flexibility and transparency of a holistic department. Institutions begin to revise policies, practices, and norms to encourage the development of holistic departments.
   This includes leadership training opportunities for department chairs. It
   also includes developing mechanisms for reporting departmental goals—
   which both aggregate and contribute to individual work plans—and accomplishments to the administration beyond program reviews.

2. Institutions engage in discussions about the ways in which teaching,
   scholarship, and service have been transformed on their campuses. Each
   institution has its own culture and mission, and the approach to faculty
   evaluation must be compatible with that culture and mission.

3. Departments, led by their chairpersons, modify their decision-making processes to be more transparent and collaborative, particularly in the development of faculty work plans. Departments also need to develop collaborative
   processes for departmental agenda setting and assessing departmental
   effectiveness. Departments will approach a holistic management style in different ways depending on the discipline, numbers of faculty members and
   students, and other institutional factors. Smaller departments have to be more
   selective than larger departments and programs about how they respond to
   some campuswide initiatives and how they participate in the community
   beyond the campus. Some departments, such as those of education, social
   work, and criminal justice, may be more active in civic engagement than
   English or philosophy departments. Departments in the sciences are likely
   to put more emphasis on proposal writing and collaborative research than
   humanities departments are. Departments need the flexibility to develop an
   approach that works for them. Administrators need to know that departments
   are meeting their goals and responding to the institutional mission.

4. Faculty members and administrators need to discuss the expanded
   definition of faculty workload and come to an agreement on how much

flexibility individual departments should have in creating work assignments, and which of those assignments will be included in the direct evaluation of faculty productivity. For example, an institution may decide that all faculty members must serve as academic advisors rather than allow department-level decisions about which faculty members do this work or whether nonfaculty academic advisors should be used. At the same time, the institution may or may not decide to have an annual evaluation of the quality of individual faculty members' work as academic advisors.

5. Faculty members discuss how teaching or learning, scholarship, and service can be merged for evaluation purposes into a holistic process. Compared to current approaches in the academy, a holistic approach to evaluation is a more effective way of recognizing the totality of faculty work. However, it is also a more complex approach to evaluation, and it is critical for faculty members and administrators to understand and agree on new approaches for evaluating faculty work.

6. Faculty members revise student evaluations of faculty and courses to include students' self-assessment of their contributions to the learning process. Experiential learning suggests that students need to be more engaged in their own learning process, and they should be held accountable for their own learning. In addition, when students comment on their contributions to the learning process, faculty members can increase their understanding of what pedagogical strategies are most effective for student learning.

Summary

The work of the faculty has become more integrated and holistic as the lines between teaching, research, and service have blurred. We believe that professors need to be evaluated in a holistic manner that recognizes the significant overlap and integration of the traditional evaluation categories. A holistic approach values nontraditional approaches to teaching, scholarship, and service. We also believe that the shift in emphasis from teaching to learning and the new experiential approach to student learning requires students to assume more responsibility for their own learning. Students' evaluation of faculty members should include a component of student self-assessment.

A holistic approach to evaluation recognizes that work areas differ from semester to semester. If professors are evaluated on the whole of their work, departments need to operate in a holistic manner as well. Holistic departments support the expanded definitions of faculty work in all areas and use faculty work plans to provide balance to faculty as well as ensuring that departmental and institutional goals are met. Holistic faculty evaluation and holistic departments can support student learning by encouraging pedagogical innovation;

providing faculty professional development; and expanding the definitions of teaching, scholarship, and service to include student-faculty collaborative work.

These paradigm shifts in faculty work and how universities evaluate that work have the potential to have a significant positive impact on student learning. The increased transparency of faculty work will enable departments to focus attention on student learning by increasing awareness of, and appropriately shifting priorities away from, the faculty work that is often distracting and invisible to both the faculty and the administration.

By rewarding professional development activities and a wider range of activities on the boundaries between teaching, scholarship, and service, faculty members will be encouraged to learn and implement new sets of pedagogical practices. In particular, not only will departments be more likely to implement some of the high-impact practices identified by Kuh (2008), but they will be able to do so effectively and with confidence, effective assessment and revision, and the support of the institution. The trust, autonomy, and flexibility that are part of the holistic department and learner-centered faculty evaluation developed through a collaborative process will strengthen the campus mission and its ability to meet its goals.

REFERENCES

Astin, Alexander. 1993. *What Matters in College: Four Critical Years Revisited*. San Francisco: Jossey-Bass.

Boyer, Ernest L. 1990. *Scholarship Reconsidered: Priorities of the Professoriate*. San Francisco: Jossey-Bass.

———. 1996. "The Scholarship of Engagement." *Journal of Public Service and Outreach* 1 (1): 11–20.

Fairweather, James S. 1997. *The Highly Productive Faculty Member: Confronting the Mythologies of Faculty Work*. Los Angeles: Center for Higher Education Policy Analysis, University of Southern California.

Hensel, Nancy, Lynn Hunnicutt, and David Salomon, eds. 2015. *Redefining the Paradigm: Faculty Models to Support Student Learning*. Valparaiso, IN: New American Colleges and Universities.

Hower, Mark. 2012. "Faculty Work: Moving beyond the Paradox of Autonomy and Collaboration." PhD diss., Antioch University.

Humphreys, Debra. 2013. "Deploying Collaborative Leadership to Reinvent Higher Education for the Twenty-First Century." *Peer Review* 15 (1): 4–6.

Kuh, George D. 2008. *High-Impact Educational Practices: What They Are, Who Has Them, and Why They Matter*. Washington, DC: Association American Colleges and Universities.

McMillin, Linda A., and William G. Berberet. 2002. *The New Academic Compact: Revisioning the Relationship between Faculty and Their Institutions*. Bolton, MA: Anker.

Saltmarsh, John, Kevin Kecskes, and Steven Jones. 2005. "Building Engagement Across the Campus: Creating Engaged Departments." Paper presented at the Pedagogies of Engagement Conference of the Association of American Colleges and Universities, Bethesda, MD, April.

Shapiro, Judith. 2014. "The Value of a Shared Education." *Chronicle of Higher Education*, November 17, 23–24.

Wergin, Jon. 2002. "Creating the Engaged Department." *Department Chair* 13 (2): 1–3.

Wieman, Carl. 2015. "A Better Way to Evaluate Undergraduate Teaching." *Change* 47 (1): 6–15.

10

Internationalization and Faculty Work

WILLIAM PLATER

The world has changed dramatically in the past decades. In order to keep pace with the rate and scope of change in the educational sector and with the demand for access to quality education around the world, we need to create an ecosystem for ongoing research, learning, and innovation about the future of education. (Massachusetts Institute of Technology 2014)

To respond to the skills challenge in global labor markets, the traditional model for providing . . . tertiary education will need to be transformed in both advanced and developing economies. (McKinsey Global Institute 2012)

The variety of models is reflective of diverse contexts of source and destination countries, where demand from the emerging segment of "glocal" students–who have aspirations to gain a global education experience, but want to remain in their local region/country–is creating new opportunities for institutions. (Choudaha and Edelstein 2014)

Instead, a typical student might be taking one course along with a half million other people around the world and another with three peers and a mentor in the local community. Because it doesn't cost very much money to start such a place, there are dozens of similar organizations nearby. Some may specialize in a particular subject area, offering a few extended educational programs. Others may be organized around different ideas, faiths, occupations, and philosophies of learning. (Carey 2015)

A new ecosystem for institutions offering higher education, a transformed labor market model for tertiary education staffing, and a globally flatter higher education interconnected system—these are but a few of the predictions implying that faculty work will change significantly in response to internationalization, globalization, and glocalization, all of which are accelerated by the changing technologies that make the world smaller. While these three terms are widely used to denote different things, in this chapter *internationalization* refers to the intentional steps that institutions and faculty take to reflect intellectual interdependence; *globalization* refers to external factors that affect institutions, which range from economic or political conditions to climate change and global health; and *glocalization* refers to an intentional awareness of and balance between the complex interrelationship of a local community and the rest of the world.

This chapter considers in three parts the implications of creating a new model of faculty to meet such challenges: (1) globalization factors driving change; (2) design elements for models that meet institutional needs; and (3) consideration for preserving globally aware academic professionalism. Instead of attempting to be exhaustive, each section seeks only to establish a cumulative foundation for further speculation.

Global Factors That Could Affect New Faculty Models

Among the many factors driving changes in the traditional faculty model, internationalization has been one of the least noticed but potentially most important. Internationalization has taken the form of rapidly increasing numbers of students from other nations enrolling in US institutions; even more dramatic shifts in the nationality of faculty members in engineering, mathematics, and the sciences; and curricular reforms that place a higher value on global awareness, the experience of travel wrapped in study abroad, and branch campuses in other countries. Even less visible, transnational research collaboration has also grown significantly.

The familiar, if eroding, narrative that American higher education and, therefore, its faculty members are the world's best has nonetheless encountered some surprises. Notably, US primacy may have some cracks when it comes to student success, perhaps in large part due to the realities of who faculty members have become. For example, Northeastern University (2014) found that 54 percent of 502 employers surveyed believed that the United States is behind developed and emerging nations in preparing college graduates for the workforce, a perception reinforced by test scores. The extent to which governments in different nations—and in very different ways—are shifting funding either to or from higher education as a public good or as an instrument of economic competition further complicates the picture. If the fundamental purpose of tertiary education is preparing highly competent graduates, then the US higher education community ignores global competition at its peril.

Curriculum

Like their counterparts in the European Union (EU), Asia Pacific, and South America, most US-based higher education associations have created international curricular initiatives in response to the perceived benefit of increased global awareness and experience, often bolstered by studies affirming the value of study abroad, second-language learning, and recognition of global interdependencies. In brief, globalization drives internationalization.

One of the clearest statements of the explicit value of internationalization in the curriculum is the Lumina Foundation's Degree Qualifications Profile (DQP), which includes global and civic learning as one of its five primary areas of competency (Adelman et al. 2015). Qualifications frameworks in many other regions of the world similarly explicitly include some form of global competence, and Lumina's DQP draws heavily and specifically on the EU's Bologna Process and so-called tuning. The near-term implication for academic work in the United States is that faculty members must be able to place their disciplinary student-learning outcomes in a global context.

Beyond their global reach, new media and educational technologies have begun to explore the potential of social media to reshape learning as a concurrent, globally collaborative experience unbounded by enrollment, as students themselves import into courses both materials and fellow learners from other nations—for example, as in CourseNetworking (n.d.). The impact of students' acting without faculty direction or control to expand context and engage learners outside the enrolled course will require faculty members to learn new skills—and tolerances—since their authority and expertise may be surpassed by students' academic crowd sourcing. This underappreciated but radical shift to truly learning-centered education—with global reach—by itself will eventually require new approaches to both the function and competence of faculty.

Curricular models reflecting internationalization have been growing for many years. Study abroad, for example, has subtle but real implications for faculty competence as international students bring foreign perspectives to the domestic classroom and returning US study-abroad students display new awareness of their own locales. The growing prospect of joint and dual degrees depends on faculty engagement and reliable knowledge about counterpart cultures and learning environments.

Collaborative "2+2" programs and their variations, including those at the graduate level, are based on students in a university or college in another nation studying locally for the first two years in a curriculum designed to match that of a US, institution where they complete their degree in the second two years. Faculty involvement in these programs' curricular design, admissions decisions, pre-transfer virtual mentoring, post-transfer support, and many other elements of internationalization depend on increasingly sophisticated faculty knowledge, expertise, engagement, and adaptability.

While still relatively new, joint programming that combines degrees with competency-based certification necessary or useful for transnational employment will have many of the same features, but with the further requirement of cross-cultural expertise among faculty members who can situate disciplinary mastery in other cultural and regulatory contexts. As competency-based learning increases in response to employer demands, faculty members should expect to meet new requirements for their own transnational qualifications.

Faculty Appointments

The internationalization of curricula and transnational student mobility may be helpful to prepare faculty members for changes in the nature of their appointments, especially as job announcements begin to include international competence as a desired qualification. However, institutions and their faculties face an increasingly dizzying array of new challenges accelerated by globalization, including rapid changes in curricula to meet employer needs; industry's even faster generation of new information and applications, which require faculty members to catch up; and citizen graduates who can help their local communities adapt quickly to changing global impacts.

Ironically, the growth of the adjunct model contains key elements of institutional responses, since faculty expertise and competence can be changed much more quickly when appointments are of a fixed term and specific to courses, certifications, and even research projects. Through technology, appointments can tap a global labor market, especially when hiring an already well-employed expert to teach a single online course (or perform a specific research task) to meet a specific curricular (or research) need.

While not solely or even primarily the consequence of internationalization, a new faculty model may be built on a small cadre of full-time, tenured (or long-term contract) faculty members who manage the essential elements of the core curriculum and then augment unchanging foundational knowledge with specialized knowledge, competence, or experience as needed through short-term appointments.

Internationalization is thus a stimulus for thinking creatively about the adjunct, part-time, and entrepreneurial aspects of evolving faculty work when the potential labor market is worldwide and virtual. The successful model of the future will have the flexibility to allow a faculty member to be a complete scholar at one institution while concurrently serving as an adjunct at another institution in a highly unbundled role. Moreover, the core faculty members who ensure curricular stability and integrity will necessarily acquire new skills in finding, assessing, and integrating into their institution colleagues who may come from a variety of sectors outside academe and countries outside the United States.

Faculty Mobility and Autonomy

Institutions must necessarily manage their human capital—their faculty, specifically—as a resource constrained by resources, laws, missions, and the like. When viewed as positions—full-time and part-time equivalents—required to achieve specific ends instead of people with names and ambitions, faculty can be treated as functions or means, as ciphers and statistics. But as human beings with self-awareness and self-interest, faculty members do not always align their work with institutional needs.

Technology enables all faculty members—full or part time, contingent or tenured—to be international, global, and glocal. Institutions can expect and require any and all academic workers to act in an internationalized context. But expertise, preference, and temperament are highly individual, personal, and changeable. The autonomy and discretionary control of time traditionally enjoyed in the currently fading faculty model have become negotiable attributes of the conditions of work, not rights.

When a mismatch of institutional and personal interests occurs, especially when the academic workforce is mostly contingent, greater faculty (virtual) mobility may emerge as a new characteristic of faculty models, especially as the academic workforce is perceived as global instead of national. The predominance of faculty members born outside the United States in some highly visible and economically critical fields is only the first stage of global mobility.

Nationality may now have a dual meaning: where one was born and where one earned a PhD. Faculty members born or educated in the United States may find more opportunity and more flexibility in academic positions located in other nations—even if for only for a few years in a long career, or for a short-term virtual appointment for a specific assignment that does not compromise full employment elsewhere. As cross-border education assumes new forms, ranging from the expansion of US colleges and universities into other nations with joint or stand-alone branch campuses to virtual faculty teaching online from almost anywhere in the world, assumptions about faculty and geography (and mobility) need to be reassessed.

While US academic senates are debating the efficacy of foreign branch campuses and the role of the faculty members who work there, they may not be aware of the growing interest of institutions in other nations in opening campuses in the United States (why not a Mexican university in South Texas, or an Indian university in Silicon Valley?). Or they may not appreciate the potential of for-profits (such as the University of Phoenix and Laureate International) and nonprofits (for example, the University of the People or the Open University

USA) to recruit faculty from a global talent pool—which has expanded to accommodate people who wish to come and go from industry, government, or nonprofits, not just academe.

Industry-Influenced Global Faculty Qualification Frameworks

The consequence of professions' creating global expectations for competency in their respective fields is already playing a role in models of faculty work, and it will reach eventually into the liberal arts disciplines. Professions in the United States have long had influence over both the curricula and the nature of faculty appointments (such as credentials required of faculty members, percentages of full-time faculty members, and the extent of continuing professional development). As many disciplinary accreditors have internationalized, the understanding of what determines competence at varying degree levels has also internationalized, along with expectations about who is competent to serve as a faculty member.

The approach taken by AACSB International, for example, is indicative of how a globalized view of faculty competence may play out. The accrediting body does not require that faculty be full time, tenured, or even have the program as the principal employer: "Faculty contractual relationships, title, tenure status, full-time or part-time status, etc., can help to explain and document the work of faculty, *but these factors are not perfectly correlated with participation or with the most critical variables in assessing faculty sufficiency, deployment, and qualifications*" (AACSB 2015; emphasis added).

Some fields, notably law and medicine, have US accrediting bodies that have declined to internationalize, while accrediting bodies in engineering, technology, business, education, and other fields have forged ahead. Of the roughly fifty program accreditors recognized by the US Council for Higher Education Accreditation (CHEA), over two-thirds have expanded beyond the United States—often in response to the needs and demands of industries that are transnational and depend on the same levels of competence among potential employees worldwide. Some global companies contract with institutions in the nations where they operate to hire faculty members who can offer curricula designed to meet accredited industry standards as the most efficient way to ensure a qualified future workforce.

Credentialing

Economic competitiveness (the proven role of education as the ladder of personal social and economic advancement) and vocationalism (the highest priority of credentialing) combine to exert demands first on the curriculum and then on faculty members' preparation, competency, and performance. Education and certification are no longer the monopoly of educational institutions. When higher education institutions—and their faculty members—cannot deliver, other providers can. An example is Minerva, a newly established global university whose faculty members can live anywhere: all they need is an Internet connection (Wood 2014).

Society's and employers' tolerance for new forms of credentialing has become one of the most potent catalysts for intentionally creating new models of faculty work and appointments. Higher education globally has entered a transitional (and most likely transformative) period in which credible evidence of competence and the ability to perform relevant tasks—whether those of work at a hierarchy of levels and skills or of citizenship across a range of sophistication—have become unbundled, along with faculty work.

Taking a variety of names—certificates, badges, MOOC certification, specializations, nanodegrees, prior learning assessment, lifelong learning, and so forth—alternative ways of quantifying, aggregating, transferring, and applying learning as well as certifying competence have broken free from the monopoly of degree-granting institutions.

Degrees continue to carry considerable value—especially as a function of the prestige of the awarding institution—but other credentials are being recognized at the sub-degree level and as a validation of lifelong learning, now made essential in many endeavors where knowledge and techniques change so quickly. The inevitability of alternative credentialing has led CHEA to call for the creation of a quality assurance system for these new kinds of credentials and providers: "The technological breakthroughs of the past decade now enable both traditional institutions and alternative postsecondary providers of education offerings to provide unparalleled access to students, offering multiple opportunities for learning. *The world is witnessing a rapidly emerging national and international campus without boundaries.* New alternative providers are entering the educational marketplace, joining the ranks of traditional, established providers and gaining acceptance" (Council for Higher Education Accreditation 2014; emphasis added). If there is a borderless global campus, then there is likely to be an unprecedented model of faculty members who staff it.

In brief, people recognized as valid individual providers of learning and credentialing—that is, alternative faculty members—need not be employed by degree-granting institutions that are approved and certified by conventional accreditors or by ministries of higher education or other traditional guarantors of quality. Competence and expertise can trump pedigree and tradition when the labor market is global.

There will be a growing role for unaffiliated individuals who can market themselves as educational providers via technology and global communications. This group will probably include a new class of superstars who can leave academe (or another sector) with enough personal credibility to serve as an accepted certifier of competence. The enormous uncertainty of the forms and means of alternative credentialing precludes any but the most preliminary estimate of the impact on traditional faculty models, but it is clear that any new, deliberately designed model of faculty for the institutional setting must accommodate a still shadowy cadre of providers who may function as independent contractors or entrepreneurs with highly variable contractual relationships, scaled according to the perceived value of and demand for the offering.

For example, why shouldn't underemployed doctoral students at US institutions (and others) accept concurrent virtual part-time employment at colleges in emerging economies? If Uber can match drivers and riders worldwide, could a new Google-like entity match teachers and learners? While not yet a model for educational entrepreneurs or universities, the Amazon Mechanical Turk is a provocative innovation that leads to speculation about what may be possible. It "provides an on-demand, scalable, human workforce to complete jobs that humans can do better than computers"—like teaching, perhaps (Amazon 2015). Established in 2005, the Amazon Mechanical Turk has over 500,000 workers in 190 countries (Amazon Web Services 2011) and a system giving employers access to optional qualification tests that can be used to select competent workers (Amazon Web Services n.d.). It is not too much of a stretch to imagine an academic "mechanical Turk" serving a global clientele of institutions by providing on-demand, precertified (and accredited) faculty members for jobs big or small, long or short, specialized or general.

Glocalism

The reality of the uneven and changing development of nations creates a dynamic and even an energy for considering the interplay of local interests, understandings, and needs with the influences of remote places and things. As students are likely to be glocal—wanting a globally informed education with aspirations to the highest possible levels of quality even as they expect to live their lives and use their learning in one or a few places—there are implications not only for curriculum, credentialing, and concepts of quality, but also for the organization of those who teach, create new knowledge, and apply it for the betterment of the people with whom they live. The internationalization of professional societies—both scholarly and accrediting—is only one example.

Values

The traditional faculty model has claimed several shared values that are closely linked to tenure, ranks, classifications, titles, disciplinary allegiance, and autonomy. Principal among them—and topics for exploration in this volume—are academic freedom; shared governance; professional development as a corollary to career advancement; and discretion in the allocation of time to meet responsibilities in teaching, research, and service.

However, both globalization and internationalization have brought these conditions of work—long assumed to be integral to the US faculty model—into sharp relief as cross-border education, the rise of transnational for-profit companies, the flattening tendencies of online learning, and the realities of a largely part-time and contingent academic workforce reveal the weak spots in values espoused but less and less frequently practiced. As filtered by glocalisms, academic freedom and other values may no longer be expedient in new faculty models.

A "flatter" higher education world upends or at least levels the organizational hierarchies on which all of these values are based—hierarchies such as faculty ranks, administrative and economic levels, and tenure status. In a briefing on the future of work in the *Economist*'s first issue of 2015, the lead article noted: "Firms [and, arguably, colleges and universities] make sense when the cost of organising things internally through hierarchies is less than the cost of buying things from the market; they are a way of dealing with the high transaction costs faced when you need to do something moderately complicated" (*Economist* 2015).

In the face of the massification of education worldwide and the attention to the cost of higher education in the United States, the fundamental model of educational organization is fair game, and—as the increased adjunctification of the faculty has documented—the faculty model is especially vulnerable. How much shared governance is possible with a largely contingent and significantly part-time workforce? How real is academic freedom when reappointment is discretionary, or the threat of retribution by a group in another country limits what faculty members profess? How is the return on investment in professional development calculated?

Higher education has resisted commodification for a very long time, but politicians, venture capitalists, technologists, and the disenfranchised are chipping away. What values remain—and for how long—will clearly be a function of economic issues first, but globalization will surely be a factor as outsourced services (such as advising, grading, tutoring, curriculum development, content acquisition, and publication) proliferate. With greater globalization of services and hence greater interaction with other value systems, fundamental values (especially academic freedom) may be replaced with personalized contract provisions instead of institutionally guaranteed rights, and with insurance instead of due process.

Design Elements of New Faculty Models

From the institution's perspective, any new model has to enhance its capacity to achieve its mission in spite of resource constraints, ensure sustainability, and create competitive advantage (or at least avoid loss). Elements to be considered include the topics discussed in the following sections.

Mission

Cost considerations tend to narrow the institution's mission, more clearly identify its market position, and reduce its offerings. A narrowed mission with a proportionately shrunk core faculty can reduce costs while protecting quality and brand. Core content may require core faculty members who are full time and employed in a way to ensure stability without permanence and thus the use of longer-term (for example, ten-year rolling) contracts. In contrast, collateral content can be completely outsourced via technology; offered by faculty members with less of an institutional commitment (for example, those with contracts of only one to three years); or supplied in specialized areas by experts drawn from industry, governments, nonprofits, or educational institutions anywhere in the world (who typically have no contract beyond that for a single offering). Selective collaboration with institutions from around the world through curricular innovations such as dual degrees or competency-based certificates can preserve a comprehensive range of offerings while providing flexibility. Most probably, there will be a combination of these approaches.

Recruitment

With a global talent pool, global communications, and globalizing standards of acceptable performance for learning outcomes, institutions can risk faculty mobility and any lack of institutional loyalty in favor of maximum flexibility and cost control. Disciplinary expertise and loyalty are market factors, not the building blocks of transformed institutions, which can free some parts of the institution from the hegemony of departments.

For all but core content areas on which their reputation is based, institutions will benefit from a just-in-time labor supply made possible by communications technologies and standardized learning objectives and by going global, with appreciable cost savings. Basic skills courses—for example, those in communication, quantitative reasoning, and information literacy—may attract mostly providers from a global labor market, but so will costly, time-intensive teaching in cases where individualized approaches and frequent feedback can be segmented into modules, even at advanced levels. The routinization of professional knowledge and the commodification of educational services translate into flexibility for institutions based on globalized, nonhierarchical labor markets.

Tenure and Stability

Tenure is local. Competence is global. In the emerging reality in which local issues and practices are always linked to the global, tenure may give way to new relationships between individual faculty members and their employers. In a new model of globalized faculty work, institutions may eventually offer only contracts, replacing tenure with degrees of loyalty. Investments in the institution's overall success can be purchased with longer and more robust contracts for some faculty members. Leadership and management are then differentiated with varying performance metrics and reward structures.

Professional development is differentiated. For those with longer-term contracts in core areas, it is provided as a part of their contracts. For the more fluid and contingent workforce, professional development is a personal responsibility and a by-product of work outside of academe. With a globalized, highly contingent labor market, institutions can acquire the expertise they need—at the desired level of competence and cost—without investing in professional development.

As disruptive as this scenario (or even parts of it) might be to the traditional faculty model, it may have advantages. Long constrained by disciplinary hegemony, interdisciplinary fields may have greater acceptance and greater possibilities for knowledge building through transnational collaborations and exchanges. New fields of inquiry and practice may find accelerated pathways for recognition supported by new forms of global peer review. Individual scholars may more easily find collaborators in a transnational environment.

And as for-profit and hybrid universities are linked in global networks (such as Laureate International, Alliant, and the Open University) and nonprofits form voluntary alliances, new transnational faculty development projects may emerge as an alternative to tenure. Such initiatives might focus on disseminating the latest research, new technologies to advance student learning, or curricular developments to meet industry needs. Relevance, competence, and readiness are likely to become better forms of employment security for many global faculty members than tenure.

Academic Freedom and Intellectual Property

For institutions, academic freedom will become congruent with free speech since the contractual nature of appointments ensures institutional flexibility, which will give management the capacity to reshape the teaching, research, and service directions of the academic workforce as needed through contract renewal or nonreappointment. The freedom to speak and write will be as broad as freedom of speech (and the legal system) allow instead of a function of institutional policy and values.

A global standard may not be possible, but what has already become clear is that current negotiations (as of early 2015) to establish the Transatlantic Trade and Investment Partnership and the Trade in Services Agreement have signaled the reality of globalized higher education, the lack of clarity on how trade rules might affect public, private, and for-profit education in transnational interactions, and the impact on autonomy of national and regional governments to regulate their own or exported educational services, including intellectual property.

In the EU there are worries that US for-profit institutions might proliferate there, bringing in their faculty models as well as business practices. Because the United States has not yet been much of a target for exported educational services, few US educators seem worried about the implications of a globalized, commodified range of services. However, with the United Kingdom's Warwick University, India's Amity University, and Mexico's CETYS University all expressing interest in opening branch campuses in California, that situation may change.

The European University Association has issued a statement that says, in part: "Current trade negotiations have the potential to impinge not only on the learning and teaching mission of universities, but also on other aspects of H[igher] E[ducation], such as research and development, data collection and data flows, intellectual property, e-commerce, and the recognition of professional qualifications" (2015). Startled by the thought that their professional knowledge can be commodified, academics would be stunned to think that their work could not only be covered by an international trade agreement but actually be regulated as trade.

Quality

While the cumulative quality of individual faculty members' work has long been the basis of institutional quality, the fluidity of the workforce will enhance the role of external and third-party quality assessment. The US model of combined, mandated institutional assessment and accreditation augmented with elective specialized program accreditation is likely to evolve, as CHEA already anticipates.

In the not so distant future, institutional assessment will most likely focus exclusively on operational integrity—much as other regulated industries face external validation—while quality assessment will rest on a combination of program accreditation based on globalized industry standards and new systems of validation of individual providers (faculty members) drawn from a global market (perhaps accelerated by the ongoing negotiations over international trade agreements that include educational services). Clearly, a new breed of educational service providers—for-profit, nonprofit, and individual entrepreneurial—has led policy makers in several nations to consider a new regulatory approach in the face of global competition.

Amid a widespread belief among financial institutions that the current US higher education model is unsustainable (such as the TIAA-CREF Institute's conclusion that "the model is in need of fundamental change and [many] are seriously concerned about the ongoing viability of the industry" [quoted in *ICEF Monitor* 2014]), there have been many predictions about what might emerge from the future. For example, Ernst and Young foresee three new models: a "streamlined status quo," "niche dominators," and "transformers" (ibid.). All of these models assume higher education's partnering with many other sectors and with significantly different workforces.

Academic Professionalism as the Foundation of a New Model

The *Economist* article about the future of work noted that globalization and computerization are the principal factors in the unbundling of the concept of a job—being an employee in an organization with a defined place of work, defined roles and mutual responsibilities, defined career paths, and defined benefits, all of which is similar to what characterizes the traditional faculty model. There is a coming collapse in the structure of careers, the *Economist* argues, because "the knowledge economy is subject to the same forces as the industrial and service economies: routinisation, division of labour and contracting out. A striking proportion of professional knowledge can be turned into routine action, and the division of labour can bring efficiencies to the knowledge economy" (2015).

While many—perhaps most—in the academy would be incredulous that their professional knowledge could be routinized, the continuing unbundling of faculty roles suggests otherwise. Moreover, the decades-long trend toward specialization in graduate education; research; and vying for narrowly focused, upper-level courses instead of the more general introductory courses ironically makes it easier to replace these narrower specialties in a culture grown used to component parts that can be used to "plug and play."

All of the catalytic factors discussed in this and other chapters in this volume will ameliorate some problems even as they aggravate others. In brief, an intentional model designed—as the editors of this volume intend—to support student learning and higher education's full mission will tend toward modeling principally the interests of either the institution or the faculty. Thus far, the impact of adjunctification, technologically based delivery, and the market entry of for-profit providers have addressed institutional interests and paid only grudging attention to the interests of casualized academic labor.

What elements constitute a proper model—that is, one that considers the interests of the institution and the individual equally—is amorphous, as other chapters make clear in their variety and differing degrees of suggested probability. There is no international model per se for the US faculty, only the influence of internationalization on the mission and operation of institutions, the nature of appointments and roles, the talent pool of people to fill roles, and the environment (since competition, prestige, and peer pressure tend to drive most institutions toward a mean). But there is a sense that the faculty role is defined and perhaps protected by academic professionalism, however hard that is to describe.

For all of its complexity and ambiguity, the traditional faculty model has core elements that tend to underlie other professions as well, such as adequate preparation, an understanding of the rules or patterns of professional conduct, being subject to peer scrutiny, continuing current competence in the field of one's practice, personal integrity and ethical conduct, and a duty to the public good (Shaker 2015).

All of these elements—and more—will be challenged by new models that begin with the current, largely contingent workforce. It is unrealistic to design models that ignore current trends. The extent to which faculty work remains that of a profession may be an open question—especially a profession with a duty to the public good. In some other professions where professional knowledge is being routinized, such as medicine, concerns about professionalism are growing proportionate to the change in working conditions that prioritize the interests of the institution. But if we were able to design a new model that harnessed the change factors to increase the amelioration of adverse conditions while reducing the aggravations, what might we imagine? And how might internationalization impact the model?

Contracts Vary by Mission

Appointments are likely to be contracts of varying length that depends on the centrality of the discipline to the mission of the institution and market conditions. An increasing number of opportunities are likely to be virtual. Most faculty members—including those who are part time—will have documented their competence to practice their professions and advance their disciplines in a globally competitive academic environment. Core faculty members can expect longer-term contracts with full-time employment; periodic adjustments of responsibilities among teaching, research, service, and administration; opportunities for professional development to better meet institutional needs; a direct but not decisive role in shaping the curriculum and hiring new faculty members; and a proliferation of titles intended to reflect the greater diversity of the academic workforce.

Little Change for Core Faculty Members;
Greater Diversity of Roles for Others

Core faculty members at elite institutions, along with most of the supporting faculty members there, can expect relatively little change except for a steady increase in the number and variety of part-time and outsourced educational providers as colleagues. And those providers themselves will find an evolving and rapidly changing range of employment opportunities, from working at institutions in the United States and other countries that will hire them from intermediaries and brokers that will function as academic "temp agents" to serving as new, high-performing providers specializing in select specialties and working at new kinds of globalized institutions like Minerva.

What is the specific role or impact of internationalization on the institutional model of faculty: Opening a global labor market that requires institutions to seek out new intellectual advances worldwide through the people they hire to retain competitiveness and to prepare students (for whatever credential) with documented global competitiveness based on learning outcomes recognized and validated by industry. In the era of computer-based on-demand employment and hyper-specialization, most faculty members will find themselves working for more than one employer at a time, and only one of those employers may be a college or university.

Conclusion

There is little doubt that globalization, internationalization, and glocalization will be factors in any new models of faculty work, whether intentional or not. These factors will not be determinate or, finally, the most important because other factors and catalysts are already overwhelming. Some elements of the model will enhance the quality of faculty life while some detract from it; some will ameliorate problems while others aggravate them.

In many ways, this picture is not very different from current conditions, given that so much change has occurred in the nature of faculty work over the past two decades with little public notice or concern. What is at risk and thus needs to be the focus of an intentional model is ensuring respect for faculty members as academic professionals, with clear expectations for how faculty members themselves honor the profession across political, cultural, religious, economic, and linguistic differences when issues such as academic freedom, prestige, and conditions of work are so very different. In this sense, globalization will certainly aggravate emerging problems. If there is only one ameliorating factor, it may be the renewal and reaffirmation of institutions' support for a faculty duty to the public good—however that good may be defined locally—with the understanding that the world in the vastness of its different and ever-changing societies shares a public good and a common future.

As the academic workforce is globalized, so too must be the principles underlying an evolved concept of a profession transformed by forces it cannot resist. No credible voice has yet emerged to articulate the principles that will define an academic profession that takes as its highest duty ensuring that there even *is* a public good—global, local, or glocal. But that voice is needed, and soon.

REFERENCES

AACSB International. 2015. "Eligibility Procedures and Accreditation Standards for Business Accreditation: Engagement, Innovation, Impact." January 31. Accessed December 13, 2015. http://www.aacsb.edu/~/media/AACSB/Docs/Accreditation/Standards/2013-bus-standards-update-jan2015.ashx.

Adelman, Cliff, Peter Ewell, Paul Gaston, and Carol Geary Schneider. 2015. "The Degree Qualifications Profile." Lumina Foundation. Accessed December 13, 2015. http://www.luminafoundation.org/dqp.

Amazon. 2015. "Amazon Mechanical Turk: Getting Started Guide." Accessed December 13, 2015. http://docs.aws.amazon.com/AWSMechTurk/latest/AWSMechanicalTurkGettingStartedGuide/Welcome.html.

Amazon Web Services. n.d.. "Amazon Mechanical Turk: Developer Guide: Creating and Managing Qualifications." Accessed January 9, 2016. http://docs.aws.amazon.com/AWSMechTurk/latest/AWSMechanicalTurkRequester/Concepts_QualificationsArticle.html.

———. 2011. "Discussion Forum." Accessed January 9, 2016. https://forums.aws.amazon.com/thread.jspa?threadID=58891.

Carey, Kevin. 2015. "One Vision of Tomorrow's College: Cheap, and You Get an Education, Not a Degree." *Washington Post*, February 20.

Choudaha, Rahul, and Richard J. Edelstein. 2014. "Towards Quality Transnational Education." *University World News*, October 15. Accessed December 13, 2015. http://www.universityworldnews.com/article.php?story=20141015210003860.

Council for Higher Education Accreditation. 2014. "Quality Assurance and Alternative Higher Education: A Policy Perspective." August. Accessed February 13, 2016. http://www.chea.org/pdf/Quality_Assurance_and_Alternative_HE_7x8.5.pdf.

CourseNetworking. n.d. Home page. Accessed December 13, 2015. https://www.thecn.com/.

Economist. 2015. "There's an App for That." January 3. Accessed December 13, 2015. http://www.economist.com/news/briefing/21637355-freelance-workers-available-moments-notice-will-reshape-nature-companies-and.

European University Association. 2015. "EUA Statement on TTIP and TiSA." January 30. Accessed December 13, 2015. http://www.eua.be/Libraries/Publication/EUA_Statement_TTIP.sflb.ashx.

ICEF Monitor. 2015. "Growing Questions about the Business Model for Higher Education in the US." February 24. Accessed December 13, 2015. http://monitor.icef.com/2015/02/growing-questions-business-model-higher-education-us/.

Massachusetts Institute of Technology. 2014. "Institute-wide Task Force on the Future of MIT Education: Final Report." July 28. Accessed December 13, 2015. http://web.mit.edu/future-report/TaskForceFinal_July28.pdf.

McKinsey Global Institute. 2012. *The World at Work: Jobs, Pay, and Skills for 3.5 Billion People*. June. Accessed December 13, 2015. http://www.mckinsey.com/~/media/McKinsey/dotcom/Insights%20and%20pubs/MGI/Research/Labor%20Markets/The%20world%20at%20work/MGI-Global_labor_Full_Report_June_2012.ashx.

Northeastern University. 2014. "Northeastern University Business Elite National Poll." Accessed December 13, 2015. http://www.northeastern.edu/innovationsurvey/pdfs/Pipeline_toplines.pdf.

Shaker, Genevieve. 2015. *Faculty Work and the Public Good: Philanthropy, Engagement, and Academic Professionalism*. New York: Teacher's College Press.

Wood, Graeme. 2014. "The Future of College?" *Atlantic*, September. Accessed December 13, 2015. http://www.theatlantic.com/features/archive/2014/08/the-future-of-college/375071/.

11

The Future of Faculty Work

Academic Freedom and
Democratic Engagement

R. EUGENE RICE

By the 1980s, it was widely acknowledged that there was a dramatic mismatch between faculty priorities and the primary institutional missions of American colleges and universities. As early as 1983, Ernest Lynton, a distinguished physicist and the provost at Rutgers University, drew our attention to the "crisis of purpose" in our institutions of higher education. Then Lynton and Sandra Elman published a book containing a penetrating accusation that resonated widely across the academy: "Many universities are striving to be what they are not, and falling short of what they could be" (1987, 8).

In 1990, the Carnegie Foundation, under the leadership of Ernest Boyer, published the influential *Scholarship Reconsidered: Priorities of the Professoriate*. Provosts worked so vigorously to institutionalize a broader definition of scholarship that some faculty members began to complain about being "Boyerized." From 1992 to 2002, a national Forum on Faculty Roles and Rewards, sponsored by the American Association of Higher Education (AAHE), pursued the realignment of faculty work and institutional purpose.

The years surrounding the emergence of the twenty-first century were replete with robust reform efforts of all sorts focusing on faculty work, driven largely by external factors—financial pressures, the call for accountability, the availability of radically new technology, and global challenges. Internally, concerns about the quality of student learning, program assessment, and community engagement led to the development of a strong and talented leadership, a rich associational life, and numerous journals.

Most of the work, while genuinely creative and scholarly in its own way, focused on the expansion and enrichment of what was already being done. It was an approach to reform—institutional change—that was largely additive and instrumental. By 2006, it was clear that this approach was seriously limited and would not suffice. In that year, an issue of *Liberal Education*, a journal published by the Association of American Colleges and Universities (AAC&U), was organized around the theme "Faculty Work and the New Academy." I observed in that issue that "the growth of untenured full-time positions, the use of adjunct faculty, and the demographic shifts in non-tenured faculty are the result of arbitrary, expedient, short-term decisions rather than thoughtful planning for a different future" (Rice 2006, 6).

This collection of essays, in its effort to respond to the heavy reliance on what are now called "contingent faculty" and the decline in the number of full-time appointments of full-time tenured professors, has made the press for a more transformative approach to faculty work a critical imperative. The editors are to be commended. Now that the number of instructional faculty members at US colleges and universities has grown well beyond the majority, the issue of the contingent faculty has turned from being a source of contentious debate over salary and benefits to what David Scobey identifies as a serious "moral issue" (2014, 6)—a public embarrassment of major proportions. The time has come for restructuring the academic workplace and profoundly rethinking the professoriate. Two central elements that need to be addressed in restructuring the role of the faculty for the twenty-first century are the place of academic freedom and democratic engagement.

Academic Freedom and Democratic Engagement

John Gardner was one of the great public intellectuals of the twentieth century. He provided leadership in both the public and private sectors and is best known for founding Common Cause. When pressed for a succinct definition of a democratic society, he replied: "Liberty and duty. Freedom and responsibility. That is the deal" (quoted in Shulman 2005, xv).

As we look forward, the social compact that the new academy makes with a changing democratic society will need to incorporate these two essential elements. As a new ecology of American higher education evolves, the polar strengths of "liberty and duty, freedom and responsibility" will need to be solidly institutionalized. Our universities and colleges can then, and only then, provide the global leadership to which we aspire.

E. J. Dionne, one of our most thoughtful journalists, recently published an influential book titled *Our Divided Political Heart* (2012), in which he analyzes the struggle throughout American history to sustain the balance between individual liberties and a strong commitment to democratic community. In the decades surrounding the beginning of the twentieth century, this tension between individual freedom and social responsibility loomed large in the struggle to define what came to be called the new American university. At the core of the formation of the modern university—with the emergence of the disciplines and the new graduate schools marked by laboratories, seminars, and expanding PhD programs—was the broader societal tension between academic freedom and civic engagement.

In 1915, a key document defining what faculty members in American colleges and universities might regard as a guiding statement of what it meant to be an academic professional emerged from the founding of the American Association of University Professors (AAUP). In 1940, that document was expanded to become the influential "Statement of Principles on Academic Freedom and Tenure" (American Association of University Professors 1940) developed jointly by the AAUP and the association now known as AAC&U. The statement formed the basis for the academic profession's social compact that incorporated both academic freedom and the social responsibilities of the faculty.

This effort to articulate a comprehensive vision of the faculty role in the American university was a part of what Talcott Parsons, a leading social theorist at Harvard, identified as the "process of professionalization" (1968, 545). It was a cohesive vision that Parsons would describe in the middle of the twentieth century as "the most important single component of the structure of modern societies" (ibid.). Parsons and others studying the emergence of the professions began to argue that the keystone in the arch of the professionally oriented society is the modern university, and that "the professional *par excellence* is the academic". It was a professional vision that was celebrated in the title of Christopher Jenks and David Riesman's *Academic Revolution* (1968). By the time that book appeared, the faculty was seen as dominant. This was true particularly in the research universities and their graduate schools, where most of the faculty members had been prepared and socialized. These were the faculty members who at the time were regarded as the envy of the world.

A consensus emerged that I later referred to as "the assumptive world of the academic professional" (Rice 1996, 4). Despite serious flaws that would later become starkly evident, such as siloed departments, too narrowly specialized disciplines, and a hierarchical status system driven by a debilitating prestige economy, this professional vision held in balance the precarious tension between academic freedom and responsibility for the public good. It was a conception of the academic profession that—despite its limitations—called for individual and institutional autonomy, shared governance, and peer review. It made room for the scholarly independence, creativity, and innovation that became the hallmark of American higher education. But it also emphasized the faculty's responsibility to serve the democracy. The original 1915 AAUP statement contains these words: "the responsibility of the university teacher is primarily to the public itself" (American Association of University Professors 1915, 295). In 1908, Charles Elliot, then president of Harvard University, emphatically declared: "Most of the American institutions of higher education are filled with the democratic spirit. Teachers and students alike are profoundly moved by the desire to serve the democratic community" (quoted in Kuehnemann 1909, 56).

This consensus that bridged the gap between the commitment to academic freedom and democratic engagement was widely shared, although it was hotly contested in state legislatures, church delegations, and boards of trustees. Fortunately, one of America's leading philosophers, John Dewey, played a key role in the 1915 AAUP articulation of the importance of academic freedom and then spent most of his professional career providing the basic rationale for democratic engagement in the learning process. In one of his most memorable quotations he said: "Democracy has to be born every generation, and education is its midwife" (1993, 122). In 1952, Supreme Court Justice Felix Frankfurter argued in *Wieman v. Updegraff*, a case about academic freedom: "To regard teachers . . . as the priests of our democracy is . . . not to engage in hyperbole. It is the special task of teachers to foster those habits of open-mindedness and critical inquiry which alone make for responsible citizens, who in turn make possible an enlightened and effective public opinion" (quoted in Fish 2014, 46). Obviously, the bridge between academic freedom and civic engagement had strong support.

In the closing decades of the twentieth century, the social fabric that had shaped this consensus regarding faculty freedoms and responsibilities began to unravel. The rapid growth and expansion of higher education beginning in the 1960s cultivated the image of the isolated ivory tower, and faculty members began to see themselves as autonomous actors—individual entrepreneurs in a competitive academic market. Academic freedom began to mean something different. As most of this book contends, American higher education is moving into a new era, with a radically different academic workforce, student population and a changing technological base. As we look forward, I do not think that any of the contributors to this book are prepared to provide a detailed vision of the future of the faculty role, but the task of thinking through what the essential elements might look like must begin.

Academic Freedom Reconsidered

One of the many changes that will have an impact on the faculty of the future is the tension that has been growing in recent years between the collegiate culture of the faculty and the managerial culture whose power and influence has been increasing throughout the academic world. Both cultures have essential strengths that need to be sustained, and both have serious liabilities.

Academic freedom as understood in the academy during most of the twentieth century was rooted in a collegial culture that can be traced back to the ancient Athenian philosophers (Kimball 1986). However, it was not until the

years surrounding the opening of the twentieth century that academic freedom was fully defined in the US context. As graduate students returned from
advanced studies in Europe, particularly Germany, the new American university
took form. With the conception of the research university—with its disciplinary specialties, laboratories, and seminars—came the idea of *Lehrfrieheit*. The
historian Fredrick Rudolph defined *Lehrfrieheit* as "the right of the university
professor to freedom of inquiry and to freedom of teaching, the right to study
and to report on his findings in an atmosphere of consent" (1962, 412).

It was understood that the "consent" comes from the collegium—the community of scholars. To be a faculty member was to be incorporated into the
collegium. It was not long before the faculty role was surrounded and supported
by an elaborate institutional culture and organizational structure. Disciplinary
associations were formed, journals established, and conferences held. Publications of original, legitimate knowledge were adjudicated by peers, who were
also members of the collegium. Because most of the colleges and universities
in nineteenth-century America had been established by religious institutions,
the unfettered pursuit of knowledge was often contested. The primary purpose
of the college or university at that time was frequently seen as indoctrinating
students into the beliefs and practices of the founding denomination or sect,
not the open pursuit of truth in the classroom or research laboratory.

By 1915, faculty members in the disciplinary associations recognized the
need for a national faculty group to protect academic freedom from internal
and external influences, which led to the formation of the AAUP. An elaborate organizational structure was introduced to protect the freedom of faculty
members to pursue new knowledge and disseminate it. Admission to the community of scholars was carefully refined. Called tenure, it was an extended,
up-or-out induction process conducted by qualified peers. Winning tenure
was embedded in a collegial culture that could be highly competitive (depending on the disciplinary employment market), prestige driven, and hierarchical. Tenure functioned best during the period of rapid growth in US higher
education that followed World War II. Often it was used as an incentive in the
recruitment process, or to retain the most talented faculty members. When
the appointment market turned down in the mid-1970s, in many places tenure became an oppressive, highly contentious process in which concurrence
with the dominant disciplinary theory, methodology, or sometimes ideology
took precedence over the open exchange of ideas: dissent was discouraged.
"Consent" took on a dark tone, and the academic freedom of the tenure candidate was seldom invoked (Rice 1982). Ironically, those most in need of the
protection of academic freedom were the early career faculty members on the
tenure track.

The collegial culture was composed of tenured faculty, protected ideally by
academic freedom. The generation of knowledge was monitored by the review

of peers, and even institutional accreditation was assumed to be dominated by peer review. From this perspective, institutional leadership rose from peers selected from the collegium—individuals who ascended through the professorial ranks. Also, there was every expectation that institutional governance would be shared, but only by those selected to join the community of scholars—faculty with tenure.

In the 1980s, corporation life in the United States experienced a managerial revolution, and in colleges and universities a strong managerial culture arose in contrast to the dominant collegial culture. The institutional authority of the faculty declined as the professorial occupation with academic merit judged by peers was challenged by the need for institutional worth. Faculty priorities and what was both valued and needed by the institution moved in competing directions. Institutional discourse among administrators and trustees shifted to the bottom line, accountability, efficiency, and a different kind of productivity. The selection of leadership moved from the pool of academic peers to the more technically qualified—often corporate executives and lawyers.

Managerial professionals began to emerge with their own credentials and authority (Rhoades 1998). In the AAHE's Forum on Faculty Roles and Rewards, the debate about the unbundling of the faculty role was beginning to gather steam. The autonomy of the faculty had been clearly challenged by the emerging culture. In fact, teaching, research, institutional leadership—virtually everything—was being challenged. For faculty members, what had at one time been "my work" was becoming "our work." The autonomy and prestige that academic freedom and tenure were seen to provide were being questioned. By the opening decade of the twenty-first century, it was clear that both academic freedom and tenure would have to take on new meanings and different forms.

As we look to the future, it is evident that both cultures are seriously flawed. The collegial culture is preoccupied with the prestige economy, concerned with departmental and institution-wide rankings, and academic status that can be destructively disaggregating and competitive. The managerial culture is largely driven by a market economy and is instrumental, overly pragmatic, and reliant on short-term strategies.

What will be needed in the years ahead is a collaborative culture that builds on the best of the two. From the collegial, that might be a sense of community—a community of scholars—with enough institutional memory to sustain the best and avoid the worst. I doubt that tenure, as we now know it, will survive, but there needs to be a permanent faculty of a critical mass that can provide coherence and institutional continuity. Academic freedom must also be sustained, but as a freedom that goes beyond individual autonomy and guaranteed rights, and one that recognizes the responsibilities that go with freedom, which is understood more precisely as professional and institutional independence.

The managerial culture is here to stay. By now we have learned that the faculty can no longer be oblivious to issues of accountability, efficiency, and productivity. The collegial culture, however, will have to provide a balance to the powerful incentives of the market economy. The reconceptualization of academic freedom could serve as a significant check on the excessive pressures of the market and preserve essential academic values that might otherwise be lost.

A New Focus on Responsibility and Student Learning

In 2006, academic freedom became a national subject of political contention—from both the left and the right. David Horowitz (2003), the conservative activist and founder of Students for Academic Freedom, proposed an academic bill of rights to protect conservative students from what was seen as the overbearing influence of the biases of liberal faculty members. Legislation in several states was introduced to politically monitor the scholarly work of faculty and academic program development. On the left, antiwar protesters disrupted speeches with the intent of silencing speakers with whose points of view they disagreed, rather than engage in open public debate. AAC&U took up the challenge and revisited the basic principles adopted in the 1940 statement on academic freedom. The association issued a formal declaration titled *Academic Freedom and Educational Responsibility* (Hamilton and Gaff 2009). The authors of the new document found in the 1940 statement little emphasis on the responsibilities of faculty members and, particularly, their obligation to attend to the connection between academic freedom and student learning. They wrote: "Academic freedom is necessary not just so faculty members can conduct their academic research and teach their own courses, but so they can enable students—through whole college programs of study—to acquire the learning they need to contribute to society" (Association of American Colleges and Universities 2006, 1). They placed special emphasis not only on the acquiring of knowledge, but also on the students' development of "independent critical judgment," concluding: "This too is an essential part of higher education's role both in advancing knowledge and sustaining a society that is free, diverse, and democratic" (ibid.). This more recent statement on academic freedom draws a direct connection between academic freedom and the democratic engagement of colleges and universities.

Over the past several decades, American higher education has learned a great deal about how people learn (Barr and Tagg 1995). There has been a major revival of Dewey's (1938) principal tenet, that learning is the reconstruction of experience. As noted above, Dewey was a contributor to the original AAUP statement on academic freedom, and he redefined our understanding of the key elements of democracy—freedom and equality—and gave them new meaning. Freedom became not just freedom from (for example, from oppression) but also freedom to (for example, to grow and develop and to learn as individuals, institutions, and a society). Much of the AAC&U's 2006 statement on academic freedom prefigures the association's later report, *A Crucible Moment: College Learning and Democracy's Future* (National Task Force on Civic Learning and Democratic Engagement 2012). The emphasis has shifted from "freedom from" to "freedom to." The faculty role in the future will need to encompass not only freedom to engage in unfettered inquiry and teaching as individuals, but responsibilities to protect and support open inquiry, tolerance of difference, and encouragement to raise what Max Weber called "inconvenient facts" (1946, 147) on the part of students and the growing list of participants in the learning process—on campus, in the local community, and in the larger democratic society.

This broader view of academic freedom and responsibility is being challenged on a variety of fronts. Most vocal and particularly thoughtful is a new book by Stanley Fish, *Versions of Academic Freedom* (2014). In the popular press, Fish has been adamant in setting forth his view that the role of the professor is "just a job" and his views on why academic freedom must not be confused with "saving the world" (ibid., 9). Obviously, I reject his position that is widely shared in the ivory tower but is rapidly passing. His recent book, however, presents a typology of stands on academic freedom, providing a framework for considering a different understanding of academic freedom appropriate for the emerging academy in the new century. His typology ranges from his own "it's just a job" school to "the road to revolution." (ibid., 104).

Fish defines his own approach to the role of the professor and academic freedom as "teaching and research in accordance with the standards of the discipline of which I am engaged" (2014, 65). To argue for the strength and authority of the discipline is to defend one of the serious weaknesses of the established view of the professorial role. Those people most vocal in attacking the present university structure have used the term *silo* so often that it has become a cliché. What is being referred to directly here is the disciplinary structure: a self-protective process of boundary maintenance that discourages debates about competing ideas and promotes gatekeeping in the selection of colleagues. It represents the past, not the future.

Many of the new ideas and inventions appear at the edges of a discipline or are interdisciplinary. Also, if engagement is taken seriously, new knowledge will be generated by the inclusion of practice in the larger external community. When Fish sets forth his democratically engaged type in posing competing perspectives, he is speaking of shared governance within the confines of the university. Our understanding of expert knowledge—or, to use Robert Post's phrase, "democratic competence" (2012, 34)—requires collaboration and the inclusion of people beyond the walls of the university.

Any discussion of the future of the American faculty has to be placed in a larger global framework. I know that task has been put in William Plater's able hands in this volume. However, the topic of academic freedom requires special mention when the international context is addressed. In my own experience—and in my discussions with others invited to address the changing faculty roles in other countries such as China, Saudi Arabia, and Brazil, where financial resources are available—the question of academic freedom in the American university invariably surfaces. Economic productivity and a variety of other instrumental achievements are of interest, but the topic of greatest concern to faculty members early in their careers is how the American university has been able to foster an ethos of creativity and a climate that whets the imagination, thus making innovation and the generation of new ideas possible. Academic freedom is seen as a pivotal asset. As we move into a new era, maintaining that asset in a radically different context will be of paramount importance.

Being Professional

Among those writing about the future of the faculty role there is widespread concern about the loss of a social compact between the academy and the larger society. Neil Hamilton and Jerry Gaff (2009) attempt to capture the meaning of the academic profession's social compact set forth in the 1915 declaration of the AAUP. The profession's "high calling," as it was referred to, was to provide "knowledge creation and teaching critical inquiry and analysis" in a way that would "lead to public acceptance that the professors' work both contributes to a transcendental public good and is grounded in a body of theoretically based knowledge requiring a high degree of discussion" (quoted in Hamilton and Gaff 2009, 9). The authors of the declaration concluded: "This is the precondition for the professions' social contract" (quoted in ibid., 10).

The older social contract framed in the 1915 statement has largely disintegrated. As Boyer (1990) frequently reminded us, American higher education has gone through a fundamental shift, from functioning in the interests of the public good to being primarily concerned with private benefits. Currently the academy in general and the faculty in particular are perceived by the public as having made this shift. In the years ahead, a new social compact will have to be constructed, with greater attention being paid to community engagement and the common good (Shaker 2015).

As the faculty of the future struggle with constructing a new and more appropriate social compact, one that fits the radically changing context, they will need to articulate a new vision of the academic vocation. I find even the term *higher calling* appropriate. Academic freedom is very important not only for higher education in this country, but globally.

Much of the current discussion of the faculty work of the future acknowledges the need for a new conception of academic professionalism (Shaker 2015; Sullivan 2005). I am reluctant to use the word *professionalism* because in the history of the development of the disciplines, it too often evolved into a form of market monopoly. As a field became more commercially profitable, professionalism became a form of academic gatekeeping—often requiring the establishment of professional licensure. The best example is in the field of psychology, where professional psychotherapy became a source of billable hours and clinical psychology separated—or was pushed out—from psychology as a scientific discipline. I prefer the phrase *being professional*, understood as engaging in a vocation in the sense that Weber intended in his famous essay "Science as a Vocation" (1946).

In taking this position I find myself siding in several ways with the more traditional Fish. Academic freedom takes on special meaning for the faculty member. It carries not only special privileges, but also obligations and responsibilities. The new academic compact will need to address what those obligations and privileges are, and what they are not. In reference to political issues, Fish cites William Van Alstyne's argument: "If academics are functioning not as academics, but as political advocates, then they do not merit academic freedom" (quoted in Fish 2014, 19).

I want to maintain the sense of vocation for the academy—including the privileges and responsibilities of academic freedom—but also argue that politicians, ministers, lawyers, and other professionals have their own professional guidelines. They, too, have vocations, every bit as important as that of the professor. And collaboration in a larger learning community requires that their special sense of vocation be honored. When professors launch into partisan harangues or attempt religious indoctrination in the classroom, they are not functioning as academics.

When the discussion of academic freedom shifts to a context in which the engaged university is taken seriously, a wide range of new concerns emerge: What is the role of the disciplinary expert? Who are the peers? What is the role of the practitioner, and what is the place of experience and practice in the larger community? What does it mean to be intentionally collaborative in a learning environment that is more open, more democratic, and less hierarchical than in the past. This would foster a different kind of individuation, creative freedom, and—most important—professional responsibility for the autonomy of the university itself, in contrast to the dominance of the state, church, or corporation.

Scholarship and the Engaged University

Twenty-five years have passed since *Scholarship Reconsidered* (Boyer 1990) was published and distributed widely. Since then, colleges and universities around the globe have made gallant efforts to broaden the definition of scholarship in a variety of ways. The tired old debate of research versus teaching was challenged and a new paradigm proposed. The definition of the scholarly work of faculty would be enlarged to encompass four separate yet overlapping meanings: the scholarship of discovery—the research agenda—continued to play a vital role as part of a larger whole, but it was expanded to include the scholarship of teaching, the scholarship of integration, and the scholarship of application. From the beginning these different forms of scholarly work were seen as an interdependent whole, or, to use Lynton's words, "an ecosystem of knowledge" (quoted in Saltmarsh et al. 2011).

Important and enduring work has been done on the scholarship of teaching and learning (Hutchings, Huber, and Ciccone 2011). When Lee Shulman became president of the Carnegie Foundation, he and Pat Hutchings led the way in turning teaching and learning into a scholarly field. Teaching and learning were made a matter of open, public reflection and serious assessment. AAC&U became the leading national forum on the integration of the scholarly enterprise. Its flagship journal, *Liberal Education*, has as its primary focus the critical issues of coherence and integration.

As the broader view of scholarly work penetrated the deliberations among the disciplinary associations (Diamond and Adam 1995), the meaning of the scholarship of application was seriously contested. Questions were raised about that scholarship, in which the assumption is that knowledge is generated in the academy and then applied to the problems of the larger world. This was increasingly seen as potentially exclusive, privileged, and hierarchical.

In the midst of this debate, Donald Stokes, of the Woodrow Wilson School at Princeton, published a very influential book called *Pasteur's Quadrant* (1997). In it he challenged the core compact between academic science and government that established the relationship between pure and applied research. This compact, proposed by Vannevar Bush, shaped funding practices by the National Science Foundation and defense spending during the Cold War, the golden age of scientific research following World War II. This emphasis on basic research gave preference to work purely driven by curiosity—knowledge for knowledge's sake—over the applied and immediately relevant. This priority in turn had a widespread impact not only on funding priorities in higher education, but also on determining what counts toward the awarding of tenure and promotion. Even the meaning of academic freedom was swayed. Freedom to follow one's curiosity where it led, irrespective of pragmatic needs or public utility, was given preference. Academic responsibilities were a secondary concern.

Donald Schön, a professor at the Massachusetts Institute of Technology, pulled the debate in another direction in his important book titled *The Reflective Practitioner* (1983). Schön joined directly in the discussion of the new scholarship and called for an alternative epistemology—that is, a different approach to knowing (1995). The original formulation in *Scholarship Reconsidered* (Boyer 1990) of the scholarship of application reflected the older, established expert model and assumed a distance between the university and the external community. New knowledge was created in the university and then applied in the larger society, out there—the image of the ivory tower still obtained.

While a body of scholarship about scholarship was emerging, a genuine movement related to issues of engagement was also gathering energy. Civic engagement—the community involvement of students—was nourished by Campus Compact (a national organization promoting academic engagement). Service learning aimed at integrating community service and academic inquiry attracted foundation support and broad campus/community participation. The place of service learning in a pluralistic democracy became a major issue, and the role of community participants as partners in the service-learning process was forcefully insisted on. It became increasingly clear that community engagement could not be separated from increased democratic participation and the commitment to an inclusive democracy. Democratic engagement as a movement had taken off. The scholarship of engagement soon emerged as having substance and a constituency, and it was adopted as an alternative to the scholarship of application. In a recent book on the future of faculty work, the title of the first chapter is "The Arc of the Academic Career Bends Toward Publicly Engaged Scholarship" (Eatman 2012).

As we reflect on the possible contours of the faculty role in a radically changing academy, the call for a different epistemological approach becomes increasingly salient. In fact, all the established elements of faculty work shift dramatically. Teaching—particularly the professor's relationship with students— is being altered. Faculty members are no longer seen as the purveyors of expert knowledge to a largely passive audience. Most effective approaches to learning are already viewed as active and experience-based. Much student learning is relational, building on a different kind of collaboration with faculty and staff members, student peers, and community partners. If we examine the National Survey of Student Engagement Project and George Kuh's report on high-impact practices (2008), we find that almost every practice making a notable difference in the quality of student learning is active, engaged, and collaborative. With the transformative impact of digital learning, faculty members have become more involved in course design and the process of learning, instead of simply being the content specialist and presenter. Even research—the generation of knowledge—is being substantively altered. Often it is community-based or collaborative-action research. The relationship between local and cosmopolitan knowledge is being widely debated (Rhoades et al. 2008). And the connection of faculty members to community partners is different: it has become more collaborative, reciprocal, and inclusive. Following Shulman, the emphasis is on honoring the wisdom of practice.

For the faculty members of the future, the sources of ego gratification are going to be different; there will be fewer calls for what is known as the sage on the stage, and the performance standards for those selected will be markedly higher. A different kind of person is going to be attracted to an academic career. The unbundling of the faculty role will be a special challenge. Working together in a more collaborative, democratic way will shake the status system cultivated over the years and still perpetuated in most graduate programs.

A New Model of Academic Excellence

Rethinking the meaning of academic freedom and making the walls of academic institutions more permeable—in other words, taking the engaged university seriously—calls for a different understanding of academic excellence. In the history of American higher education, two comprehensive views of excellence have been successfully institutionalized and, over time, come to dominate our thinking about the work of faculty and how it ought to be organized and rewarded. The first is the liberal arts college, and the second is the research university. Until recently, these two models have served the United States well.

Other configurations have been proposed, such as the land-grant college model with its outreach mission and extension programs. For a time, when agriculture and industrialization were dominant concerns in an emerging nation, this vision thrived. Following World War II and the generous federal funding of pure research described above, the mission of the land-grant college gave way to the overarching power and prestige of the research university model. As we look to the future and the changes in the work of faculty discussed in this chapter, a new approach to the meaning of success is intimated. Are characteristics of excellence emerging that can take us in a new direction—a new prototype of academic success? Let me suggest several.

Integration/Beyond Differentiation

The research university model thrives on specialization, and top research is on the cutting edge of the field: if the work is not original, it does not count. Our future will be built on learning communities with a wide range of contributors: faculty members, students, digital specialists, course designers, community partners, and others. Integration will be central. For some time now it has been clear that differentiation has gone about as far as it can go; specialization pressed beyond its limits can lead to fragmentation and isolation. It is time for a new integration.

Collaboration/Beyond Hierarchy

In the research university as it often functions, the achievement of academic excellence is an individual accomplishment. In the new complex environment—technically driven, global, and engaged—collaboration will be a pivotal requirement for success. In an article titled "Battle for German Brains," Scott Jaschik notes that "science today depends on international networks" (2011). Germany now virtually requires international postdoctorates in the sciences. Placements in US universities are preferred because of the free flow of ideas and techniques among faculty and staff members, practitioners, and particularly students. In Germany, the controlling authority of the senior professors often stifles the exchange of insights, new ideas, and discoveries. In the American universities where the star system informs the way faculty members are appointed, high-achieving faculty members are increasingly acting as individual entrepreneurs, and the academic unit is made more internally confrontational, exclusive, and hierarchical.

Gary Rhoades, Judy Marquez Kiyama, Rudy McCormick, and Marisol Quiroz have explored at length how high quality is connected to high exclusivity in the American university (2008). Scholarly expertise will always have its place in the university. However, attention needs to be paid to a more reciprocal, less hierarchical scholarship of engagement in which inquiry and learning take place in a more open and democratic environment.

Inclusion/Beyond Diversity

The widespread acknowledgment in American universities that diversity is an educational value and catalyst is a major accomplishment. But the demographic shifts in the student population and the influx of international students require that we move beyond diversity—honoring the other—to comprehensive, structural inclusion (Sturm 2006). Universities in a pluralistic democracy require a shift of this sort, toward a new kind of excellence.

Engaged and Open/Beyond Walls and Silos

Academic freedom in the ivory tower came to mean freedom from interference and often individual isolation. The engaged university calls for a different orientation—looking outward, across boundaries, and bringing people together. Serious questions are being raised about the way we organize academic work. Putting together individual discretion and community engagement is a critical democratic challenge.

Networked/Beyond the Separation of Content and Process, Content and Context

Fortunately, the twenty-first century has opened with an explosion—or, as Clayton Christensen and Henry Eyring would say, the "disruption" (2011)—of digital breakthroughs, new ideas, cost-saving strategies, online learning techniques, for-profit schemes, new credential proposals, and learning incubators of all sorts. Not enough can be said about the profound influence of technology and networking on what we know and how we learn. The new generation of students is already interconnected and becoming global in orientation. The whole world of social media is challenging the way we think, create, organize, make meaning, and relate to one another. In the new world of learning where Google is a verb, thought and action are intertwined and all the participants in the learning process are interdependent actors: all are experts, all are learners, and all are teachers. Stanford University's Daphne Koller, the founder of Coursera, makes the point by arguing that "content is about to become free and ubiquitous" (quoted in Wood 2014, 60).

In the networked world, process and content will be fundamentally interconnected. Faculty members will no longer dominate as content specialists. Also, content and context will be substantially interrelated. As Douglas Thomas and John Seely Brown contend, "meaning emerges as much from context as content. This truly opens a new dimension of meaning creation" (2011, 5). A new form of academic excellence is emerging. More than ever, the academy will require intellectual freedom and critique, as well as a rich imagination and openness to innovative approaches to inquiry and a new kind of learning.

During the years 1988 and 1989, I was senior scholar in residence at the Carnegie Foundation in Princeton, New Jersey. I had been invited to study the changing nature of faculty work. The title of the first draft report on that project was "The New American Scholar." After I left to become dean of the faculty at Antioch College, the title was changed to *Scholarship Reconsidered: Priorities of the Professoriate* (Boyer 1990). It was an audacious title that struck at the heart of the academic enterprise. This year is the twenty-fifth anniversary of that Carnegie report. After years of contentious debate, the case for a broader definition of scholarship still stands—a major achievement. Regrettably, the reward structure for faculty has not changed, and the prestige economy supporting the narrower view of scholar as content specialist and expert (standing apart from the larger world) persists.

Looking Forward: The Democratization of Scholarship

As we look toward the future, an enlarged and more encompassing vision of academic work will be required, a new epistemology that honors the wisdom of practice and welcomes the engaged practitioner who attends to the changing process and context of what we know and how we make meaning—that is, the democratization of scholarship itself. We will need a faculty to lead a changing democracy marked by—again in Gardner's words—"Liberty and duty. Freedom and responsibility. That is the deal" (quoted in Shulman 2005, xv).

To speak of the democratization of scholarship itself sounds extreme, even radical. Unless the older established view of scholarship is reconsidered in a more substantive way, however, the alignment of faculty priorities with basic institutional purposes and conditions will become increasingly inadequate. The narrow conception of scholarship as only disciplinary research conducted by an increasingly exclusive group of self-selected experts cannot be sustained in an educational ethos—an ecology of knowing—that is rapidly becoming more diverse, inclusive, collaborative, and engaged.

A broader definition of scholarship must include the scholarship of discovery, but that cannot continue to dominate in the ways in which it has. It must be acknowledged that the established view of scholarship has been richly productive and needs to be built upon, but it is rooted in an organizational context that is restrictively elitist, hierarchical, top-down—anchored in a reward system and protocols that are no longer viable.

Scholarship Reconsidered got us off to a good start. Over the past twenty-five years, higher education has gone through a genuinely transformative period. Serious scholarly work by talented academic leaders has taken the rhetoric of that foundation report and struggled to build a new vision of scholarship into the structures and procedures that shape the way lives are lived—day to day—in our colleges and universities, despite ingrained resistance.

Attention to the quality of student learning and the transformative role of technology has generated widespread public acknowledgment and acceptance. As the walls of the university become increasingly permeable; students learn in new, active ways; and practitioners of all sorts contribute to the generation of new knowledge and its assessment, a new epistemology is emerging from work on the scholarship of engagement. Scholarly work leading to new discoveries and inventions will continue to surge ahead, but increasingly research will rely on collaboration, global networking, and democratic engagement. Rigorous ways of assessing these different forms of scholarship will require serious investment, and special attention will need to be paid to the integration of this broader and more inclusive vision.

Following World War II, it was commonly argued that the American university had become the envy of the world primarily because of its capacity to generate cutting-edge research that could be translated into military and commercial innovations. The statement of adulation—the envy of the world—fits nicely into the Cold War narrative used to justify the rich support of research funding for faculty members and the expansion and dominance of the research university. Underlying this generous surge in funding was a reward system that emphasized a particular kind of faculty work. It was a vision of academic excellence that was part and parcel of the larger argument for American exceptionalism— an image that was competitive; hierarchical; exclusive; and, in the academic world, obsessed with rankings.

In his speech at the Edmund Pettus Bridge on the fiftieth anniversary of the march from Selma to Montgomery, President Barack Obama began to explore a new and very different view of American exceptionalism. He did not reject that idea, as some have contended, but called for an alternative—"the true meaning of America" (Obama 2015). It is a conception of American exceptionalism that focuses more on the future than on the past and that calls for collaboration, more than individual competitiveness; and inclusion, more than separation. Rather than emphasizing the exercise of power and dominance in the world, the alternative he is articulating values shared leadership and enabling the disadvantaged. The stress is on equal opportunity for all.

In this very special speech Obama labors to reenvision what it means to say America is exceptional. With reference to the rich and growing diversity of the nation, he highlights what might be accomplished working together and claims that "the single-most powerful word in our democracy is the word 'We.' 'We The People'" (Obama 2015). The faculty of the twenty-first century can have a leading role in shaping this vision, but it will need a conception of academic freedom that goes beyond the protection of individual rights and privileges and cultivates a notion of scholarship that aggressively fosters democratic engagement—not just my work, but ours.

REFERENCES

American Association of University Professors (AAUP). 1915. "1915 Declaration of Principles on Academic Freedom and Academic Tenure." Washington: AAUP. Accessed February 12, 2016. http://www.aaup.org/NR/rdonlyres/A6520A9D-0A9A-47B3-B550-C006B5B224E7/0/1915Declaration.pdf.

——. 1940. "Statement of Principles on Academic Freedom and Tenure." Washington: AAUP. Accessed December 8, 2015. http://www.aaup.org/report/1940-statement-principles-academic-freedom-and-tenure.

Barr, Robert B. and John Tagg. 1995. "From Teaching to Learning—A New Paradigm for Undergraduate Education." *Change* 27 (6): 12–26.

Boyer, Ernest L. 1990. *Scholarship Reconsidered: Priorities of the Professoriate*. Princeton, NJ: Carnegie Foundation for the Advancement of Teaching.

Christensen, Clayton, and Henry J. Eyring. 2011. *The Innovative University: Changing the DNA of Higher Education*. San Francisco: Jossey-Bass.

Dewey, John. 1938. *Experience and Education*. Toronto: Collier-Macmillan Canada.

——. 1993. "The Need of an Industrial Education in an Industrial Democracy." In *John Dewey: The Political Writings*, edited by Debra Morris and Ian Shapiro, 121–24. Indianapolis, IN: Hackett.

Diamond, Robert M., and Bronwyn E. Adam. 1995. *The Disciplines Speak I: Rewarding the Scholarly, Professional, and Creative Work of Faculty*. Washington: American Association for Higher Education.

Dionne, E. J., Jr. 2012. *Our Divided Political Heart: The Battle for the American Idea in an Age of Discontent*. New York: Bloomsbury.

Eatman, Timothy. 2012. "The Arc of the Academic Career Bends Toward Publicly Engaged Scholarship." In *Collaborative Futures: Critical Reflections on Public Graduate Education*, edited by Amanda Gilvin, Craig Martin, and Georgia M. Roberts, 25–48. Syracuse, NY: Syracuse University Press.

Fish, Stanley. 2014. *Versions of Academic Freedom: From Professionalism to Revolution*. Chicago: University of Chicago Press.

Hamilton, Neil W., and Jerry G. Gaff. 2009. *The Future of the Professoriate: Academic Freedom, Peer Review, and Shared Governance*. Washington: Association of American Colleges and Universities.

Horowitz, David. 2003. *Battle for Academic Freedom*. Los Angeles: Center for the Study of Popular Culture.

Hutchings, Pat, Mary Taylor Huber, and Anthony Ciccone. 2011. *Reconsidering the Scholarship of Teaching and Learning*. San Francisco: Jossey-Bass.

Jaschik, Scott. 2011. "Battle for German Brains." *Insider Higher Ed*, September 7. Accessed December 14, 2015. https://www.insidehighered.com/news/2011/09/07/germany_woos_its_postdocs_in_the_u_s_to_come_home_with_goal_of_reforming_universities.

Jenks, Christopher, and David Riesman. 1968. *The Academic Revolution*. Garden City, NY: Doubleday.

Kimball, Bruce. 1986. *Orators and Philosophers: A History of the Idea of Liberal Education*. New York: Columbia University Press.

Kuehnemann, Eugen. 1909. *Charles W. Eliot: President of Harvard University (May 19, 1869– May 19, 1909)*. Boston: Houghton Mifflin.

Kuh, George D. 2008. *High Impact Educational Practices*. Washington: Association of American Colleges and Universities.

Lynton, Ernest A. 1983. "A Crisis of Purpose: Reexamining the Role of the University." *Change* 15 (7): 18–53.

Lynton, Ernest A., and Sandra E. Elman. 1987. *New Priorities for the Universities*. San Francisco: Jossey-Bass.

National Task Force on Civic Learning and Democratic Engagement. 2012. *A Crucible Moment: College Learning and Democracy's Future*. Washington: Association of American Colleges and Universities.

Obama, Barack. 2015. "Remarks by the President at the 50th Anniversary of the Selma to Montgomery Marches." White House Office of the Press Secretary, March 7. Accessed June 9, 2015. https://www.whitehouse.gov/the-press-office/2015/03/07/remarks-president-50th-anniversary-selma-montgomery-marches.

Parsons, Talcott. 1968. "Professions." In *International Encyclopedia of the Social Sciences*, edited by David L. Sills, 12:536–547. New York: Macmillan and Free Press.

Post, Robert C. 2012. *Democracy, Expertise, and Academic Freedom: A First Amendment Jurisprudence for the Modern State*. New Haven, CT: Yale University Press.

Rhoades, Gary. 1998. *Managed Professionals: Unionized Faculty and Restructuring Academic Labor*. Albany: State University of New York Press.

Rhoades, Gary, Judy Marquez Kiyama, Rudy McCormick, and Marisol Quiroz. 2008. "Local Cosmopolitans and Cosmopolitan Locals: New Models of Professionals in the Academy." *Review of Higher Education* 31 (2): 209–35.

Rice, R. Eugene. 1982. "Dreams and Actualities: Danforth Fellows in Mid-Career." In *To Improve the Academy: Resources for Student, faculty and Institutional Development*, edited by Stephen Scholl and Sandra Cheldelin Inglis, 19–37. Orinda, CA: John F. Kennedy University.

———. 1996. *Making a Place for the New American Scholar*. Washington: American Association for Higher Education.

———. 2006. "From Athens and Berlin to LA: Faculty Work and the New Academy." *Liberal Education* 92 (4): 6–13.

Rudolph, Frederick. 1962. *The American College and University: A History*. New York: Vintage.

Saltmarsh, John, Elaine Ward, and Patti H. Clayton. 2011. "Profiles of Public Engagement: Findings from the Ernest A. Lynton Award for the Scholarship of Engagement for Early Career Faculty." Dublin: Dublin Institute of Technology. Accessed February 13, 2016. http://arrow.dit.ie/cgi/viewcontent.cgi?article=1027&context=cserrep.

Schön, Donald. 1983. *The Reflective Practitioner: When Professionals Think in Action.* New York: Basic.

———. 1995. "Knowing-in-Action: The New Scholarship Requires a New Epistemology." *Change* 47 (6): 26–34.

Scobey, David. 2014. "Technology, Education, Democracy: Elements of an Emerging Paradigm." *Diversity and Democracy* 17 (1): 4–8.

Shaker, Genevieve G., ed. 2015. *Faculty Work and the Public Good: Philanthropy, Engagement, and Academic Professionalism.* New York: Teachers College Press.

Shulman, Lee S. 2005. Foreword to William M. Sullivan, *Work and Integrity: The Crisis and Promise of Professionalism in America,* ix–xv. 2nd ed. San Francisco: Jossey-Bass.

Stokes, Donald E. 1997. *Pasteur's Quadrant: Basic Science and Technological Innovation.* Washington: Brookings Institution.

Sturm, Susan. 2006. "The Architecture of Inclusion: Advancing Workplace Equity in Higher Education." *Harvard Journal of Law and Gender* 29 (June): 247–334.

Sullivan, William M. 2005. *Work and Integrity.* 2nd ed. San Francisco: Jossey-Bass.

Thomas, Douglas, and John Seely Brown. 2011. *A New Culture of Learning: Cultivating the Imagination for a World of Constant Change.* Accessed January 20, 2016. www .newcultureoflearning.com/newcultureoflearning.pdf.

Weber, Max. 1946. "Science as a Vocation." In *From Max Weber: Essays in Sociology,* edited and translated by H. H. Gerth and C. Wright Mills, 129–56. New York: Oxford University Press.

Wood, Graeme. 2014. "The Future of College?" *Atlantic.* September, 51–60.

12

Aspirations and Inclinations among Emerging and Early-Career Faculty Members

Leveraging Strengths, Imagining Possibilities

LESLIE D. GONZALES

AIMEE LaPOINTE TEROSKY

For several years, policy and economic leaders as well as prominent media figures have accused faculty members of not focusing enough on teaching and student learning and of being distracted by futile research that lacks real-world application (Allen and Seaman 2011 and 2013; Conrad 2004; Maier 2012; McQuiggan 2012; Seaman 2009). There are a number of ways in which one can interpret these long-running critiques. One interpretation is that these attacks reflect techno-rationalism and neoliberalism—philosophies that suggest that anything (including cultural processes like teaching, learning, and knowledge creation) can or should be made into easy-to-capture outputs and utilitarian tangibles. Alternatively, these critiques might be understood as the result of frustration over the failure of academics to adequately communicate the value of their work, the unique nature of faculty workloads and work, and the diversity of work that the professors perform. In any case, a response is needed.

We suggest that a response might be found in the unique strengths afforded by emerging and early-career faculty members, who are increasingly diverse in terms of gender, race, age, class, and college generation (having previous family members, especially parents, who attended college). Specifically, we argue that emerging and early-career faculty members have strengths that, if marshaled and adequately supported, provide starting points for creatively redesigning faculty roles as well as hiring and evaluative practices. We suggest that several of the reforms noted throughout this book—such as customized and differentiated faculty roles; a focus on (and reward) for teaching, student development, and community engagement; the incorporation of technology into many realms of faculty work; and more flexible work arrangements—are aligned with the strengths embodied by emerging and early-career faculty members.

A Snapshot of Emerging and Early-Career Faculty Members: Demographics

In this section, we present a demographic summary of emerging and early-career faculty members. For the purposes of this chapter, we define *emerging faculty members* as doctoral students who are in the latter phase of their doctoral programs and aspiring to academia as well as recent graduates who are about to enter their first positions. Included in our definition of *early-career faculty members* are two groups of professors who are within the first five years of their initial academic appointment: those in the tenure stream who do not yet have tenure and non-tenure-stream, contingent faculty members. Because the vast majority of new faculty hires are for non-tenure-stream positions, we felt it important to consider both subgroups in this chapter, but because the two subgroups clearly have different working conditions, we differentiate between the two when appropriate. An important caveat: to our knowledge, no agency collects demographic data for the groups that we have defined as emerging or early-career faculty members. Therefore, in developing this chapter, we drew from various sources that offered information on graduate or doctoral students and pretenure or contingent faculty members in general. As a result, these groups, as defined in other studies, did not perfectly align with the definitions we developed. Thus, readers should read the demographic snapshot, offered below, in the context of other sources.

In 2013, there were 2.9 million postbaccalaureate (master's and doctoral) students enrolled in US colleges and universities (National Center for Education Statistics 2015). Continuing a long-running trend, the vast majority were women. More than half of these graduate students were identified as white; black, Hispanic, Asian, American Indian, and Pacific Islanders constituted the other 50 percent. Although far from equitable, this racial portrait of graduate students (and potential future faculty members) does reveal significant changes—particularly among black and Hispanic students, whose "enrollments nearly quadrupled" between 1990 and 2014 (ibid.). In terms of people with doctoral degrees, the National Center for Education Statistics (NCES) found that 74 percent of the 2010 doctorate earners were white, with blacks, Hispanics, Asians, and American Indians or Native Americans accounting for the remaining 26 percent. Again, continuing a decade-long trend, women constituted the majority of doctorate earners across all racial groups.

In 2013 there were 1.5 million faculty members across all US postsecondary institutions (National Center for Education Statistics 2014). About half of these held full-time appointments, while the other half held part-time appointments. The full-time faculty members were spread across all ranks, including non-tenure-track lecturers, tenure-track assistant professors, associate professors, and full professors. Although it is difficult to estimate the number of early-career faculty members, as we define them, since the NCES collects information only by rank and not by number of years worked, assistant professors held 166,056 of the full-time positions. Again, though, it is important to note that statistics related to time in position are not kept for full-time non-tenure-track or part-time faculty members. Of the full-time faculty members in 2013, the large majority (79 percent) were white (43 percent were white males). The remainder were black (6 percent), Hispanic (5 percent), Asian/Pacific Islander (6 percent), and American Indian/Alaska Native or those who identified themselves as multiracial (less than 1 percent). Plainly there is a great distance to go before equity is reached, but it is important to note that the number of racial and ethnic minority faculty members has increased in recent years, with some significant gains among women of color. Specifically, black, Latina, and Native American women accounted for about 10 percent of all assistant professors in 2010 (Turner Kelly and McKann 2014). It is not suprising, though, given their persistent underrepresentation—especially at the higher, more powerful ranks—that women, women of color, and men of color face marginalization and a lack of fit in their institutional or departmental settings (Delgado-Bernal and Villalpando 2002; Ponjuan, Conley, and Trower 2011; Zambrana et al. 2015).

In addition to the changes—however slow—in gender and race demographics, increasing numbers of professors are also from working-class backgrounds and are first-generation college students. This is a shift from the past, when most academics came from the middle or upper middle class and had parents who had also gone to college (Cerecer et al. 2011; Ostrove, Stewart, and Curtis 2011; Ryan and Sackrey 1996). Sizable percentages of these working-class academics come from racial or ethnic minority groups, which suggests that emerging professors occupy multiple marginalities (Cerecer et al. 2011; Gutiérrez y Muhs et al. 2012; Hernández and Gonzales 2015) that inevitably shape the kinds of experiences that they bring with them to academia (Gonzales 2012 and 2014; Gonzales, Murakami, and Núñez 2013; Huckaby 2007). Another interesting, and potentially influential, fact is that emerging and early-career faculty are more likely to have been educated at some point at a minority-serving institution (MSI)—which, broadly defined, is an institution that enrolls a sizable percentage of students from racial or ethnic minority groups. This is important because, to some extent, faculty members' views and experiences of academia—and, thus, their preferences and insights into the roles and responsibilities of faculty members—are determined in part by the types of institution in which they were educated (O'Meara, Bennett, and Neihaus 2016; Terosky and Gonzales 2016).

According to the National Center for Education Statistics, the majority of doctoral recipients were in their very late twenties or early thirties, meaning that early-career faculty members fall between generation X and the millennial generation. According to the generational theorists Neil Howe and William Strauss (2000) and Arthur Levine and Diane Dean (2012), much can be learned about individuals by accounting for major historical events, experiences, and shifts that took place during their formative years. The formative experiences of the members of generation X, born in the late 1970s and early 1980s, include growing up in a labor and trade market that was rapidly and significantly changing and amid public informational campaigns related to sex, sexual identity, gender, and HIV. Because millennials were born in the early to mid-1980s, some of the distinguishing features of their formative experiences are said to include 9/11 and the dominance of technology (Twenge 2010). Millennials are particularly well known for viewing technology as a natural part of life, and they seem to rely seamlessly and heavily on it for social, professional, and academic needs (Howe and Strauss 2000). Overall, generational researchers have found that both the members of generation X and millennials tend to have more progressive views on issues related to identity and diversity, are generally more inclusive of diverse experiences and peoples, and seem more open to fluidity in terms of their work lives (for example, in terms of how work is accomplished). Indeed, according to the NCES, a large number of today's graduate students have experienced online coursework, meaning that today's early-career faculty members have the advantage of having experienced teaching and learning in ways that greatly differ from those of the past.

Distinctive Aspirations and Inclinations among Emerging and Early-Career Faculty Members: Seeing the Possibilities

Above, we sketched out key demographics of emerging and early-career faculty members. In this section, based on the premise that a person's history and contextual experiences inevitably shape—but do not determine—that person's aspirations, inclinations, interests, and worldviews (Archer 2007; Gonzales 2014), we highlight the unique strengths of emerging and early-career faculty members.

Thus, although diversity is often framed as challenging or problematic—meaning that there is an almost immediate attempt to reshape or at least have people of racial and ethnic minoritized background or marginalized statuses (gender, class, sexuality) fit dominant institutional histories and expectations (Núñez, Murakami, and Gonzales 2015)—we assume a very different perspective. Specifically, we argue that there is much to be gained by considering what emerging and early-career faculty members bring to the profession, and we suggest that these strengths are aligned with the current context of academic work and provide fertile ground for responding to some of the criticisms that academics face.

Aspirations: Balance and Meaningful Work

In 2002, Ann Austin published a study that revealed three very important insights about graduate students. First, countering the suggestion that scholars prioritize and prefer research above any other activity, the students in Austin's study were deeply committed to teaching and aspired to achieve a balance between teaching and research (also see Bieber and Worley 2006). Second, these students wanted to craft a life in which they could have a healthy balance between work life and personal life. Third, because of their commitment to establishing a life of balance, many of the students in Austin's study felt that academia was not a good fit and therefore, ruled the profession out or were considering doing so.

The 2010 National Survey of Doctoral Recipients showed perhaps even more clearly emerging faculty members' aspirations for balance. Specifically, when asked to list their motivations for choosing an academic position, 2010 doctoral recipients ranked options in the following order: (1) obtaining a position that entailed meaningful work, (2) a balance between teaching and research, (3) a balance between work and family/personal commitments, and (4) a quality of life that allowed for affordable housing and good elementary and secondary schools (Finkelstein 2015). It is noteworthy that the desire for balance, particularly between work and family, is a concern not only for female faculty members, but also for males, and especially for fathers (Sallee 2014). This pronounced desire for balance represents an interesting turn, in that faculty roles were designed for—and to a large extent remain oriented toward—the ideal worker and patriarchal norms (Ward and Wolf-Wendel 2012; Winslow 2010). How might such aspirations for balance be considered a strength? How might different policies or practices be forged out of such aspirations?

As KerryAnn O'Meara and Lauren DeCrosta argue in chapter 8 of this book, we suggest that the creation of flexible roles built around individualized faculty work plans and commitments is a good starting point. For example, although hiring growing numbers of contingent (non-tenure-stream) faculty may be an irrevocable trend, it might be possible to leverage the desire for balance among emerging and early-career faculty members and redirect a hiring and employment pattern that has led to mostly negative consequences. For example, when it is time to hire a new faculty member (whether or not for a tenure-stream position), current faculty members should seriously consider the needs of the department and develop a position description that lists the needs and skills that the new hire must possess. Working from this information, new hires, with the assistance of their department chairpersons or senior members of the evaluation committees, could build a customized work plan that not only serves departmental and college needs but also allows them to map out a semester's or academic year's worth of work. For instance, a department might need support in program coordination and quantitative methods, and these needs should, then, be a central part of the customized faculty work plan. Such customized work plans could offer relief to new hires who want to achieve balance, and because the work plans would be systemically integrated into the evaluative process, this might make academia more attractive to those who might otherwise opt out due to lack of clarity in expectations or burnout due to too many expectations. In other words, by tying specific work expectations more explicitly to evaluative practices and honing in on the strengths of new hires, achieving balance seems more realistic.

Martin Finkelstein (2015) noted that male and female faculty members are now equally likely to be married, and Margaret Sallee (2014) found that both men and women desire a balance between their work life and family life. Therefore, another way to honor the desire for balance amid the reality of declining tenure-stream positions is to develop positions that allow dual-career academic couples to share roles as described by Colleen Flaherty (2015). For example, in a previous study, we interviewed two pretenure professors who were married and who shared one tenure-stream position. While one partner taught, advised students, and conducted research, the other stayed at home to care for their children and manage household matters. The following semester, the couple switched all responsibilities. In other words, the university had two bright, early-career scholars who shared one salary and one set of benefits, and the couple struck a balance between work and home with which they were extremely satisfied. The situation may have been ideal because the two professors had a similar research program and were in the same department, but the arrangement provides a good example of creative position design.

Besides a desire for work-life balance, recent doctoral recipients noted that having a career in which they can accomplish meaningful work is a high priority. Indeed, researchers often characterize the millennial generation as committed to serving the greater good (Clydesdale 2015; Finkelstein 2015; Howe and Strauss 2000). Of course, there is no single definition of meaningful work, and we do not intend to prescribe one here. However, what we can do is briefly compare what emerging and early-career faculty members seem to define as meaningful work with the work that tends to be rewarded in most evaluation systems or called for by administrative and policy leaders.

In short, there is a well-established body of literature that highlights how research and research-related activities are given preference in most faculty reward systems (Boyer 1990; Gonzales 2012b; O'Meara 2002; Terosky 2005). These preferences are often held by academics themselves, as well as by university administrators who reward scholars for the publications, awards, or grants that they receive, since these research accomplishments yield prestige to the university (Melguizo and Strober 2007). And although policy and economic leaders generally assume that most faculty members are distracted by futile research, they are quick to praise professors whose research attracts economic resources.

However, for the most part, studies (Austin 2002; Bieber and Worley 2006; Gonzales 2012a and 2012b; O'Meara and Braskamp 2005; Terosky 2005; Wright 2005) show that a vast number of faculty members choose academia because they want to teach in a discipline they love and because they enjoy working with students. Indeed, studies of female, racial and ethnic minority male and female, and working-class faculty members—all groups that are growing— describe these professors' serious commitments, outside of their research and publication, to having an immediate and actionable impact through teaching or working with communities (Baez 2000; Gonzales 2012a and 2014; Terosky 2005; Wright 2005). For instance, in a collection of essays edited by Kenneth González and Raymond Padilla (2008), many Latino and Latina professors from working-class backgrounds described how they see their work as academics as, first and foremost, an opportunity to serve their communities, especially by mentoring upcoming Latino and Latina students and forming research agendas that respond to local community needs—even if those community needs are not aligned with issues in current disciplinary conversations (also see Gonzales 2014; Núñez, Ramalho, and Cuero 2010). One Latina professor noted, "This has never been about me, getting full professor, or whatever. It has always been about my community" (Gonzales 2012a, 133). More recently, J. Luke Wood, Adriel Hilton, and Carlos Nevarez (2015) verified that faculty members of color tend be involved in more community-based service than their white counter- parts and urged senior tenured faculty members and administrators to reassess the ways that service is valued in faculty reward systems. What else can be done, though, to nurture these diverse conceptions of meaningful work, held by a growing number of emerging and early-career professors? And why do we argue that these conceptions are strengths?

The fact that emerging and early-career faculty members articulate a clear desire to work closely with students or at least to have a balance between teach- ing and research is a narrative that must be presented to the larger public and included in conversations with critics who believe that faculty members have little interest in student learning. We suggest that faculty members, institu- tional researchers, and media relation specialists work together to create cam- paigns that highlight the diverse interests and work of faculty members across an institution. Such campaigns should produce short pieces that highlight faculty and student relationships in the context of teaching and research and showcase the diverse kinds of work that faculty might engage in with students (for example, in laboratory settings and during undergraduate advising and graduate school or career advising).

Taking this one step further, institutional leaders could invest in faculty-led action research projects that trace innovative teaching activities, curricular transformations, and their impacts on students. By working with local news outlets or organizing showcases of this work during graduation or convocation ceremonies, the diverse work and interests of faculty members would be communicated to a much broader audience. In some cases, if and when appropriate, students might be asked to describe how a small classroom project grew into a publication, or faculty members might be interviewed about their most powerful teaching experience. Work in the community might be highlighted in similar ways, with community members asked to discuss changes or improvements that have been made via partnerships with college or university faculty members. Indeed, sharing work with broader audiences builds on other strengths of emerging and early-career faculty members: their desires to work in groups and to engage—in a variety of ways—with diverse audiences.

Inclinations: Collective Work and Social Engagement

In addition to the research highlighting emerging and early-career faculty members' desire for balance and meaningful work—which often revolves around teaching and community service—other studies show that this cohort of faculty enjoys working with others, characteristics that bode well with the recommendations offered in this book by Ann Austin and Andrea Trice and by Richard Gillman, Nancy Hensel, and David Salomon. Indeed, women and African American, Latino, and Native American communities as well as millennials (Kezar and Lester 2010)—all of whom are increasingly entering academia—often express an inclination toward collective work. Enjoying and even desiring to participate in teamwork can help achieve many goals. Working in collectives might start new conversations within academia, perhaps across departments (Gonzales and Terosky 2015), and also between academia and local communities, the policy world, and other audiences (Kiyama, Lee, and Rhoades 2012). However, collective work will become ever more important as the number of tenure-stream professors declines. Tenure-stream and non-tenure-stream faculty members will have to work together to handle the growing, increasingly complex work demands (such as those related to technology and government accountability) expected of college and university faculty.

Finally, and relatedly, we find that a notable strength among emerging and early-career faculty members is their familiarity with technology (Glass 2012). Indeed, the technological capabilities of early-career faculty members have already been shown in the ways that academics are reaching out to a broader public via Twitter, online publications such as the *Huffington Post*, virtual chat sessions, and other similar forums. Perhaps even more important, though, having an interest in and being comfortable with technology are tremendous strengths when it comes to teaching and serving today's student body, many of whose members are not of traditional college age, are working, and/or have complex familial responsibilities—and who often require online or hybrid learning opportunities. Reforming and reinvigorating teaching methods in higher education has never been so important. With emerging and early-career faculty members already inclined to use technology as part of their everyday lives, the professoriate is and will be better positioned to provide learning opportunities in ways that reflect students' needs, knowledge, and preferences (Bain 2004; Bransford, Brown, and Cocking 2000; Merriam and Bierema 2014).

Conclusion

The long-running critiques of the professoriate and the hiring trends within academia require an agile response. The aspirations and inclinations of today's emerging and early-career faculty members provide the foundation for many possibilities, but most of these possibilities will require change from within the profession. We suggest that processes be set in place to give emerging and early-career faculty members the opportunity to articulate their aspirations and inclinations, and that current faculty members, administrators, and other interested stakeholders listen closely and imagine what the professoriate could be, if we leveraged the strengths of emerging and early-career faculty.

REFERENCES

Allen, I. Elaine, and Jeff Seaman. 2011. *Online Education in the United States 2011: Going the Distance.* Newburyport, MA: Sloan Consortium.
———. 2013. *Changing Course: Ten Years of Tracking Online Education in the United States.* Newburyport, MA: Sloan Consortium.
Archer, Margaret S. 2007. *Making Our Way through the World: Human Reflexivity and Social Mobility.* Cambridge: Cambridge University Press.
Austin, Ann E. 2002. "Preparing the Next Generation of Faculty: Graduate School as Socialization to the Academic Career." *Journal of Higher Education* 73:94–122.
Baez, Benjamin. 2000. "Race-Related Service and Faculty of Color: Conceptualizing Critical Agency in Academe." *Higher Education* 39 (3): 363–91.
Bain, Ken. 2004. *What the Best College Teachers Do.* Cambridge, MA: Harvard University Press.
Bieber, Jeffrey P., and Linda K. Worley. 2006. "Conceptualizing the Academic Life: Graduate Students' Perspectives." *Journal of Higher Education* 77 (6): 1009–35.
Boyer, Ernest L. 1990. *Scholarship Reconsidered: Priorities of the Professoriate.* Princeton, NJ: Carnegie Foundation for the Advancement of Teaching.
Bransford, John D., Ann L. Brown, and Rodney R. Cocking. 2000. *How People Learn: Brain, Mind, Experience, and School.* Washington: National Academies Press.
Cerecer, Patricia D., Lucila D. Quijada, Iliana Alanis Ek, and Elizabeth Murakami-Ramalho. 2011. "Transformative Resistance as Agency: Chicanas/Latinas (Re) Creating Academic Spaces." *Journal of the Professoriate* 5 (1): 98–129.
Clydesdale, Tim. 2015. *The Purposeful Graduate: Why Colleges Must Talk to Students about Vocation.* Chicago: University of Chicago Press.

Cole, Darnell. 2007. "Do Interracial Interactions Matter? An Examination of Student-Faculty Contact and Intellectual Self-concept." *Journal of Higher Education* 78 (3): 249–81.

Conrad, Dianne. 2004. "University Instructors' Reflections on Their First Online Teaching Experiences." *Journal of Asynchronous Learning Networks* 8 (2): 31–44.

Delgado-Bernal, Dolores, and Octavio Villalpando. 2002. "An Apartheid of Knowledge in Academia: The Struggle over the 'Legitimate' Knowledge of Faculty of Color." *Equity and Excellence in Education* 35 (2): 169–80.

Finkelstein, Martin J. 2015. "Do I Still Want to Be a Professor and, If So, Can I? Entering the American Academic Profession in the First Decade of the Twenty-First Century." In *Young Faculty in the Twenty-First Century: International Perspectives*, edited by Maria M. Yudkevich, Phillip G. Altbach, and Laura E. Rumbley, 45–73. Albany: State University of New York Press.

Flaherty, Colleen. 2015. "More Than Adjuncts." *Inside Higher Ed*, February 27.

Glass, Christopher R. 2012. "Digitally-Mediated Teaching and Professors' Professional Worlds and Identities: A Faculty Learning and Professional Growth Perspective." Paper presented at the annual meeting of the Association for the Study of Higher Education, Las Vegas, NV. November.

Gonzales, Leslie D. 2012a. "Stories of Success: Latinas Redefining Cultural Capital." *Journal of Latinos and Education* 11 (2): 124–38.

———. 2012b. "Responding to Mission Creep: Faculty Members as Cosmopolitan Agents." *Higher Education* 64 (3): 337–53.

———. 2014. "Framing Faculty Agency Inside Striving Universities: An Application of Bourdieu's Theory of Practice." *Journal of Higher Education* 85 (2): 193–218.

Gonzales, Leslie D., Elizabeth Murukami, and Anne-Marie Núñez. 2013. "Latina Faculty in the Labyrinth: Constructing and Contesting Legitimacy in Hispanic Serving Institutions." *Journal of Educational Foundations* 27 (1–2): 65–88.

Gonzales, Leslie D., and Aimee LaPointe Terosky. 2015. "Exceeding Instrumentalism: Relationships for Learning within Academia." Paper presented at the annual meeting of American Education Research Association, Chicago, IL, April 10.

González, Kenneth P., and Raymond V. Padilla, eds. 2008. *Doing the Public Good: Latina/o Scholars Engage Civic Participation*. Sterling, VA: Stylus.

Gutiérrez y Muhs, Gabriella, Yolanda Flores Niemann, Carmen G. González, and Angela P. Harris. 2012. *Presumed Incompetent: The Intersections of Race and Class for Women in Academia*. Logan: Utah State University Press.

Hernández, Susana and Leslie D Gonzales. 2015. "*Testimonio* for Living and Learning in Academia: Caring for Mind, Body, and Soul." In *Abriendo Puerta, Cerrando Heridas: Latinos and Latinas Findings Work Life Balance in Academia*, edited by Frank Hernandez, Elizabeth Murkami-Ramalho, and Gloria M. Rodriquez, 56–70. Charlotte, NC: Information Age.

Howe, Neil, and William Strauss. 2000. *Millennials Rising: The Next Great Generation*. New York: Vintage Press.

Huckaby, M. Francyne. 2007. "A Conversation on Practices of the Self within Relations of Power: For Scholars Who Speak Dangerous Truths." *International Journal of Qualitative Studies in Education* 20 (5): 513–29.

Kezar, Adrianna, and Jamie Lester. 2010. "Breaking the Barriers of Essentialism in Leadership Research: Positionality as a Promising Approach." *Feminist Formations* 22 (1): 163–85.

Kiyama, Judy Marquez, Jenny J. Lee, and Gary Rhoades. 2012. "A Critical Agency Network Model for Building an Integrated Outreach Program." *Journal of Higher Education* 83 (2): 276–303.

Levine, Arthur, and Diane R. Dean. 2012. *Generation on a Tightrope: A Portrait of Today's College Student*. San Francisco: Jossey-Bass.

Maier, Linda. 2012. "What Are Online Teaching Faculty Telling Us About Building Community?" *Community College Journal of Research and Practice* 36 (11): 884–96.

McQuiggan, Carol A. 2012. "Faculty Development for Online Teaching as a Catalyst for Change." *Journal of Asynchronous Learning Networks* 16 (2): 27–61.

Melguizo, Tatiana, and Myra H. Strober. 2007. "Faculty Salaries and the Maximization of Prestige." *Research in Higher Education* 48 (6): 633–68.

Merriam, Sharon B., and Lauren L. Bierema. 2014. *Adult Learning: Linking Theory and Practice*. San Francisco: Jossey-Bass.

National Center for Education Statistics. 2014. "Digest of Education Statistics." Accessed February 13, 2016. https://nces.ed.gov/programs/digest/d14/tables/dt14_315.20.asp.

———. 2015. "Postbaccalaureate Enrollment." Accessed February 13, 2016. http://nces.ed .gov/programs/coe/indicator_chb.asp.

Núñez, Anne-Marie, Elizabeth T. Murakami, and Leslie D. Gonzales. 2015. "Weaving Authenticity and Legitimacy: Latina Faculty Peer Mentoring." *New Directions for Higher Education* 2015 (171): 87–96.

Nuñez, Anne Marie, Elizabeth Murakami Ramalho, and Kimberly K. Cuero. 2010. "Pedagogy for Equity: Teaching in a Hispanic-Serving Institution." *Innovative Higher Education* 35 (3): 177–90.

O'Meara, KerryAnn. 2002. "Uncovering the Values in Faculty Evaluation of Service as Scholarship." *Review of Higher Education* 26 (1): 57–80.

O'Meara, KerryAnn, Jessica Chalk Bennett, and Elizabeth Neihaus. 2016. "Left Unsaid: The Role of Work Expectations and Psychological Contracts in Faculty Careers and Departure." *Review of Higher Education* 39 (2): 269–97.

O'Meara, KerryAnn, and Larry Braskamp. 2005. "Aligning Faculty Reward Systems and Development to Promote Faculty and Student Growth." *Journal of Student Affairs Research and Practice* 42 (2): 369–86.

Ostrove, Joan M., A. J. Stewart, and Nicola Curtis. 2011. "Social Class and Belonging: Implications for Graduate Students' Aspirations." *Journal of Higher Education* 82 (6): 748–74.

Ponjuan, Luis, Valerie Martin Conley, and Cathy Trower. 2011. "Career Stage Differences in Pre-Tenure Track Faculty Perceptions of Professional and Personal Relationships with Colleagues." *Journal of Higher Education* 82 (3): 319–46.

Ryan, Jake, and Charles Sackrey. 1996. *Strangers in Paradise: Academics from the Working Class*. Albany: State University of New York Press.

Sallee, Margaret W. 2014. *Faculty Fathers: Toward a New Ideal in the Research University*. Albany: State University of New York Press.Schuster, Jack H., and Martin J. Finkelstein. 2006. *The American Faculty: Restructuring Academic Work and Careers*. Baltimore, MD: Johns Hopkins University Press.

Seaman, Jeff. 2009. *Online Learning as a Strategic Asset*. Vol. 2: *The Paradox of Faculty Voices: Views and Experiences with Online Learning*. Washington: Association of Public and Land-Grant Universities.

Terosky, Aimee LaPointe. 2005. "Taking Teaching Seriously: A Study of University Professors and Their Undergraduate Teaching." PhD diss., Teachers College, Columbia University.

Terosky, Aimee LaPointe, and Leslie D. Gonzales. 2016. "Re-Envisioned Contributions: Experiences of Faculty Employed at Institutional Types That Differ from Their Original Aspirations." *Review of Higher Education* 39 (2): 241–68.

Terosky, Aimee LaPointe, and Chris Heasley. 2014. "Supporting Online Faculty through a Sense of Community and Collegiality." *Online Learning* 19 (3): 147–61.

Turner Kelly, Bridget, and Kristin I. McKann. 2014. "Women Faculty of Color: Stories behind the Statistics." *Urban Review* 46: 681–702.

Twenge, Jean M. 2010. "A Review of the Empirical Evidence on Generational Differences in Work Attitudes." *Journal of Business and Psychology* 25 (2): 201–10.

Ward, Kelly, and Lisa Wolf-Wendel. 2012. *Academic Motherhood: How Faculty Manage Work and Family*. New Brunswick, NJ: Rutgers University Press.

Winslow, Sarah. 2010. "Gender Inequality and Time Allocations among Academic Faculty." *Gender and Society* 24 (6): 769–93.

Wood, J. Luke, Adriel A. Hilton, and Carlos Nevarez. 2015. "Faculty of Color and White Faculty: An Analysis of Service in Colleges of Education in the Arizona Public University System." *Journal of the Professoriate* 8 (1): 85–109.

Wright, Mary C. 2005. "Always at Odds? Congruence in Faculty Beliefs about Teaching at a Research University." *Journal of Higher Education* 76 (3): 331–53.

Zambrana, Ruth Enid, Rashawn Ray, Michelle M. Espino, Corinne Castro, Beth Douthirt Cohen, and Jennifer Eliason. 2015. "'Don't Leave Us Behind': The Importance of Mentoring for Underrepresented Minority Faculty." *American Educational Research Journal* 52 (1): 40–72.

13

Resonant Themes for a Professoriate Reconsidered

Consensus Points to Organize Efforts toward Change

ADRIANNA KEZAR

DANIEL MAXEY

For the past several years, the Delphi Project on the Changing Faculty and Student Success has convened major stakeholder groups and thought leaders in higher education to take part in a dialogue about the need for collective effort to facilitate short- and long-term change in the professoriate. In those discussions, it has generally been much easier for stakeholders to conceive of the ways we could come together to improve working conditions for non-tenure-track faculty members in the short term and a much greater challenge for them to imagine what the professoriate might look like if we endeavored to create new faculty models for the future.

Envisioning a different future for the professoriate is not easy; it appears that we have been so deeply socialized into the current model, which has emerged over roughly 120 years and been a dominant fixture for close to 50 years, that we struggle to imagine a future with different facets. Yet we must engage in discussions about the future of the faculty—about the types of faculty positions that are needed, the roles of faculty members in serving our students, our institutions' missions, and the increasingly complex expectations of our society. The Delphi Project and its committed partners representing stakeholder groups across the higher education enterprise have been building the foundation for such an expanded discussion about our shared future. We published a report, titled *Adapting by Design: Creating Faculty Roles and Defining Faculty Work to Ensure an Intentional Future for Colleges and Universities* (Kezar and Maxey 2015), that emerged from dialogues with thought leaders on faculty issues in higher education. The report articulates the need for change and describes a process that institutions can use in developing new faculty models to meet their many needs.

This book emerged as another product of that dialogue and ongoing discussions about what are some key features that we believe need to be considered as efforts to reimagine the professoriate move forward. Editing this book and inviting a distinguished panel of authors to contribute their expertise and vision to it has been an attempt to try to piece together some of the various ideas that emerged about a future faculty model—if only as fragments of a whole—to create a vision for the future. While our thinking is still nascent and catalogued throughout the chapters in this book, several important themes and points of consensus are worth emphasizing in this final chapter.

Reorienting Faculty Models to Achieve Our Goals and Fulfill Core Missions

The first point of consensus is that any future faculty models need to be created in the context of what the higher education enterprise overall and individual institutions with different missions are trying to achieve. We cannot disaggregate the goals of the enterprise or our institutions from the roles of faculty if we are to achieve them; the two are inextricably linked. So academic leaders have to ask what are the major goals, and how can faculty work be best aligned with them to ensure that we achieve them? Thinking along these lines emphasizes the importance of teaching and learning, since they are the most central and foundational goals of higher education shared across the enterprise: learning is a core mission regardless of the type of institution. Yet institutions have various other missions, which suggests the need for faculty models to be differentiated and diversified to best serve a range of missions and needs. Achieving differentiation may be a challenge, though, as survey results from a recent national study by the Delphi Project (Kezar, Maxey, and Holcombe 2015) suggest that stakeholders fear that existing hierarchies would be exacerbated by such a shift. But this tension only highlights another important goal: greater equity for faculty members and respect for their contributions, no matter what sort of institution or discipline they serve or what roles they play. If differentiation and diversification can be achieved alongside this additional goal of greater respect and equity, much could be gained. This is certainly an area where we need to do more thinking and make more progress.

Accommodating a Changing Higher Education Landscape

Second, future models will almost certainly need to accommodate changes in the broader landscape that will reshape the profession, whether we like it or not. Several of these changes were purposefully included in this book, such as the internationalization and globalization of the academy; the rise of technology and its ability to change various areas of faculty work, such as faculty development; the changing demographics of society and the increasingly diverse racial, gender, ethnic, and socioeconomic makeup of student bodies; and the changing financial realities and accountability or productivity mandates that are challenging higher education. These external forces mean that institutions and their faculties will be subjected to different sets of expectations than in the past.

Restoring Academic Professionalism in the Professoriate

Third, there is consensus that professionalism in faculty roles—or, as Eugene Rice prefers, hallmarks of vocation—must be a priority. This ideal has suffered as a result of the growing reliance on contingent labor over several decades, and significant changes need to occur to revitalize the academic profession. Non-tenure-track faculty members, particularly those employed on a part-time basis, have too often received very little compensation for their labor, lacked access to benefits, and been excluded from participation in shared governance and decision making about matters affecting their work. They have also lacked access to professional development and have not had the opportunities for evaluation and promotion that would allow them to improve and advance in their careers. These are just a few issues that need to be addressed moving forward.

Fostering Commitments to Core Values

Fourth, and following the idea that there is a real need for greater professionalism among the full faculty, there is also consensus that a core set of values should undergird future faculty positions. These values include greater equity, flexibility, collegiality, professional growth, and a renewed commitment to academic freedom; they also call for a more collaborative orientation to faculty work, collective responsibility, and developing faculty members' primary identity as scholarly educators.

In this chapter, we briefly review these four areas of consensus that have emerged throughout this volume. We hope that they will help to provide a vision and set of priorities to guide efforts to reconsider faculty models and roles moving forward.

Goals, Missions, and Faculty Roles

We cannot adequately reimagine the faculty model and faculty roles without ensuring that they are closely aligned to the goals and objectives of institutions and the higher education enterprise overall. As we pointed out above, the two are inextricably linked. Many of the problems we encounter with today's faculty arrangements, which were reviewed in the opening chapters of this book, have emerged because we have either lost sight of those goals or failed to keep them at the forefront of our efforts by ensuring that faculty roles are intentionally designed and deployed to meet them. One problem in making changes has been our collective unwillingness or inability to break the dominance of the traditional model of the tenure-track faculty that has focused so many academics on tripartite roles of research, teaching, and service. Ernest Boyer tried to expand our thinking to value multiple forms of scholarship over twenty years ago, in *Scholarship Reconsidered* (1990). While we have come a long way, it seems we still have a long way left to go.

As so many of the authors in this volume point out, there is no one-size-fits-all approach that will work for every faculty member at every institution. First, higher education, as an enterprise, is composed of a very diverse set of institutions with very different missions. These conditions require a greater diversity of faculty roles than currently exists. William Mallon provided us with a review of this reality as it is already unfolding in his discussion of how medical school faculties have evolved to meet a diverse range of needs; the example and lessons of this series of changes can help inform efforts elsewhere. But second, a one-size-fits-all approach may not work for faculty members, either. As Ann Austin and Andrea Trice, KerryAnn O'Meara and Lauren DeCrosta, and Richard Gillman, Nancy Hensel, and David Salomon all point out in their chapters, diversified, flexible, and customized arrangements and faculty roles that engage faculty members in a range of scholarly pursuits over the course of their careers, while also engaging them in directly helping meet departmental and institutional goals, will be an important characteristic of the future faculty.

With an eye to the future, as well as the differentiation and diversification of faculty roles, several of the chapters in this volume point to a need to restore the focus on student learning and development as a priority in faculty work across the enterprise. Today's students need a more active and engaged faculty member. Arleen Arnsparger and Joanna Drivalas highlighted students' perspectives about priorities for faculty work as mentors and experts in teaching and learning. In moving forward, we might need to restore some aspects of faculty roles that have moved down the list of priorities for faculty work, particularly things like providing mentoring and advising to students, to create opportunities for faculty members to have more participation in the lives of students. And we need to figure out how to do that while serving many more students than faculty members generations ago did.

As many authors in this volume caution, though, a broader view of faculty roles than just a focus on teaching and learning will be necessary to meet the missions and mandates of higher education in the future. Above, we discussed how faculty roles need to be more oriented to promoting and fostering student success. Like teaching and learning, scholarship is another important part of the core mission of many institutions. Thus, research will continue to be a major part of the work of many faculty members in the future. This is imperative: knowledge creation or translation and synthesis play vital roles in promoting the betterment of our society and communities, as well as in ensuring that our institutions and the American higher education enterprise overall remain competitive globally. While we believe the emphasis on research that pervades so much of the faculty today is far too intense to sustain while meeting our teaching and learning goals in the future, there is absolutely no question that scholarship remains a priority for institutions and the enterprise.

Understanding the Opportunities and
Threats Posed by External Forces

Faculty models and roles have already been dramatically affected by changes in the broader landscape. Dwindling finances and changing budgetary priorities contributed to today's growing reliance on part-time appointments. Technology has affected the ways faculty members do their work and will continue to do so, perhaps altering their roles more fundamentally in coming years. Greater pressure for accountability and productivity have led to the rise of post-tenure review and may very well continue to prompt calls for change in the faculty from external stakeholders. Not every force for change in the environment requires the assent of the faculty or necessitates change; creating and maintaining the best faculty to meet the needs of our institutions and the enterprise will demand that we resist those changes that threaten our values and missions. However, in general, there is a greater need for the faculty to be more responsive and open to change than it has often been. Throughout this volume, authors have repeated over and over again that we need to be aware of changes in the external environment and their implications for the faculty so that we can respond collectively and more intentionally.

Several important trends have been outlined in this book that cannot be ignored and should be embraced and explored as the faculty is reimagined; others may demand our opposition. For example, technology and its integration in faculty work ought to be a priority. We have grown more accustomed in recent years to hearing about ways technology can be more effectively used as a tool for enriching learning opportunities for students. Malcolm Brown discussed how technology can also be better used to improve opportunities for faculty development and lifelong learning. William Plater reviewed ways that the internationalization of higher education will continue to provide faculty members with exciting opportunities for greater mobility and can enrich faculty work lives. And, as Eugene Rice pointed out, an emerging shift in conceptualizations of American exceptionalism toward collaboration and inclusion has the potential to help make positive changes in how we think about our collective responsibilities as faculty members and to cultivate a notion of scholarship that more completely fosters democratic engagement. For the most part, these forces create exciting opportunities. As the first chapter pointed out, though, forces like economic constraints and corporatization that have affected the professoriate in ways that have intruded on our values will need to be countered; they have sometimes been ignored, which has put the enterprise at risk. External forces—whether they create opportunities, threats, or both—need to be carefully monitored, and their implications must be discussed and debated with greater regularity so that we can better understand their implications for the profession and respond accordingly.

Academic Professionalism and Faculty Roles

Throughout the history of higher education in the United States, our institutions have flourished because a strong foundation of academic professionals—the faculty—had the means and support to contribute to those institutions, the community of scholars in the professionals' fields of study, and the greater public good. Half of all faculty members today, those holding part-time or adjunct appointments, have working conditions that lack the most basic attributes of professionalism. Although many adjunct faculty members have received the same specialized training as their tenure-track peers, they typically are not afforded the same status, working arrangements, or opportunities to make contributions to advance their institutions and the public good—at least not beyond what their tireless work with students inside the classroom will allow. The chapter that we coauthored with Elizabeth Holcombe and that summarized the findings of a national survey of stakeholders in higher education called attention to widespread interest across the enterprise in taking steps to improve or restore professionalism across the professoriate and to ensure the faculty role is a career. This is an imperative.

For adjunct faculty members—who often lack job security and stability, opportunities for growth, involvement in decision making that affects their work, and opportunities to remain engaged as scholars—restoring professionalism is an immediate priority. However, the shift toward greater contingency and other changes have placed strains on tenure-track faculty roles (such as increased service and scholarship), which may very well threaten the professionalism of those faculty members, too. We must attend to these shifts, identify the problems and find potential solutions, and take steps to restore the professionalism of all faculty members, regardless of their rank or position, to ensure the vitality of the professoriate. And it is important for us all to recognize that having a professional identity as a faculty member and fulfilling a professional role need not be linked to tenure or conducting research. Professionalism can be achieved through a wide variety of possible future faculty models.

Another cornerstone of professionalism—inside and outside of the academy—has been an obligation to serve a larger public good; this has been an historic part of the mission of higher education and faculty roles. Typically, this notion has been seen as guiding faculty members toward contributing to knowledge generation, providing social critique, and working with the community to help solve pressing societal problems. Eugene Rice's chapter invites us to think more broadly about what faculty members' professional responsibilities should be as they pertain to the larger public good and to develop a new social contract for our role in a changing society. Adrianna Kezar, Tony Chambers, and John Burkhardt (2005) similarly suggested that a discussion among various higher education stakeholders is needed and that a new social compact needs to be developed; Rice's contributions are vital to informing such a discussion as we move ahead.

Although the theme of the public good has emerged in various places throughout this volume, in general the book does not focus specifically on responsibilities associated with academic professionalism as they relate to the public good. We recommend a recent book by Genevieve Shaker, *Faculty Work and the Public Good* (2015), which considers how the public good roles of faculty members can be supported in the future. Shaker suggests that the increasing participation of faculty members in community engagement is a promising trend and demonstrates strong support for aligning faculty roles to serving the larger public good. Yet the book also stresses that strains created by the rise of contingent faculty members, pressures on the dwindling tenure-track faculty members to be more productive, prevailing rewards structures, and current declines in funding for higher education at the state level make working for the public good increasingly difficult. We have to consider how our obligations to the public good are being diminished and take steps to ensure that this remains a key part of academic professionalism in the future.

Core Values Undergirding the Professoriate

A set of essential elements reflecting core values for the professoriate that are well integrated into the work and roles of faculty members of all types and ranks should be at the core of any attempt to redesign the faculty. Many of these values, discussed throughout this volume, are not new; rather, they mirror values articulated in the literature over the past several decades. Some, but not all, are part of faculty members' roles today; others are still ideals invoked but not yet fully realized in the academy. Authors in this volume have suggested a variety of values that could be invoked to strengthen the roles and contributions of faculty members in the future. Ann Austin and Andrea Trice, for example, guided us through important values such as equity, academic freedom, flexibility, professional growth, and collegiality, all centered around respect and a culture of reciprocal and mutual relationships between faculty and their institutions; many of these core values have been cited throughout this chapter and many others. These values are organizing principles that will help us to ensure that a redesign of the faculty provides satisfaction for faculty members, helps meet the institutional mission, fosters commitment to the institution and to its mission, enhances the capability of institutions to recruit and retain talented faculty members, and optimizes the use of human and intellectual capital and potential possessed by the faculty as a whole.

Collective responsibility and collaboration also emerged as a resonant theme and core value throughout the volume. Autonomy has long been a part of the value system associated with faculty work, although the way that it has been conceived as fostering individualism to a fault is something that authors in this volume have rejected as hindering knowledge creation by discouraging interdisciplinarity, community engagement, and collaborative efforts to meet departmental and institutional goals and objectives. Rather, as several authors have suggested, a less individualistic and more collective and collaborative orientation is a necessary characteristic of the faculty of the future. Austin and Trice, for example, have emphasized the development of a reciprocal and mutual relationship between faculty members and their institutions that would promote greater satisfaction of personal and shared goals. Richard Gillman, Nancy Hensel, and David Salomon discussed the potential of holistic departments to ensure that faculty members are able to participate in a range of scholarly activities, while also ensuring that the broader needs of their academic units and institutions are continuously met. Eugene Rice helped us understand academic freedom as not just an individual protection, but a value that calls us to acknowledge and honor the responsibilities that it demands of us in serving our academic communities and beyond. Leslie Gonzales and Aimee Terotsky provide evidence that new faculty members desire a more collaborative commitment. We know from our survey, though, that more senior faculty members highly value autonomy and individuality and eschew aligning their roles with departmental or institutional goals. We may have much work to do to shift this focus.

Another core value that emerged is the importance of developing a more cohesive identity for faculty members as scholarly educators. We purposefully put the word *scholarly* in front of *educators* to suggest, as many of the chapter authors have, the importance of establishing a scholarly identity that values faculty members' connections and contributions to their disciplines—ensuring opportunities for them to engage in scholarship in any of its many forms. This is as much a priority for professors with more traditional tenure-track faculty roles as it is for the majority of contingent faculty across the enterprise, whose roles primarily involve them in teaching. Faculty members should value knowledge about how students learn and become experts in pedagogy. As the survey data we summarized in chapter 3 suggest, stakeholders across higher education see engagement in scholarship as an important part of future faculty roles. But that scholarship has to look different from the traditional form with a single focus on discovery through empirical research.

Broader definitions of faculty work are also welcome among women and faculty members of color, who often find that the narrow definitions of faculty work can exclude important work that they think should be the focus of institutions of the future. In fact, Gonzales and Terotsky's chapter notes how the values of women and faculty members of color are aligned with the future directions we have outlined in terms of being more committed to focusing on student learning, finding teaching a meaningful faculty role, having time and opportunity to advise and mentor students, and participating in community engagement to support and enrich local and regional communities. Research and writing over the past thirty years have demonstrated that women and faculty members of color feel that the current construction of the faculty is not aligned with their own value systems or with what they think the enterprise should focus on. As we diversify the faculty, there may be greater synergy between new faculty members' views and the broader definitions of faculty work described in this volume.

Organizing Themes into a Model for the Future of the Faculty

We were reluctant to organize the various characteristics of the future faculty into any single model. As we have emphasized throughout this volume, there is a need for variation in faculty work and roles based on institutional missions, changing external forces affecting higher education, and the evolving needs of students. Yet we also wanted readers to understand that there are several key issues that need to be considered as they seek to rethink faculty roles. We offer a brief summary in figure 13.1 as a way to capture the main areas that we think warrant review.

At the center is the fundamental concept of the scholarly educator, embodying the essential emphasis on student success. As we noted above, most faculty members across the enterprise have roles that are focused in one way or another on student learning. Even when their roles do not primarily involve teaching, such as in the clinical faculty roles in medical schools or in the roles of the increasing numbers of research faculty members in the sciences, individuals still have important contributions to make to the education of students by providing advising (whether formal or informal), mentoring, and support. For example, research faculty members are increasingly being asked to oversee research conducted with undergraduate students. Thus, enabling and encouraging the identity of the scholarly educator is a main consideration for future faculty models: it is at the core of faculty work, regardless of the

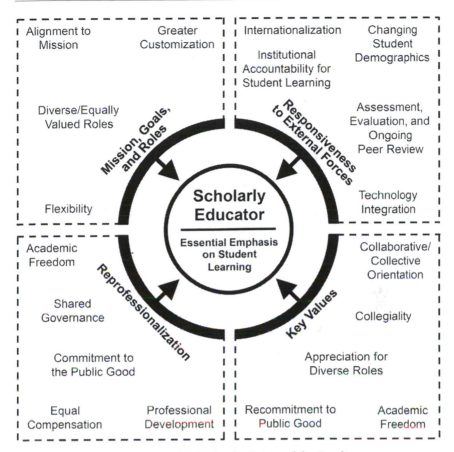

FIGURE 13.1 A Model for the Future of the Faculty

particulars of the individual position. Efforts at redesigning faculty roles ought to attend to elaborating and emphasizing responsibilities for teaching or the mentoring and advising of students. Connected to this core concept, there are four arcs of influences around which this chapter is organized: mission, goals, and roles; responsiveness to external forces; reprofessionalization; and key values. These are essential issues that must be considered and integrated into the future faculty.

The first arc—mission, goals, and roles—emphasizes the need to design and develop faculty roles and contracts that are better aligned with the diverse needs of our higher education system, which is composed of various types of institutions striving to achieve a range of outcomes. Essential considerations include a greater customization of roles that allows for faculty work to be more closely aligned to institutional missions; roles must also involve greater flexibility and be diverse enough to meet multiple, complex needs while also valuing the contributions that all faculty members make equally. Throughout this book, authors have emphasized these three qualities—flexibility, diverse roles, and equal value—as needing attention in future faculty designs.

The second arc encompasses the various external forces to which faculty redesign must respond, facilitating adaptations that allow the faculty to keep pace with the changes facing our institutions. For example, external trends impel us to consider the integration of technology into all facets of faculty work, assessment in response to growing concerns about educational quality and accountability of institutions for learning, the opportunities for and benefits of ongoing peer review and evaluation, the implications of internationalization, and how to ensure that adequate support is available to an ever changing and increasingly diverse student population through faculty involvement in advising.

The third arc involves the reprofessionalization of the professoriate, which is necessary to help faculty members contribute to their own success and that of their institution, discipline, and students through their roles. This includes their participation in professional development and shared governance, the guarantees of academic freedom, more equitable compensation, and other factors discussed in more depth in this chapter and others in the volume. As has been highlighted repeatedly, the current adjunct and contingent roles held by the majority of faculty members today typically lack basic conditions of professionalism and modes of support that allow most mainline, tenure-track faculty members to perform effectively. Professionalization has a distinct impact on the capability of faculty members to support students, their own continued learning, and institutional mission and goals. However, accompanying the rights associated with being a professional are responsibilities. Chief among them in the context of faculty work is maintaining a commitment to support the public good. Historically, as noted in this book, faculty members have done this by speaking out on issues of social or political importance; contributing to the resolution of local, regional, or national problems and policy development; public service; and conducting and publishing research that is available to the public.

Lastly, the fourth arc attends to reinforcing—and, in some cases, restoring—certain values such as facilitating a more collaborative or collective orientation to faculty work, a recommitment to the public good, and a greater appreciation of diverse roles, reversing the hierarchy that has privileged research roles at the expense of teaching and service. It is no coincidence that many of these values also correspond or overlap with priorities for reprofessionalizing the faculty, such as ensuring academic freedom or professional growth.

We see these areas as making up some of the essential elements of a future faculty.

Conclusion

We have been engaged in the work of rethinking the professoriate for a relatively short time. Many of the contributors to this volume have made numerous contributions to advance thinking about the direction of change in faculty
roles for many years. For example, Eugene Rice, Ann Austin, KerryAnn O'Meara,
and William Plater have worked tirelessly on issues related to the faculty for
decades. We are humbled and honored by their contributions to this volume,
as well as their continuous attention and care to improving the faculty. Many
ideas that have been articulated throughout this volume help make the case
for change and begin to establish some sort of vision for our future. We hope
that these ideas will be met with an openness to change. Our dialogues with
many stakeholders and thought leaders across the enterprise and the findings
from our research suggest that the time for a conversation about the future of
the faculty has finally come. And there is evidence of an emerging consensus
about some priorities and a future direction. This volume has helped to provide
the basis for a shared vision. Now it is time to come together and take action.

REFERENCES

Boyer, Ernest L. 1990. *Scholarship Reconsidered: Priorities of the Professoriate.* Princeton, NJ:
    Carnegie Foundation for the Advancement of Teaching.
Kezar, Adrianna J., Tony C. Chambers, and John C. Burkhardt, eds. 2005. *Higher Education for
    the Public Good: Emerging Voices from a National Movement.* San Francisco: Jossey-Bass.
Kezar, Adrianna J., and Daniel Maxey. 2015. *Adapting by Design: Creating Faculty Roles and
    Defining Faculty Work to Ensure an Intentional Future for Colleges and Universities.* Delphi
    Project. Accessed December 15, 2015. http://adaptingbydesign.thechangingfaculty
    .org/.
Kezar, Adrianna J., Daniel Maxey, and Elizabeth Holcombe. 2015. *The Professoriate
    Reconsidered: A Study of New Faculty Models.* New York: TIAA-CREF Research Institute.
Shaker, Genevieve. 2015. *Faculty Work and the Public Good: Philanthropy, Engagement, and
    Academic Professionalism.* New York: Teachers College Press.

ABOUT THE CONTRIBUTORS

ARLEEN ARNSPARGER works with educational organizations whose leaders are striving to improve student success. She developed the Initiative on Student Success at the Center for Community College Student Engagement at the University of Texas at Austin and led the center's qualitative work for more than a decade. In that role, she worked with community colleges throughout the country, conducting focus groups and interviews with students to learn about their college experiences, interviewing presidents, and listening to faculty and staff members. Arnsparger is a coauthor of the book and the producer of the companion video *Students Speak—Are We Listening? Starting Right in the Community College*. She has also published numerous articles related to student success and is the producer of the video *Aspirations to Achievement: Men of Color and Community Colleges*. Since her early career as a television and radio reporter and newscaster, Arnsparger has been a professional listener. She asks questions that get to the heart of people's perceptions, experiences, and actions. She has served as an administrator at community colleges in New York and Colorado; an adjunct faculty member at two- and four-year institutions; and an education policy advisor, working with governors, state leaders, higher education systems, and school districts throughout the country on education improvement. Arnsparger has also worked with organizational leaders who seek to bridge generational differences in the workplace. She is a coauthor of *Millennials@Work: Engaging the New Generation* and *4genR8tns: Succeeding with Colleagues, Cohorts, and Customers*.

ANN E. AUSTIN is a professor of higher, adult, and lifelong education at Michigan State University. She is currently on leave to serve as a program director in the Division of Undergraduate Education at the National Science Foundation (NSF) in Washington, D.C. Her research is related to faculty careers and professional development; teaching and learning in higher education; the academic workplace; organizational change; doctoral education; and reform in science, technology, engineering, and mathematics (STEM) education. She is a fellow of the American Educational Research Association and past president of the Association for the Study of Higher Education, and she was a Fulbright fellow in South Africa (1998). She has also served for a decade as the co–principal investigator of the Center for the Integration of Research, Teaching, and Learning, funded by the NSF, and has been the principal investigator on an NSF-funded grant to study organizational change strategies that support the success of women scholars in STEM fields. Her publications include *Rethinking Faculty Work: Higher Education's Strategic Imperative* (2007) and *Educating Integrated Professionals: Theory and Practice on Preparation for the Professoriate* (2008), as well as other books, articles, and chapters on higher education issues in the United States and in international contexts. She has worked with colleagues at the national and institutional levels on higher education issues in a number of countries outside the United States, including Australia, China, Egypt, Finland, Malaysia, Oman, the Philippines, South Africa, Thailand, the United Arab Emirates, and Vietnam.

MALCOLM BROWN has been director of the EDUCAUSE Learning Initiative (ELI) since 2009 and has initiated major ELI undertakings such as the Seeking Evidence of Impact program and the Learning Space Rating System. Prior to assuming the directorship of the ELI, he was director of academic computing at Dartmouth College, overseeing a team active in instructional technology, research computing, classroom technology, and pedagogical innovation. During his tenure at Dartmouth, he worked actively with the ELI, contributing chapters to EDUCAUSE e-books, helping plan focus sessions, and serving on the ELI Advisory Board. He has been a member of the EDUCAUSE Evolving Technologies Committee and was the editor of the New Horizons column for the *EDUCAUSE Review*. He has served as a faculty member of the EDUCAUSE Learning Technology Leadership program. He has been on the advisory board for *Horizon Report* since its inception in 2004 and served as chair of the board of the New Media Consortium. He is currently serving ex officio as a member of the board of IMS Global. Brown holds a pair of BA degrees from the University of California, Santa Cruz; studied in Freiburg, Germany, on Fulbright scholarships; and has a PhD in German studies from Stanford University. He has taught several academic courses on Nietzsche and maintains the *Nietzsche Chronicle* website. He has given presentations in Australia, Japan, and the United Arab Emirates and has spoken most recently at Columbia University, Penn State University, and the University of Central Michigan.

LAUREN DeCROSTA is a doctoral student in the international education policy program at the University of Maryland. As a graduate research assistant for the university's ADVANCE Program for Inclusive Excellence, she assisted KerryAnn O'Meara with qualitative research related to the program's focus on improving work environments and retention and advancement of women faculty members in ways that improve the culture for all faculty members. Prior to beginning the PhD program, she worked as a teacher trainer and taught English as a second language, both in Washington, D.C., and in Barcelona, Spain. Her professional experience also includes work in both the public and nonprofit sectors of international development. DeCrosta holds a master's degree in international training and education and a graduate certificate in peace building from American University, as well as a dual bachelor of arts degree in international affairs and Spanish from the George Washington University.

JOANNA DRIVALAS is a dean's fellow in the urban education policy PhD program at the University of Southern California's Rossier School of Education. She serves as a research assistant at both the Center for Urban Education and the Pullias Center for Higher Education at the school. Her research interests include access, readiness, and retention of underrepresented students; transitions within the K–16 pipeline; and institutional climate, culture, and responsibility. She has taught as an adjunct faculty member and is currently studying the impact of national education associations on pedagogy and cultural change at four-year research institutions. Drivalas holds an MS in higher education from the University of Pennsylvania's Graduate School of Education and a BA in theatre and creative writing from Florida State University.

RICHARD ALAN GILLMAN is a professor and associate provost for faculty affairs at Valparaiso University. He has also served as assistant dean for sponsored research and faculty development, was the founding director of the university's Celebration of Undergraduate Scholarship conference, and was chair of the Department of Mathematics and Computer Science. Gillman has edited two volumes published by the Mathematical Association of America (MAA), *A Friendly Competition* and *Current Practices in Quantitative Literacy*, and serves as chair of both the MAA's Problem Series Editorial Board the MAA's Committee on Sections. He coauthored *Models of Conflict and Cooperation*, also published by the American Mathematical Society. Gillman completed his undergraduate work at Ball State University and earned his doctorate of arts at Idaho State University in 1986.

LESLIE D. GONZALES is an assistant professor of higher education in the College of Education at Michigan State University. Her research agenda consists of three overarching lines of inquiry: legitimacy in academia; the relations of power that govern the recognition of knowledge and knowers; and the possibility of agency among academics. She received her BA in political science, with a minor in sociology, from New Mexico Highlands University; and her MA in political science and her EdD in higher education from University of Texas at El Paso.

NANCY HENSEL became the first president of the New American Colleges and Universities on November 15, 2011. Previously she served for seven years as chief executive officer of the Council on Undergraduate Research, in Washington, D.C.

During her tenure there, she was principal investigator for seven National Science Foundation grants to help faculty and institutions develop undergraduate research programs. She initiated an undergraduate research program at the University of Maine at Presque Isle, where she served as president. Prior to her presidency, she was provost at the University of Maine at Farmington and a professor of education and department chair at the University of Redlands. Hensel holds a doctorate in early childhood education from the University of Georgia, master's degrees in theatre and early childhood education from San Francisco State University, and a bachelor of arts degree in theatre, also from San Francisco State. In 2003, Hensel was inducted into the Maine Women's Hall of Fame for her work in promoting higher education in Maine and supporting the role of women in higher education. She is the author of several articles on the issues of family and work, creativity in young children, and diversity in education.

ELIZABETH HOLCOMBE is a provost's fellow and doctoral research assistant at the Pullias Center for Higher Education at the University of Southern California. Her current research interests include reform of science, technology, engineering and math (STEM) education; teaching, learning, and assessment; faculty issues; and leadership in higher education. Before beginning her doctoral work, Holcombe held a variety of roles in student affairs. These included working with a college access partnership, managing an academic advising and mentoring program, and leading a co- and extracurricular assessment initiative. Prior to her career in higher education, Holcombe was an elementary school teacher with Teach for America in Atlanta. She holds a bachelor of arts in political science and Spanish from Vanderbilt University and a master of arts in politics and education from Teachers College, Columbia University.

ADRIANNA KEZAR is a professor of higher education at the University of Southern California and codirector of the Pullias Center for Higher Education. She holds a PhD and an MA. Kezar is a national expert on change, governance, and leadership in higher education, and her research agenda explores the change process in higher education institutions and the role of leadership in creating change. An international expert on the changing faculty, she is director of the Delphi Project on the Changing Faculty and Student Success. She has published eighteen monographs, over a hundred journal articles, and over a hundred book chapters and reports. Her recent books include *How Colleges Change* (2013), *Enhancing Campus Capacity for Leadership* (2011), *Embracing Non-Tenure-Track Faculty* (2012), and *Understanding the New Majority of Non-Tenure-Track Faculty* (2010).

WILLIAM T. MALLON is senior director of strategy and innovation development at the Association of American Medical Colleges (AAMC), in Washington, D.C. He received his bachelor of arts degree, and one master's degree from the

University of Richmond, and a second master's degree and a doctorate degree from Harvard University. His doctoral thesis, an examination of how US colleges abolish or institute systems of academic tenure, was awarded the Dissertation of the Year Citation of Excellence from the Association for the Study of Higher Education. Mallon publishes regularly on the management, organization, and leadership of higher education and academic medicine. He is the author of thirty-five journal articles, book chapters, and monographs as well as ten teaching case studies, and his peer-reviewed research has appeared in journals such as *Science*, *Academic Medicine*, *Innovative Higher Education*, and *New Directions in Higher Education*. Mallon also leads the development of the AAMC's overall strategy, organizational performance analytics, and organizational learning and innovation. He led the expansion of the AAMC's portfolio of executive leadership programs for administrators and faculty members at medical schools and teaching hospitals. Mallon is the author of *The Handbook of Academic Medicine: How Medical Schools and Teaching Hospitals Work* and coauthor of *Finding Top Talent: How to Search for Leaders in Academic Medicine*. He co-created Faculty Forward, a program that strengthens medical schools' capacity to improve faculty satisfaction and engagement. In 2013–15, Mallon was a visiting professor of medicine at the Geisel School of Medicine at Dartmouth College. Prior to joining the AAMC, Mallon was a researcher at Harvard University.

DANIEL MAXEY is the former codirector of the Delphi Project on the Changing Faculty and Student Success. He is currently provost's fellow at Santa Clara University, where he works on strategic initiatives and policy development in the Office of the Provost. Prior to beginning his work at Santa Clara University, Maxey spent four years at the University of Southern California (USC), where he was a dean's fellow in the Rossier School of Education and founded the Delphi Project, with Adrianna Kezar. In this capacity as codirector of the Delphi Project, Maxey established himself as an authority on postsecondary faculty issues. He has coauthored numerous articles and reports and made presentations at national conferences and workshops on issues related to trends in the changing composition of postsecondary faculty, the implications of faculty policies and practices, and potential strategies and approaches for collaboratively reimagining or redesigning faculty work. In addition to his scholarship on faculty issues, his publications include works on higher education policy and governance, the politics of higher education, civic engagement, and the public roles and responsibilities of colleges and universities. Prior to beginning a career in higher education, Maxey had an accomplished career in public policy, government affairs, and politics at the state and federal level. He received a PhD in urban education policy at the University of Southern California in 2015. He also holds a BA in government from the College of William and Mary in Virginia and an MA in higher and postsecondary education from Arizona State University.

KERRYANN O'MEARA is a professor of higher education, director of the ADVANCE Program for Inclusive Excellence, and an affiliate faculty member in women's studies at the University of Maryland. Her research examines organizational practices that support or limit the full participation of diverse faculty members and the legitimacy of diverse scholarship in the academy. Her recent work examines how work environments influence faculty agency and departure, the role of peer networks in advancing equity and inclusion, and gender equity in workload and distribution of campus service. Her work has been published in the *Journal of Higher Education*, *Review of Higher Education*, *Research in Higher Education*, and *Gender and Education*, among other venues. She consults with higher education institutions interested in reforming their promotion and tenure policies to acknowledge broader definitions of scholarship and reform workload, retention, and faculty development systems.

WILLIAM PLATER is executive vice chancellor and dean of the faculties emeritus at Indiana University–Purdue University Indianapolis (IUPUI) and Indiana University Chancellor's Professor Emeritus of public affairs, philanthropic studies, and English. From 2012 through 2014, he was senior advisor for international affairs of the Western Association of Schools and Colleges (WASC) Senior Colleges and Universities Commission, where he served as a commissioner from 2005 through 2011. Plater served Indiana University as dean of the School of Liberal Arts (1983–87), executive vice chancellor and dean of the faculties (1987–2006), acting chancellor (2003), and director of the Workshop on International Community Development (2006–10). From 2011 to 2012, he served as senior advisor for education strategies at Course Networking, a learning-technologies company that provides global networking services. He was a director of the management committee of Epsilen, a learning-technologies company owned by the *New York Times*, and senior advisor for education at Epsilen from 2010 to 2011. Plater served as a member of the advisory boards for the Carnegie Community Engagement Classification, the Indiana University Center on Global Health, the Council of Adult and Experiential Learning, the Children's Museum in Indianapolis, WFYI public radio and television stations, the Indiana Humanities Council, and numerous other community boards. In 2006 the American Association of State Colleges and Universities established the William M. Plater Award for Civic Engagement, the first national award of any kind to recognize provosts. Plater has been awarded honorary doctorates by Purdue University and the National Institute of Development Administration in Thailand.

R. EUGENE RICE is a senior scholar at the Association of American Colleges and Universities. He received his PhD in religion and society from Harvard University and is a graduate of the Harvard Divinity School. In Washington, D.C., Rice served for ten years as director of the national Forum on Faculty Roles and Rewards, as well as of the New Pathways projects on the changing faculty career at the American Association for Higher Education (AAHE). Before moving to AAHE he was vice president and dean of the faculty at Antioch College, where he held an appointment of professor of sociology and religion. Earlier, Rice was a senior fellow at the Carnegie Foundation, where he was engaged in the national study of the scholarly priorities of the American professoriate and collaborated with Ernest Boyer on the influential Carnegie Report *Scholarship Reconsidered*. Rice began his career as professor of sociology and religion at the University of the Pacific, where he helped initiate the first of its experimental "cluster colleges"—Raymond College—and served as chairperson of the Department of Sociology. His teaching and research focus on the sociology and ethics of the professions and the workplace. His special interest is in the scholarship of engagement, and recently he has taken this work internationally, including to Brazil, Liberia, the West Bank, Saudi Arabia, and the United Kingdom. In *Change* magazine's survey of leadership in American higher education, Rice was recognized as one of a small group of idea leaders whose work has made a difference nationally and globally.

DAVID A. SALOMON is a professor of English at the Sage Colleges in Troy and Albany, New York. In addition to teaching courses in medieval and Renaissance literature, he is the director of general education, undergraduate research, and study abroad. His research specialties include medieval religious literature and the intersection of technology with philosophy and religion. Among his other publications, he is the author of *An Introduction to the Glossa Ordinaria as Medieval Hypertext*, published in 2013. He is also coeditor of and a contributor to *Redefining the Paradigm: Faculty Models to Support Student Learning*, published in 2015. His current work examines the concept of the self in Augustine and Carl Jung.

AIMEE LaPOINTE TEROSKY is an assistant professor of educational leadership at Saint Joseph's University, in Philadelphia. She received her BS in secondary education (social studies) from the Pennsylvania State University, her MA in school leadership from Villanova University, and her EdD in higher and postsecondary education from Teachers College, Columbia University. Her research focuses on higher education and K–12 settings with a concentration on teaching, learning, career management, faculty development, instructional leadership, and educational or professional experiences of girls and women.

ANDREA G. TRICE earned her doctorate in 1998 from the University of Michigan. She has worked as a research scientist at Northwestern University and as a faculty member at Purdue University. For the past nine years, she has used her research and consulting skills to help numerous universities, government agencies, and other nonprofits achieve greater organizational effectiveness. Her articles and two coauthored books reflect her interest in organizational effectiveness as well as cross-cultural dynamics.

INDEX